Beyond Elemental Loss

SUNY series in Environmental Philosophy and Ethics

J. Baird Callicott and John van Buren, editors

Beyond Elemental Loss
Shifting Constellations of Water, Fire, Air, and Earth

M<small>ARJOLEIN</small> O<small>ELE</small>

Published by State University of New York Press, Albany

© 2025 State University of New York

All rights reserved

Printed in the United States of America

No part of this book may be used or reproduced in any manner whatsoever without written permission. No part of this book may be stored in a retrieval system or transmitted in any form or by any means including electronic, electrostatic, magnetic tape, mechanical, photocopying, recording, or otherwise without the prior permission in writing of the publisher.

Links to third-party websites are provided as a convenience and for informational purposes only. They do not constitute an endorsement or an approval of any of the products, services, or opinions of the organization, companies, or individuals. SUNY Press bears no responsibility for the accuracy, legality, or content of a URL, the external website, or for that of subsequent websites.

EU GPSR Authorised Representative:
Logos Europe, 9 rue Nicolas Poussin, 17000, La Rochelle, France
contact@logoseurope.eu

For information, contact State University of New York Press, Albany, NY
www.sunypress.edu

Library of Congress Cataloging-in-Publication Data

Name: Oele, Marjolein, author.
Title: Beyond elemental loss : shifting constellations of water, fire, air, and earth / Marjolein Oele.
Description: Albany : State University of New York Press, [2025] | Series: SUNY series in environmental philosophy and ethics | Includes bibliographical references and index.
Identifiers: LCCN 2024039357 | ISBN 9798855801682 (hardcover : alk. paper) | ISBN 9798855801699 (ebook) | ISBN 9798855801675 (pbk. : alk. paper)
Subjects: LCSH: Environmental psychology. | Loss (Psychology) | Environmental degradation—Psychological aspects. | Human ecology—Philosophy. | Environmental sociology—Philosophy. | Four elements (Philosophy)
Classification: LCC BF353 .O335 2025 | DDC 155.9/15—dc23/eng/2024

For Gerard

For moving me past zones of comfort
For traveling with me around the world
For always pulling me close
And holding me in and beyond loss

Contents

Acknowledgments	ix
Introduction	1
Chapter 1. **Water**—Living and Speaking Oceanic Loss: On Extinction, Migration, and Language(s)	23
Chapter 2. **Fire**—Pyrogenic Creation and Destruction: Contemplating the Meaning of Fire, Affect, and Loss in the Pyrocene	43
Chapter 3. **Air**—The Breath of Decaying Constellations: A Phenomenology of Loss, Illness, Allergies, and Bad Air	61
Chapter 4. **Earth**—Silent Tremors: Earthquakes and the Question of Balance and (Dis)Orientation	81
Chapter 5. **Elemental Trust**—Transforming Elemental Loss into Elemental Change	111
Notes	143
Bibliography	187
Index	205

Acknowledgments

The chapters that ultimately would become this book—*Beyond Elemental Loss*—were written against an autobiographical background full of personal loss. In April 2019, I lost my "BFF" Carole due to pancreatic cancer, and with that my first American friend who had coached me through my new academic and social life in Chicago and with whom I shared a zany take on life. In January 2021, I lost my brother Bas, whose larger-than-life presence in my life ended abruptly with his death due to Covid. In an anxious time before vaccines, his death in the overflowing ICU of the OLVG Hospital in Amsterdam left me speechless and broken. These losses undid me, but they also emphasized in their emotional rawness the meaningfulness of writing about loss, even if the book *Beyond Elemental Loss* is, paradoxically and explicitly, *not* about such personal losses, but about loss that pertains to shifting social-ecological constellations—shifts that appear nearly invisible because they occur at the apparent periphery of our personal and cultural consciousness.

That I was able to, somehow, *keep carrying on* and recalibrate myself is, in large part, due to the love and care of my family and friends, but also due to the consolation I have found in writing and research, which was enabled by my academic home at the time: the University of San Francisco. At USF, I was able to pursue my thinking through loss through the generous funding of the Mortimer Fleishhacker Fund for Philosophy, which allowed me to organize workshops and lectures on loss. Additionally, Faculty Development Funding enabled ample travel and research funding to present and workshop papers at various stages of progression that would become part of this book, combined with funding for research assistance. Being granted access to various writing retreats organized by the College of Arts and Sciences and being awarded the National Endowment of the Humanities Chair at USF in 2022–2023 further allowed for valuable research time to bring the manuscript toward completion. Overall, I am immensely grateful for this institutional support, without which I would not have been able to write this book. Most importantly, the encouragement I received at USF from many colleagues over the process of writing this book has been unforgettable. I would like to especially thank Ryan Van Meter, for nimbly coaching my immersion in creative nonfiction writing and hosting me in his class, as well as my colleagues in the Philosophy Department, and, of course, all the writing-and-research companions across the university whom I had the pleasure to interact with in the writing room, at writing retreats, and at other research events, over the past few years.

My new academic home, Radboud University in Nijmegen, the Netherlands, has also played a formidable role in supporting the final stretch toward publication of this manuscript. I am thankful for the Starters Grant I received enabling funding for indexing and research support, and additional aid received from the Radboud Institute for Culture and History (RICH) allowing me to publish part of this book open access. I have also benefited from interactions with my new colleagues at Radboud, specifically my colleagues of Language and Culture Studies and the Department of Metaphysics and Philosophical Anthropology.

In addition to USF and Radboud, I am thankful to yet another academic home, namely the Pacific Association for the Continental Tradition (PACT), which became an early testing ground for my ideas on elemental loss: first through a paper presentation on fire (at Yosemite National Park), and later on water (at Seattle University). I am indebted to this inspiring collegial "pact," which has intertwined friendship and philosophy in the best ways possible over the past decade, and which has shown the power of joining forces in thinking through topics in continental philosophy and doing so in a community of care. In particular, I would like to thank Kim Carfore, Russell Duvernoy, Michael Eng, Tim Freeman, Josh Hayes, Chris Lauer, Sam Mickey, Danielle Meijer, Robert Mugerauer, Shannon Mussett, Amanda Parris, David Peña-Guzman, Michael Shaw, Brian Seitz, Elizabeth Sikes, Peter Steeves, Sam Talcott, Tom Thorp, Brian Treanor, and Jason Wirth. Moreover, over the past few years I have increasingly benefited from the input of members and the executive board of the International Association for Environmental Philosophy (IAEP), and I owe special thanks to Jonathan Beever and Jonathan Maskit for their collegial empowerment of my career. I am also thankful to the feedback I received at other conferences and colloquium venues, including those of the History of Philosophy Society (HOPS), the Radical Philosophy Society, the Centre for the Study of Theory and Criticism (London, Ontario), the Critical Cultural Theory Colloquium series at the University of Amsterdam, the University of Oregon Philosophy Colloquium series, the DePaul Philosophy Graduate Conference, and the workshop "Approaching Extinction / Contesting Extinction" at Miami University.

Along the path of writing this book, earlier versions of chapters were published, and I owe gratitude to the publishers and editors of the books and journal that allowed me to reproduce that work here. An earlier version of chapter 1 was published as "Philosophizing Extinction: On the Loss of World, and the Possibility of Rebirth through Languages of the Sea," in *Contesting Extinctions: Decolonial and Regenerative Futures*, edited by Suzanne M. McCullagh et al. (Lanham, MD: Lexington Books, 2021), 85–104. An earlier version of chapter 2 was published as "Prometheus' Gift of Fire and Technics: Contemplating the Meaning of Fire, Affect, and Californian Pyrophytes in the Pyrocene," in *Philosophy in the American West*, edited by Josh Hayes, Gerard Kuperus, and Brian Treanor (London: Routledge, 2020), 29–45. A short section of chapter 5 was recently published as "Anxiety, Grief, and Trust in Times of Climate Change: A Phenomenology of Affective Constellations and Future Transformations in and beyond the Anthropocene," in *Comparative and Continental Philosophy* (2024): 1–20.

In conceiving and unfolding the argument of this book, I benefited immensely from various research assistants who were also my direct interlocutors as I formulated my ideas. In particular, I owe huge gratitude toward my inspiring editor, Daniel O'Connell, whose intellectual acumen and creative, loyal, and constructive research support over the past decade has been invaluable. I am also very thankful for my research assistants Darcy Allred, Nico González, Fleur van Schaijk, and Lincoln Stefanello for all their detailed editorial labor working through the details of this manuscript.

At State University of New York Press, I have appreciated the efficient editorial support of Michael Rinella, who deftly navigated the publication process for this book. Additionally, I am very grateful to the two anonymous peer reviewers who carefully read my manuscript and who offered thoughtful and constructive feedback.

As I reflect upon the personal background against which this book was written, I would like to thank the extended Oele and Kuperus families as well as the family of friends that have sustained me ever so caringly, humorously, and thoughtfully. In particular I would like to thank Annemieke Beekers, Mylène Berlijn, Karen Einbinder, Wim Grit, René Hansen, Rachaelle Hilhorst, Nathan Hobbs, Jannie Kuperus, Michelle Lavigne, Christian Lotz, Marie-Claire Melzer, Nicole Miglio, Katrina Olds, Corinne Painter, Ad and Angela Peperzak, Stephen and Amelia Power, Monique Roelofs, Jackie Scott, Wilma van Splunder, and Ronald Sundstrom.

Finally, I owe deep thanks to our children, Lars and Imma, for keeping me honest about *what really matters*. I have also been delighted by the playful and caring companionship of our two feline companions, Mahal and Lily, who patiently, or sometimes not so patiently, wait for me to close my laptop and play with them. The last line of this acknowledgment is devoted to my partner, Gerard, whose spirit of philosophical open-mindedness, attentive perceptiveness, humor, and loving trust continues to empower my existence. To him this book is dedicated.

Introduction

> What a fool believes is that the rock will actually ground you. Elements-as-fundamentals trigger beginnings, catalyze arrangements that resist totality, open never-ending archives, labyrinthine libraries of the not-quite-read.
>
> —Cohen and Duckert, "Eleven Principles of the Elements"

> Air fills the thorax; ten liquids circulate through the vessels and pores; fire sets the heart, the genitals and the brain ablaze; the humus models the human. How can we live without or against the four elements, without thinking like them, without turning toward them, into them, through them, for them, with them?
>
> —Serres, *Biogea*

October 2019. After working with and against the city of San Anselmo through a two-year building permit process, the home renovation was finally underway. The contractors had just started their work. They had demolished our deck, opened up the old master bedroom to the elements, and started to build the wooden frame that would soon support the new addition. I felt a sense of relief and purpose: this addition would give much-needed privacy to overseas guests staying for a number of weeks at our home, and it would give our daughter the private bedroom that she had so long wanted. But this sense of relief and optimism was clouded by news of a fire burning acre after acre north of us in Sonoma,[1] a fire that sent dangerous amounts of smoke wafting into our air. Winds picked up, and, as a precautionary measure to sparking more fires amid extreme drought conditions, the Pacific Gas and Electric Company (hereafter PG&E) announced it would cut off power. Our home was partially demolished and now powerless. The air quality index turned from orange to red. The carpenter could no longer use his power tools, so he stopped coming. The elementary school closed.

I recall one distinct scene of that time. We had just fled to San Francisco to exchange the smoke and skeletal remains of our powerless home for a breath of clean air and the comfort of a friend's apartment. But even there, at the playground in Golden Gate Park, a sense of being unsettled was inescapable:

> Does the air know walls? I asked myself as the smoke from the fire thickened the air
> and filtered the early rays of sunlight, the cypress trees turning opaque.
> The lightness of children's play now intermingled with labored breathing.
> The Golden Gate shutting on futures for play, breath, life.

Ultimately, the Kincade fire burned about 77,758 acres and destroyed 374 (residential and commercial) structures.[2] Our own home was never in the direct path of the fire, and, after the temporary stay at our friends' home, we were able to return safely to our home, which, by then, had regained power.

By the conventional account, we came out fine. I did not lose anything in particular. Our home renovation was even able to continue as it had before. It was a stark contrast to all those who did lose their homes and who would never be able to rebuild. Nonetheless, something didn't return to normal for me. I felt a profound sense of loss and disorientation, made even more unsettling given that I was *fine*. A series of questions constantly ran through my mind: Why is it that PG&E's electric wires are not more fire-resistant and can even *start fires*,[3] and how can it be that a wealthy state such as California has so poorly invested in its infrastructure that the only way out of a crisis is to cut power and close schools? Why do schools not have the wherewithal to support their students, to grant them shelter and to continue to provide learning in fire-resistant buildings? How can I carve out a future for my family in a time and place where trust in the environment and the infrastructure that orients lives (power grids, schools, etc.) is collapsing?

As my current self looks back upon the sense of loss and disorientation I felt then, in 2019, and all the questions it invoked, I realize that my inability to grasp the source of loss at that time led me on the course of writing this book. For, reflecting upon this experience of loss, I started to uncover and write about a kind of loss that lies beyond that of discrete things, beyond the loss of the animals, plants, homes, and other structures that were ablaze.

During my research, I began to understand that such discrete and individual losses are actually part of, and enabled by, a background structure. To illustrate what I mean: in megafires as I experienced them, losses of property or endangerment of species affected by megafires (such as the long-toed salamander) capture our attention from the scale and gravity of the loss. But what remains outside the usual purview of our attention and cultural consciousness is the broader context within which such megafires have come into being and can instigate loss. In the case of Californian megafires, we could point at the larger social-ecological constellation that has included factors such as fire suppression, industrialization and the rise of industrial fire, and property regimes associated with human liberty. As the world presented itself through smoky air, a powerless home, and shuttered homes, it also, upon reflection, offered a deeper disclosure of what is usually hidden, namely those broader social-ecological parameters within which we have come to orient ourselves toward and in which we call ourselves "at home."

Thus, what I have realized in writing this book is that the loss I experienced in 2019 was not oriented around discrete things being lost but had to do with shifts to these broader social-ecological constellations, to my sense of meaning-making in the world, and with the incremental inability of my cognitive and affective habitus to grasp the world and find intelligible and sentient orientation in it. It is my claim throughout the course of this book that only when we adapt and sharpen humanity's cognitive and affective habitus can we gain traction on current and future upheavals and thereby carve out, with trust, trajectories that build sustainable futures.

༄

The structural social-ecological parameters within which humans have come to orient themselves in the world is what I call, in this book, *the elemental*. And it is this, in combination with the felt sense of loss just described, that gives this book its title. As a scholar and writer trained in ancient philosophy and twentieth-/twenty-first-century continental and environmental philosophy, I have found that the theme of *the elemental*—particularly the elements of water, fire, air, and earth—can offer both synthetic clarity and material consolidation to accessing and explaining both the social-ecological structuring of the world (including its ontogenetic possibilities) and the felt sense of loss in times of anthropogenic climate change.

The three words of the book's title, *Beyond Elemental Loss*, are meant to give voice to the three main aims of this book. First, I want to fashion my own account of the *elemental* from what have been historically known as the classical "elements" (derived from the Latin *elementum*, as translation of the Greek *stoicheion*[4]) that have been sites of thinking from ancient to contemporary philosophy. Second, I want to argue that the unsettling felt *loss* experienced as part of contextual shifts, and as currently experienced in times of anthropogenic climate change, is a result of our incrementally increasing inability to cognitively or affectively render intelligible the shifts happening to these social-ecological parameters that structure the world. The sense of loss that is experienced gets at the core of who we are as habitual beings and is thus nothing but fundamental and thus *elementary*. Third, I argue that by adapting and sharpening humanity's cognitive and affective habitus through what I call "elemental trust," we can enable more sustainable futures and, thus, move *beyond* elemental loss.

When I speak of the elemental, I use it as a concept inherited from ancient Greek thought (and particularly the Presocratics) that finds renewal in twentieth- and twenty-first-century continental thinkers such as Bachelard, Sallis, and Irigaray. The appeal of the elements of water, fire, air, and earth is that they entail both very particular aspects—for instance, air is this *particular breath* I am taking—and that they are involved in co-constituting the broader world or *kosmos* we participate in—for instance, air is always a shared part of a common atmosphere co-inhabited and co-constituted by other beings. As I engage in this tradition of thought, I want to argue that the elements are not fixed, ahistorical natural entities, as scholars such as John Sallis have argued.[5] Rather, in my view, anthropogenic climate change is making it clear that ecological constellations are also social-historical constellations and are subject to change. Said otherwise, for me *the elemental is a social-ecological constellation that is holding and generative of many forms of beings: it is both subject to diachronic flux—enabling historical transformation—and open to synchronic interaction and co-creation*. I maintain that there is value in following the traditional understanding of the elements as synthetic crystallization points of our material world and to thinking of the elements in terms of four distinct and yet interconnected ways: water, fire, air, and earth. Simultaneously, however, I am reconceiving of the elemental as an ecological constellation entailing and enabling the ontogenesis of a heterogeneity of organic and inorganic beings, arguing that this constellation is subject to social and historical changes and intervention. Since it combines both so-called ecological and social factors, I conceive of the elemental as a social-ecological constellation.

In writing about the elemental, I appeal to the classic Western tradition that holds up the four elements of water, fire, air, and earth, which allows me to engage with the historical trajectory along which the elemental has traveled, along which we may discern infinitesimal changes in our relationship. However, I also appeal to other traditions (e.g., the Californian indigenous Miwok, or indigenous song and dance from the Caribbean island of Curaçao), as I am not maintaining a classificatory Western system of the elements but build out my own sense of the elemental with the goal of having the elemental speak toward our own contemporary moment. Precisely because the elemental holds the capacity to think through the co-emergence of beings at the level of the constellation or sphere, is it well suited to move us away from thinking of loss in term of individuated beings toward conceiving of loss in terms of infinitesimal and diachronic changes involving transformed relational constellations.

Accordingly, what I argue for in this book is that the elemental—as an ontogenetic and temporalizing ecological constellation—has been undergoing gradual and infinitesimal changes, due to human influences, and those changes have been mostly invisible to human perception until now. However, ultimately, these gradual changes have had a profound impact on the way the world presents itself to us, for instance, in the current form of massive species extinction, acidification of oceans, and climate emergencies such as flash flooding, extreme droughts, and so forth. These kinds of radical and drastic environmental changes are not the main subject of my argument on loss; however, I argue that these kinds of changes can, ultimately, be understood against the backdrop of incremental changes to the flux space of the elemental. Understanding this backdrop does not deny the need for specific climate action or other climate initiatives but redirects our focus toward the broader interface within which we live, and the abilities we as humans have to intervene and change our habitus within the elemental. Since this book crosses a wide range of lived experiences and tracks our relationship to the elemental over time, it offers a broader look that may precisely enable and inform a new habitus and, with that, may uncover new potentials for climate politics and affective engagement.

Thus, contemporary climate crises can be understood as consequences of changes to the conditions of the possibility of social-ecological co-emergence, that is, shifts of the elemental ontogenetic constellation. And it is due to our inability to relate to this "new normal" social-ecological presentation of the world with our usual cognitive or affective habitus that we find ourselves suffering from feelings of loss and disorientation. The final step in my argument in this book is to argue for the importance of transforming elemental loss into elemental change. In order to bring about such transformation, we need a solid epistemological grasp on the conditions of appearance and expression of the elemental. Only when we understand the various aspects of the elemental (its natural-scientific aspects, its social-historical dimensions, its narrative reconstruction in mythology and ideology, its lived phenomenology, etc.) can a sense of trust in the elemental be reinstantiated. It is my argument that reinstalling trust can set in motion the transformation from elemental loss to elemental change. Ultimately, I claim, we need to adapt and sharpen humanity's cognitive and affective habitus to carve out future trajectories embedded in trust, especially in light of current and oncoming climate upheaval.

Formulating a Theory of Infinitesimal Loss Suited for Times of Climate Change

Philosophical theories of loss are traditionally formulated around individuated beings. Starting with Plato's *Phaedo*, we find a well-known philosophical articulation of loss that ponders loss in terms of the loss of the person Socrates. The *Crito* tries to give various names to the loss—what would be lost in Socrates's death is a friend, a father, a philosopher, and a teacher. From Plato on, we find more articulations of loss, similarly thematizing loss in terms of individual beings (e.g., in St. Augustine's *Confessions*, where he mourns the loss of his mother Monica).

In twentieth- and twenty-first-century continental thought, such thinking of loss in terms of discrete entities remains strong. For instance,

Martin Heidegger's *Being and Time* addresses loss in terms of our own death, a death, however, that is fundamentally one's own and in relationship to which one may seize upon one's own innermost possibilities.[6] However, we also find in this same twentieth- and twenty-first-century continental thought other thinkers who stress the relational and contextual nature of loss. For instance, Hannah Arendt, in *The Human Condition*, builds upon, yet thoroughly reinvents, Heidegger's concept of being-in-the-world, by socializing it and diagnosing its dissipation in mass society: "The world like every in-between, relates and separates men at the same time. The public realm, as the common world, gathers us together and yet prevents our falling over each other, so to speak. What makes mass society so difficult to bear is not the number of people involved, or at least not primarily, *but the fact that the world between them has lost its power to gather them together, to relate and to separate them*."[7] As Arendt has it, modernity underpins the experience of the *fraying of* connections of the public world, dismantling the power of gathering, leading to loss in the sense of world. On a more interpersonal level, Levinas argues that we are always haunted by the loss and death of the other, and that such loss shows a commitment to a very specific, individuated other whom we lose—another with a truly human face, vulnerability, and claim for respect.[8] Another thinker worth mentioning in this regard is Martin Buber, who sees the world as lived between human beings as a relational world, established by the I-Thou;[9] the loss of loved ones thus implies the loss of such relationality.

In their work on loss, Judith Butler builds upon these ideas of relational loss as articulated by thinkers such as Buber, Arendt, and Levinas, arguing that loss confronts us with a relational sense of being that precedes and goes beyond individuality. Butler writes: "Perhaps what I have lost 'in' you, that for which I have no ready vocabulary, is a relationality that is neither myself nor you, but the tie by which those terms are differentiated and related."[10] Rather than thinking of loss in terms of individuation, loss here is formulated in terms of severed ties preceding the formation of our identities. Butler, in this formulation of grief, also returns to Freud's analyses of mourning, who, in his later writings, came to realize that mourning *can and should* include a living desire to restore the lost object, such that the "essential" task of mourning actually should be the inclusion (or "incorporation") of the lost object.[11] This implies that Freud, in his evolving theory of grief, came to acknowledge the enduring ("infinite") presence of loss and the acknowledgment of traces of loss that continue to undermine an autonomous sense of the present self.

However, it is my argument that current crises such as the climate crisis and the Covid-19 crisis challenge existing formulations of loss, even when they are inclusive of Butler's formulation of loss as involving the loss of a relationality preceding individual bonds. To focus first on Covid-19: While Covid-19 has caused the deaths of millions, the pandemic showed that loss does not just pertain to the loss of *one* being, beings, or their relationality. Suddenly, amid the lockdowns, entire lifestyles changed. Old habits broke and were lost, and entire communities dissolved. Moreover, certain communities proved more vulnerable than others based on social-economic, gender, and racial realities and accumulated vulnerabilities that had been built, slowly and incrementally, over time.[12]

In *What World Is This?* Butler grapples with understanding these shifts, seeking to understand them in terms of "world" and possibly a "common world" where the tragic, following Scheler, is occasioned by events but cannot be reduced to an event, and where grief is not singular but is understood in terms of an "atmosphere," which tells us something about the world itself.[13] Covid-19, thus, as Butler words it, makes us feel a "looming world of loss."[14] This also resonates in the work of psychologist Pauline Boss. Covid-19, she argues, has confronted us with a form of ambiguous loss that did not just include loss at the level of the individual or the family but extended to "a local community, or the global community."[15] Thus, the pandemic underlined the presence of ambiguous losses, which, in Boss's words, "are ubiquitous but rarely acknowledged because they are difficult to see, even by those of us experiencing them."[16]

If we turn to the climate crisis, which, scientists argue, is correlated with the rise of pandemics such as the Covid-19 pandemic,[17] a comparable and arguably even more poignant claim about the prevalence and meaning of ambiguous loss can be made. While it is certainly the case that anthropogenic climate change is currently threatening the loss of at least 26,500 species, and that climate-change-induced phenomena, such as excessive heat, have caused, in 2022 alone, the loss of lives of fifteen thousand people,[18] the experience of loss seems not only larger than even the sum of those parts but also qualitatively different. Having been trained to think of reality as the sum of all individuated parts has meant we find ourselves *unfit* to address an existential ecological crisis of loss that seems to go beyond the sum of such parts. Donna Haraway, in *Staying with the*

Trouble, glosses this issue this way: "What happens when the best biologies of the twenty-first century cannot do their job with bounded individuals plus contexts, when organism plus environments, or genes plus whatever they need, no longer sustain the overflowing richness of biological knowledges, if they ever did?"[19] Neither in life, as Haraway argues, nor in loss then, as I argue, does the focus on individuation-cum-context uncover the fundamental dynamics of ecological communities. This, then, has been one of the driving forces to start this project. Over and against the notion of individuated loss, I propose the notion of *ambiguous, elemental loss—that is, felt loss that does not emerge as (a) a synchronous event, or (b) as pertaining to one individuated being, but that, instead, involves (c) infinitesimal and diachronic changes that, over time, come to change the conditions of the possibility of the elemental.*

Inspired by cultural theorist Lauren Berlant's thinking on the slow, incremental, and day-to-day changes that lead to "slow death,"[20] I seek to show that a well-rounded account of ephemeral environmental loss needs to pay attention to its temporal, historical conditions. This has implications for grief. Where a singular event involving loss may jolt us into an abrupt sense of grief that centers the subject, unfolding from a synchronic snapshot of time, the meaning of grief alters when such grief traces minute historical changes building up diachronically, one at a time, with changes ultimately affecting not just one subject but many, finally translating to and informing a sense of elemental loss. It is in this regard that I find Glenn Albrecht's notion of *solastalgia* helpful in terms of thematizing the kind of (slow) grief that elemental loss brings about. The term "solastalgia" is formed from two roots: solace and desolation. The Latin suffix *algia* is added to designate pain.[21] Albrecht defines solastalgia as "the homesickness you have when you are still at home."[22] This new form of mourning is "connected to negatively perceived and felt changes to a home environment, changes that one is powerless to prevent."[23] For Albrecht, "solastalgia defines the existential, lived experience of the loss of value in the present as manifest in a feeling of disorientation, of being undermined by forces that destroy the potential for solace to be derived from the home environment."[24]

With this, we enter into the question of how to formulate an epistemology that can track such infinitesimal changes in our world, an epistemology that is fit to embrace the flux of the world while holding on to crucial notions such as *home, home environment*, or *orientation*.

Articulating an Epistemology That Can Follow the Contours of Change Undergirding Ambiguous Elemental Loss

Alongside the impetus to formulate a new theory of loss is the need to formulate an epistemology of change that can follow its contours. Especially when we talk about something like environment, nature, or life, such an epistemology is badly needed. Returning to an early formulation of nature (*physis*) in Aristotle, we find an account of nature based on the assumption of an underlying substance that remains the same throughout various changes.[25] Where Aristotle does admit modifications, he traces it in the activities (*energeiai*) or *actualizations* (*entelecheiai*) of such substances, allowing for the idea of natural beings to come into their own or, as I have put it elsewhere, for nature to "fold back upon itself."[26]

This prevailing notion, that nature, life, biology, turns around static substances that are what they are, fits with a notion that sees all of reality in terms of being rather than becoming. It fits with the aforementioned notion of individuation, insofar as that similarly sees life in discrete parts, distinct from each other, with each one being the source of its own agency. However, this view cannot do justice to life as it co-emerges together with others, in direct symbiosis and productive of affective engagement and becoming in the interface with that which touches it. Versus predominant accounts that see life in terms of insular agency or being, I therefore proposed, in my 2020 book entitled *E-Co-Affectivity: Exploring Pathos at Life's Material Interfaces*, to use the term "e-co-affectivity" to underline that life is to be understood as ontogenetic affectivity, coming into being alongside others (*co*-affectivity) within a context or home (hence *e-co*-affectivity).[27]

The theoretical underpinning for my emphasis on co-affective ontogenesis can be found in the conceptual framing of the middle voice, which allows focus on affectivity and life beyond the ontologies of being active or being passive, thereby rethinking motion in terms of a dynamic and flexible co-affective ontogenesis of the in-between.[28] With appeal to thinkers such as Gilbert Simondon, and employing a method of deconstructively reading Aristotle's categories (through what I call "categorical contamination"), I have tried to argue that life is always a place of relational affective becoming.

With this focus on relational affective becoming in the background, *Beyond Elemental Loss* continues to employ epistemologies of change and, in particular, seeks to gain traction on the ontogenetic space within which

Introduction | 11

life and loss emerges, in combination with philosophical considerations of the cultural transmission of concepts. For instance, in thematizing the loss brought about by earthquakes (discussed in chapter 4), I sketch various theoretical frameworks that build upon each other, starting with Homer and Hesiod, through Aristotle, Kant, and Voltaire, culminating in the theory of contemporary plate tectonics. In diagnosing various shifts in conceptual frameworks (e.g., from external balance to internal orientation), I seek to offer insights into a contemporary world that is increasingly shaky, both literally and metaphorically. Said differently, in this book I call to mind the historical and theoretical transformations informing our relationship to the ecological world, not merely for reasons of theoretical interest, but in order to shift our concern for, and our care of,[29] the ecological home of which we are part. In my view, it is precisely the elemental, as a social-ecological constellation that has been historically conceptualized and that needs to be deconstructed for the present, that can help us to think through this question of forming an epistemology of change and loss in times of anthropogenic climate change.

How the Elemental as a Social-Ecological Constellation Theoretically Deconstructed for the Present Helps Us to Think Through Forming an Epistemology of Ecological Change and Loss

In my effort to redefine the elemental, I appeal to three intersecting methodological pathways that inform my own epistemology: (1) the classic, Presocratic understanding of the elements, offering access to thematizing the elements in an interscalar, material way; (2) John Sallis's Heideggerian account of the elemental as a choric space of appearance, opening up to a view of the elemental as necessary background condition; and (3) Sloterdijk's account of micro and macro spheres, allowing for a sense of the elemental as a space in which we find ourselves, and which we co-create, combined with Irigaray's account of our embodied existence enabled by the elemental. Building upon these three conceptual pathways, I argue that the concept of the elemental is crucial to fashion a contemporary epistemology and ethics that can deal with infinitesimal loss in times of anthropogenic climate change.

From this point, I argue for reconceiving the elemental as a social-ecological constellation that is holding and generative of many forms of beings: it is both subject to diachronic flux—enabling historical transformation—and open to synchronic interaction and co-creation. Instead of static and atemporal, the elemental is viewed as an ontogenetic space of flux. This space of flux is currently, under the pressures of the Anthropocene, a space of incremental (and often problematic) changes that have major effects across various scales, leading to a sense of loss, both within the realm of the material-causal and logical-semantic. To investigate this site of incremental change by way of the elemental allows for grasping loss both on the microlevel (e.g., in terms of the extinction of particular species) and on the macrolevel (e.g., grasping the broader economic and technological forces that engage the earth and increase earthquake risk). The elemental thus ideally serves as an explanatory matrix for grasping various senses of loss without giving up on thematizing the broader ecological-social constellation of which we are part.

The Presocratic Elemental: Perceptive Crystallization Points Amenable to Interscalar Connections

Without focusing on one Presocratic philosopher in particular, I use some of the general content from the Presocratics to extract and radicalize ideas useful for my own analysis. For the Presocratics, the world as we see it includes material changes in the way an element presents itself, and they afford key ideas on the formal principles that rule such material change. For instance, from ice and rain to steam and ponds, water can take on different shapes; still, there are underlying formal principles that rule such change. For Heraclitus, for instance, fire serves both as material flame and as a principle reflective of *logos*.

By looking closely at all (definite) particulars in our physical world, and thinking through what (indefinitely) unites them, various Presocratic thinkers arrived at different answers, ranging from water, to fire, to air, and to earth. As the Presocratic thinker Anaximenes already indicated with regard to air, this element is both particular—it "holds us together and controls us," while air is also something that "surrounds" the entire world—and thereby holds a universal aspiration insofar as it not only constitutes one particular entity but co-constitutes the being of others, and, most importantly, the *kosmos*, as well.[30]

What I would like to keep of the Presocratic engagement with the elemental is (a) its synthetic focus on the coagulation points within which the material ecological world presents itself, enabling both organic and inorganic beings to emerge, and (b) theorizing this synthesis in four ways: water, fire, air, and earth. The explanatory power of the Presocratic elemental consists in its ability to offer a unifying synthetic material framework, while opening up to a wealth of concrete, distinct phenomena that are nonetheless part of broader networks.[31] What I will not adopt from the Presocratics is their focus on an underlying, enduring *logos*, since this is not in line with the argued historical evolution of the elemental and our co-creative engagement with it.

As I reappropriate the Presocratic elemental for my own purposes in this book, I will stress this synthetic capacity, but I will underline that my account of the elemental also seeks to gain traction on (c) our lived experience, and (d) seeks to integrate heterogeneity and the meaning of contemporary scientific insights as well. To speak first to lived experience, since the four elements offer us a "description that crystallizes what is concretely perceptible,"[32] the Presocratic elemental lends itself well to my own phenomenological engagement of the elemental, focusing on perception and lived experience. This is not to say that the elemental is not *more* than how we find it in perception or cannot be further unpacked through micro- or macrolevels; it is rather to say that humans do not know the elemental outside of their engagement in and perception of it.[33] And in thematizing their perception along four such coagulation points—water, fire, air, and earth—the Presocratics add a distilled, clarificatory lens that is both general and specific at the same time.

Moreover, speaking to my theorization of the elemental as a space that can integrate scientific studies of the material world, the elemental is both direct and concretely perceived and interacted with, yet also opens up to a broad scope of other phenomena, indexing the generative capacity of the elemental. As Stacy Alaimo helpfully writes: "Elements are not things, not objects or artifacts, but that which is the substrate for things, as well as life, to emerge."[34] In that regard, elements cannot be easily objectified, since we, as humans, participate in them, just like many other organisms. Cohen and Duckert similarly emphasize the notion that elements can connect the human with the inhuman realm: "Earth, air, fire, and water, alone and in their promiscuous combinations, function within a humanly knowable scale while extending an irresistible invitation to inhuman realms."[35] Thus, both Alaimo and Cohen and Duckert underline the notion that a turn to the elemental, hearkening back to the Presocratics, entails a turn toward what may be called *interscalar* thinking. This includes room to investigate what Cohen and Duckert call "inhuman realms" or what David Abram words as "more-than-human"[36] dimensions.

It is precisely in the aforementioned ability to accommodate interscalar thinking that I seek to push my own conception of the elemental, reinventing the elemental to suit twenty-first-century scientific thought. In my view, there are further "microlevels" (atomic and subatomic) to the elements to be considered, and natural-scientific research can thereby further inform and supplement a Presocratic account of the elemental. In this regard, I argue that the elements of water, fire, air, and earth are not only in themselves elements that entail fluidity, but their origination is in itself also subject to dynamical patterns. While this is more obviously the case when addressing fire, it is also the case for other elements. For instance, scientists have postulated that air—as we currently experience it in our atmosphere—did not exist before and has a historical beginning point in cyanobacteria creating oxygen, followed by plants producing oxygen as well.[37] This means, for my articulation of the elements, that while I take the Presocratic approach to the elemental as a helpful access point to articulating elemental loss (particularly given the Presocratic focus on synthesis), simultaneously the Presocratic approach needs to be complemented by adding examinations of lived experience and contemporary material-scientific insights to accurately deepen and complicate the layers of concrete materiality within which we live.

Moreover, I view the elemental not only in terms of ecological materiality but as materiality subject to human interpolation, such that the elements have undergone changes in meaning, in impact, in expression, alongside human evolution. This theoretical move means that I hold the view that we *are produced and enabled by the elements yet simultaneously change them as we interact with them.* This entails that the elemental, while being more-than-human and having origins outside of our existence, never simply shows up "as it is" but always emerges alongside our perception and our evolution, and it is thoroughly informed by the social-political context within which humans live.[38] It is in this way of connecting the elemental to the human, and thereby to the political, that we can grasp the elemental both as more-than-human and simultaneously as a background condition receptive to social and historical transformation, as Stephanie Clare underlines.[39]

As I reappropriate the elements to make theoretical space for their co-evolution along the lines of social-political human development, I will seek to address the role of human-caused changes in transforming the elements. I will argue that political and economic regimes have informed the way the elements appear and impact us, thus inserting an indubitable human factor in our experience of elemental loss. Small and incremental changes over time have seemed to escape notice until now, in the Anthropocene, where they confront us with a marked sense of ephemeral, elemental loss.

Thus, in short, I adopt from the Presocratics the elemental as synthetic crystallization points enabling interscalar thinking, offering both unity and diversity across the ecological world. Simultaneously, I supplement this perspective with a focus on lived experience and insights gained by science, anthropology, history, mythology, and new materialism,[40] allowing me to add to the Presocratic analysis both phenomenological and contemporary scientific insights into lived experience, the emergence and composition of the elements, as well as social-material insights speaking to the dynamics of human evolution in relationship to the elements. Through this hermeneutic exercise, I seek to imbue the elemental with a new, creative spark, enabling revival and reconstitution of the elemental in times of ecological crisis and loss.

With and Beyond Sallis: Reengineering the Choric Space of Appearance to Accommodate Material-Historical Engagement

In positioning my account of the elements as including both a micro- and a macrolevel and in speaking to both the human and the "inhuman" realm, my approach both intersects with and departs from that of John Sallis's Heideggerian interpretation of the elemental as the choric space of appearance. However, I want to revise and correct Sallis's account of the elemental, since I want to move Sallis's account in (a) a concrete, material rather than an abstract direction, and (b) seek to insert into the elemental a human/social role for interference that seems lacking in Sallis's account. The latter would allow (c) an affective-reflective role for elemental trust to be discussed in chapter 5.

Sallis's analysis convincingly shows that the elements are expansive and, phenomenologically, exceed our senses, thereby providing the notion that nature escapes the sum total of beings:[41]

> The fourfold ἀρχή consists, then, of broad earth, open sea, damp air, and bright, uranic aither. It is from these four that all the things we now look upon have become manifest. Yet

> these four, which constitute the ἀρχή of all things, are not themselves simply things; rather, they are elemental expanses within which or in the crossings or mutual limits of which things can become manifest—as when, illuminated by sunlight, an ancient temple set firmly on the promontory in the distance yet obscured by mist is glimpsed from out at sea.[42]

At the same time, Sallis's attempt to make the elements responsible for the notion of (Heideggerian) divine unconcealment, speaking of the elemental in nearly transcendental terms addressing the "brilliance of their manifestness" in which all things "shine forth,"[43] obscures the effect of human action upon and interaction with the elements, and it thus forecloses upon the notion of elemental loss so fundamental to this book's argument: the notion that, through human-caused factors, incremental changes have been set in motion that have transformed and altered the meaning and the appearance of the elements. While Sallis still wants to hold on to the Romantic image of the stone-bound temple as obscured by mist, his account does not reckon with the destructive forces of climate change that may undo the mist and scorch the earth as the temple goes up aflame in the heat of wildfires. Thus, said in different words, the so-called "brilliant" immutable elemental, choric spaces of which Sallis speaks do not exist in an atemporal, ahistorical, transcendental condition, but are prone to shifts.[44]

Hence, as Sallis addresses the enigmatic ever-expansive sky as the horizon of manifestness, his argument would suffer in the face of examining such openness for manifestness in the Anthropocene. For instance, if ozone were depleted from the sky, and plant and earth life would come to a full stop, nothing but manifestness itself is altered, thus highlighting the fundamental impact of the world of incidental, sensible changes upon the notion of the elemental as background condition.

Moreover, if contemporary phenomenological thinker Michel Serres is correct that the sky is immersed in "a space-time of communication," traversed by messengers such as "planes, satellites, electromagnetic waves from television, radio, fax, electronic mail,"[45] then the elemental space of appearance itself is thoroughly humanized, transformed, and mediated. Similarly, if earthquakes, including those caused by human action such as through gas drilling, lead to vertigo and a radical sense of disorientation, then the elemental manifestation of our material conditions also radically stands to be altered. In a world in which anthropogenic climate change wreaks havoc on our planet, not even the notion of elemental excess and manifestness is exempt from extinction. Together with our all-too-human flaws, the elemental too will be affected.

For these reasons, I seek to overcome Sallis's interpretation of the elemental, adding a more concrete, material-historical specificity to the elemental, while also inserting a distinct role for human interaction within the elemental. To fill in what I mean by this specific level of human interaction and co-engineering[46] of the elemental, addressing the broader cultural and ontological forces that produce our atmospheric and embodied conditions of living, I will turn to discuss how my account both implements and critiques Sloterdijk's and Irigaray's accounts of atmospheres and elements.

Reimagining Sloterdijk's Spheres and Irigaray's Elements to Theorize Embodied Participation in Elemental Constellations

My project on elemental loss uses aspects of Sloterdijk's spherology, particularly in Sloterdijk's helpful spatial theorization of place-making in the form of "spheres," such as bubbles—on the intimate microlevel of personal relationships—and foams—on the macrolevel of cultural, multicentered ways of living—postulating the engineering of co-created, air-conditioning atmospheres ("greenhouses") of existence.[47] However, versus Sloterdijk, I seek to dispel the purely "human-made" character of the constellations ("greenhouses") that he emphasizes. Rather, I want to intersect his project on spheres with that of the (natural-material) elemental as the Presocratics thematized it. For Sloterdijk, place and human coexistence are co-constitutive of each other:

> An inquiry into our location is more productive than ever, as it examines the place that humans create in order to have somewhere they can appear as those who they are. Here, following a venerable tradition, this place bears the name "sphere." The sphere is the interior, disclosed, shared realm inhabited by humans—insofar as they succeed in becoming humans. . . . Spheres are immune-systematically effective space creations for ecstatic beings that are operated upon by the outside.[48]

For Sloterdijk, spheres both create and structure human coexistence and are, vice versa, the products of such human coexistence. Subject to constant adaptation, spheres are "air conditioning systems in whose construction and calibration, for those living in real coexistence, it is out of the question not to participate."[49]

The advantage of adding a Sloterdijkian viewpoint on spheres to my analysis of the elemental is that it provides a comprehensive notion of humanity's role in the creation of place, home, and atmosphere. Where Heidegger focused on time, being, and solitary existence (particularly in *Being and Time*), Sloterdijk adds emphasis on place, becoming, and coexistence, thinking through the way our existence is always indebted to others, and to the co-creation of places in coexistence. This provides an important insight for my account of the elemental, as it can work to correct Sallis's approach to the elemental by stressing the fact that the elemental is not simply a place of divine unconcealment or a gift of Being, but instead a space of elemental appearing that is informed by real efforts of formal design, technical production, legal support, and political molding.[50] What is worthwhile in Sloterdijk's notion of spheres is his attempt to show that constellations are places we both find *and* build, and that we always have a mediated relationship to these spheres, as they are culturally and technologically created.

However, while Sloterdijk's account of spheres is productive for my account of the elemental in terms of adding the social-technological mediation with the elemental, what is problematic is his negligence in discussing the ecological dimensions of the places that we live in. While his articulation of warfare and airfare indicates the ways in which humans have increasingly explicitly thematized, and transformed, air, the material-ecological condition of our existence, as well as the broader role of the elemental for our systems of co-immunity and coexistence, has been omitted from his discussion. For this reason, the account of the elemental as I offer it in this book can appeal to Sloterdijk, but this book will also use more ecologically oriented accounts to supplement his omissions.

In resisting Sloterdijk's emphasis on the *mere* anthropogenic, or, in his words, "anthropotechnic" generation of our elemental spheres, Luce Irigaray's thoughts on the elemental offer recourse, since she emphasizes both the ecological dimension of the elemental as well as the way in which we, as embodied, driven humans, are experiencing the elemental. For Irigaray, "the elements represent 'natural matters' that originate our bodies and lives as well as the environment and 'the flesh of our passions.'"[51] As Irigaray writes in her reflections on Nietzsche in *Marine Lover*: "Deeper than the solid crust you must now descend to announce the meaning of the earth. Remember what happens on the inside so that you can be sure of where you are running on the outside. And realize that a solid plane is never just a solid plane. That it rests on subterranean and submarine life, on capped fires and winds which yet stir ceaselessly beneath that shell."[52] Irigaray is keen to point out the *elemental depth* that enables our embodied lives, referencing earth, water, fire, and air (in her words: "sea, sun, air, and earth") that lie beneath the surface, enabling, informing, and transforming our lives. Just as Nietzsche's mountains need a reminder of such elemental depth, at least in Irigaray's view,[53] Heidegger similarly needs a reminder that his notion of being-in-the-world is, in the first place, one of elemental becoming, namely that of becoming "airborn": "Going out of the mother, I come into the air, I enter into the world, and into the community of living beings."[54] In pointing to the forceful *forgetting* of elementals such as air (in the case of Heidegger) or water (in the case of Nietzsche), Irigaray shows that Western thinking has emphasized human domination, initiating a path toward violence: "Nature in its elemental multiplicity is already bowed to the autarchy of a power: *physis* already opened up by and for man in accordance with his needs, or desires, to appear."[55]

Irigaray's point demands underlining, in that it corrects Sloterdijk's spherological point that the atmosphere can simply be owned or engineered: the elemental, for instance in the form of air, will always be a communal space open to others—both other human and nonhuman living others as well as other inorganic substrates that are part of our world. Irigaray's access point also returns us to the strength of Sallis's account of the elemental, in emphasizing the choric space of appearance, but Irigaray does so without Sallis's problematic highlighting of the metaphysical gift of Being, rather stressing the importance of *beings* and their material, fluid, elemental ontogenesis.[56]

This is not to say that I do not find certain aspects of Irigaray's elemental problematic, such as her claims about the radical dichotomy between men and women, which is at odds with her claims regarding a shared and continuous elemental materiality.[57] Moreover, I need to distance my own account of the elemental from Irigaray's tendency to appeal to dreams and imagination for theorizing the elemental.[58] Of course, this trajectory, of connecting the elemental to imagination and to the subconscious, can be worthwhile in itself and has an important scholarly philosophical predecessor in Gaston Bachelard,[59] who wrote that "the four elements [are] the hormones of the imagination."[60] Moreover, as Bachelard clarifies the link between the imagination and the elements, our imagination regarding the elements tracks and condenses the worldly reality: "They [the elements] help in assimilating inwardly the reality that is dispersed among forms."[61]

However, versus Irigaray and Bachelard, my project is precisely *not* about pursuing the imaginary power of the elemental, not even when this imaginary elemental, according to Bachelard, tracks or assimilates the reality of the world. Since the point of gravity in my project is to discern the elemental in terms of the historically and culturally emergent ways in which ecology and society emerge, my focus will not be on the elemental as accessed through the imagination but on the elemental as materially informed and historically transformed through the *thick medium of culture and history* (which, admittedly, in that form may include cultural imagination[62]). Thus, my point here subverts Marx's claim, that matter produces ideology and culture, to argue that (cultural) historical mediation intersects with ecological factors to produce shifting meanings and appearances of the elemental.

Four Elements and Portals into Elemental Loss

The *structure* of the book follows the need for a situated focus on the losses I speak of, and traces the elements of water, fire, air, and earth. Accordingly, it is divided into four main chapters, which each analyze an element and a particular form of loss. The book begins by investigating loss as connected to oceanic extinction, migration, colonialism, and shifting relationships to the sea and its shores. The second chapter discusses fire and loss, and investigates fire both in terms of its mythological conception and in its current iteration as industrial fire and climate-change induced megafires. The third chapter is devoted to shared constellations of air, the engineering and creation of bad air, and the inequity of and rights to breathing good air. The fourth chapter is devoted to earth, earthquakes, and loss of equilibrium—this chapter asks the question of what is lost when the ground shifts, literally, and we find ourselves tumbling, disoriented, in need of orientation and recalibration.

Since the elemental in the form of water, fire, air, and earth includes such broad and deep terrain, I offer various *portals* into the elemental, moving from local aspects of the elemental to more global factors, thereby weaving together a philosophical story aimed at doing justice to the various layers of the elemental while opening up to the emerging sense of loss that has come to pervade our relationship to the elemental. The particular portals offer, as historical instantiations, access to the elements; thereby they give access to a synthetic manifold while also seeking to speak to the historical and particularized nature of living with and in the elements.

For instance, in accessing the element of water, I start with the altered seashores and intertidal life on the coast of the province of Zeeland in the Netherlands, to then discuss oceanic extinction, tracing oceanic slave-trading from Zeeland to the shores of the Caribbean, trying to find oceanic languages that can revive opportunities in the liminal connections to the water that we used to call home. For the chapter on air, I have chosen the portal of illness, particularly allergic and asthmatic illness, to access the complexities of air, air pollution, pollen, and social inequity. The portal of illness renders visible, I argue, an oscillation between particularized sensitive bodies and the airy medium in which they take part; it is through how a particular kind of participation is historically produced in the space of interaction between these two that certain bodies more than others are made subject to layers of attrition and diminution.

As for these four elements—water, fire, air, and earth—that I explore, it is important to mention that these same elements emerge in cross-cultural comparisons—for instance, in Chinese philosophy. As Macauley notes, this very overlap speaks to "both the near universality and cultural particularity of conceptions of the elements."[63] While cross-cultural comparisons could be worthwhile, given my focus on the historical transmission of concepts within the current Western worldview and relationship toward the elemental, I will, for this book, omit such comparisons.[64] Moreover, as mentioned, given the historical mediation within this tradition that has precisely given rise to our sense of loss within the climate crisis, this approach has a diagnostic value as well. Simultaneously, my account of the elemental is sufficiently elastic to include discussion of non-Western accounts of the elemental as well. Case in point is my account of indigenous Californian ways of handling fire to be used upon the land in a creative way (as discussed in chapter 2), offering a significant counterpoint to Western ways of handling and relating to fire.

In breaking up the book into four main chapters each devoted to a particular element, the book seeks to acquire conceptual depth, without denying intersection between the topics of each chapter. Already in the *Theogony*, Hesiod describes the "family" of elements, for instance in the personified elements of Earth (Gaia), mother of many, including Heaven (Ouranos) and Ocean.[65] Relatedly, as Empedocles in his writings confirms, water, fire, air, and earth constantly intermingle. Accordingly, I seek to follow the trajectory of Empedocles's philosophy, which does not prioritize one element over the others, but sees the four elements—or in his words: roots (*rhizomata*)—as equally important as they temporarily mix or are separated from each other due to the forces of love and strife.[66] Thus, the elements could arguably be said to "belong" to each other, as John Sallis shows in this analysis of the connection between sea and earth: "In a certain respect the sea is an opposite of earth, not in a purely formal sense but in a sense at once both sensible and elemental: the sea offers no support at all, in contrast to earth, which supports all, earth from which virtually all other support is, in one way or another, borrowed. And yet, sea belongs to earth, even dividing and articulating its surface."[67] Given the interaction between the elements, the senses of loss I address speak as much to the elements under discussion respectively in each chapter as to the interface and interaction *between* the elements. This means that discussions occurring in one chapter—for instance, the smoke caused by California megafires—have impact on the discussion of air in another chapter. Thus, this book seeks to offer a rigorous discussion of the elements in each chapter, while seeking to remain flexible in and open to offering cross-references that speak to interaction between the elements.

The fifth, and final, chapter functions as a conclusion, as it seeks to bring the four main chapters together. I argue that the losses that are tangibly felt in relationship to the elemental constellations have been accompanied by a loss of trust in both the elemental (material-social) constellations that provide us a home *and* in our relationship to the elemental. If it is the case that trust, when operative, is invisible,[68] and if it is the case that trust, when functioning, offers a sense of security and feeling at home in the elemental world,[69] then the historical changes underlying anthropogenic climate change have confronted us with shifts in the elemental that have left in their wake a profound loss of trust and thus a sense of disorientation. Based off Elinor Ostrom's model of communities sharing the commons collaboratively and Michel Serres's proposal for a dialogical exchange with the elemental and the communities around it, I postulate that a new kind of ethics and politics based on elemental trust can transform our sense of elemental loss into one of elemental change, moving us away from powerlessness and disorientation toward agency and reorientation.[70]

Chapter 1

Water

Living and Speaking Oceanic Loss

On Extinction, Migration, and Language(s)

To imagine a language is to imagine a form of life.

—Ludwig Wittgenstein, *Philosophical Investigations*

The environment and people always and already are given together in language.

—Robert Mugerauer, "Language and the Emergence of Environment"

The philosopher keeps watch over unforeseeable and fragile conditions, his position is unstable, mobile, suspended, the philosopher seeks to leave ramifications and bifurcations open, in opposition to the confluences that connect them or close them.

—Michel Serres, *Genesis*

My childhood is cast in the colors of the sea. There is the grayish-green of the IJsselmeer, the former Zuiderzee ("South Sea"), which became a freshwater lake after it was dammed in 1933. Close to our family home, the IJsselmeer is where we swam on hot summer days to cool off in its sweet-tasting waters. There is the grayish-blue color of the

Oosterschelde—an estuary whose waters radically changed after sea barriers were placed as part of the Deltawerken project in the province of Zeeland—where we returned each summer to the native grounds where both my parents were born and raised. I remember a day spent watching my mother there, the look into her past that place afforded:

I watch closely as my mother and her oldest sister engage in planning for their swim excursion. This must have been a daily part of their youth, of their sisterhood, of their family summer routine, freedom found amid the waves, the joy and power of their young female bodies, so constrained in so many other ways.

Their excitement at scanning the tidal schedules is palpable, contagious, even late in adulthood. It means so much more than just physical exercise. Their daily clocks lined up with the tides of the sea, they immerse and emerge. An oceanic rebirth?

The nostalgia palpable in this memory does not preclude the darkness that the same water holds. It was in these waters that close to two thousand people, in the province of Zeeland alone, drowned in the North Sea Flood of 1953. The same flood also affected Belgium, England, and Scotland, causing casualties there as well.[1] My mother, who had just recently acquired her driver's license at the time, still trembled as she recounted her chauffeuring people to safety in the days after the flood.

Thus, these transformed waters—the IJsselmeer and the Oosterschelde—inform my being with colors that go deeper than my own recollection and even that of my parents. They speak to the way a country and a culture, in this case the Netherlands, has built for its own national project—but also for the people confined within its territorial jurisdiction—a relation to the surrounding seas. What reverberates are not only personal anecdotes[2] but also stories of a country emerging out of the water, its vulnerability to water, its consequent battle to control water, and, as is the case with many colonial powers, its use of that water to subjugate other peoples. For example, in the particular case of the province of Zeeland,[3] what is important to recall is how its seafaring skills were put to service in the Dutch colonial project and the horrendous transatlantic slave trade.[4] If the sea is philosophically and historically characterized as delimiting the boundaries of the place we might call home and houses not only dynamic fluidity but also openness and infinite possibilities, then the people of Zeeland radically transformed the relationship to their sense of home. They did so by altering their relationship to the sea, both through historical (colonial) globalizing navigation and through technological interventions such as the construction of dams and dikes that changed the flow and character of the sea as much as the land itself. In both cases, the sea was instrumentalized and pushed beyond what had been the liminal spaces that offered counterpoints of potentiality in order to actualize a particular passageway that would diminish the binding sense of belonging and of home to the sea.

As I have moved across oceans the past few decades and lived nearby one of them (until recently this was the bright-blue Pacific Ocean off the coast of Marin, with its cold, uninviting waters and treacherous currents), my life's relationship to the sea comes into focus. A perhaps somewhat ungrounded but fortunate (im)migrant, I have had a hard time deciding what or who to call "home" but have settled on a preliminary answer, with home found not in the so-called solid substances such as ground or nation, but in the *connections, the shores, the transitions, and the interfaces to the open: in short, in the passageways that are made in and through the water.*

What exactly does it mean to call the interfaces with the sea one's home, however? More difficult still, what does it mean to experience home, in the words of Michel Serres, in an interface such as the sea that is dying, a sea that is dead, in foul waters full of dying fish, with depths scraped by trawl nets and then saturated with garbage?[5] How should we grasp this loss experienced at sea, losses brought on by industrialization and the expansion of capital? And what would it imply for the kind of responses we could offer?

This chapter investigates the sea and its shores as liminal spaces that offer counterpoint to our potentials and argues, following Sloterdijk and Despret, that the losses felt at sea and at its shores not only diminish *one* way of being in the world but contract the meaning of world *as* world. However, this contraction of the world of water, I want to argue, need not remain at the level of elemental loss but can be transformed once a new epistemology and semantics is generated, as Serres and Ingersoll[6] maintain. I conclude this chapter by exploring Édouard Glissant's archipelagic thinking, which enables me to turn to the Caribbean islands and to argue that the experience of shared loss as manifested on its shores and seas need not only be negative but may be generative in fostering an ethics and politics that is fundamentally organized in a multilinguistic and nonhierarchical fashion.

Extinction and Loss of World and Home

Amid the Sixth Great Extinction, we find ourselves confronted with alarming numbers of loss. It is estimated that 150–200 species of plants, insects, birds, and mammals are going extinct every twenty-four hours, and that more than 26,500 species of life are currently threatened with extinction. If we look into the future, the scenario is even more dire: "The latest governmental panel report on climate change has predicted that once the level [of carbon dioxide] reaches 450 possibly by midcentury, humans will have pushed roughly a quarter of the planet's creatures into extinction. If it reaches 500 parts per million—about double preindustrial levels—we will have caused the genetic extermination of up to 70 percent of living things."[7]

When we focus on the ocean, we can ascertain a range of effects that climate change has had and will have. Due to global warming and the rise of the concentration of carbon dioxide in the atmosphere, the volume of the sea is increasing and various chemical changes are occurring.[8] This results in changes in the levels of oxygen (a decrease) and pH (decreasing, which means water is turning more acidic), as well as warming of waters (which increases the metabolism of fish) and decreased currents (due to decreased amounts of cold water sinking).

Overall, changes in the ocean's chemistry and specifically ocean acidification may be disastrous, and, for that reason, "ocean acidification is sometimes referred to as global warming's 'equally evil twin.'"[9] Once we realize that ocean acidification was involved in "at least two of the Big Five Extinctions (the end-Permian and the end-Triassic),"[10] it is no far stretch to imagine ocean life dying out now, as it did then.

With the question of extinction comes the question of the meaning of what is (or will be) lost. Usually, when we contemplate loss, we think of the loss of individualized beings. This is a predominant conception in the philosophical tradition, typified by Heidegger's well-known account of being-toward-death, which focuses on the loss of a unique being confronted with its own finitude.[11] However, if we want to conceptualize loss from a different vantage point, one that focuses on broader material, social levels and thus has different political valances, we will need an account that goes beyond individual loss. Peter Sloterdijk offers a helpful starting point, exploring instead connections with other beings both on micro- and on macro-spherological levels. In *Bubbles*, the first volume in his *Spheres* trilogy, Sloterdijk argues that life is always lived—on the intimate level—in biune spheres bordered by semipermeable membranes that keep us both protected and open. And, when he addresses the macrolevel in *Foams*, he argues that our bonds grow deeper and older, and, as the membranes stretch thinner and become more fragile, we can speak of an increased "shared existential risk."[12]

Thus, in Sloterdijk's rearticulation of loss, even if it is still confined to a certain class of beings, we begin to see the first outlines of a theory that addresses loss in terms of the falling apart of a constellation, with special attention for the effects of such dissipating spheres on the (former) inhabitants of such a constellation. As Sloterdijk states: "What Heidegger called being-toward-death means not so much the individual's long march into a final solitude anticipated with panic-stricken resolve; it is rather the circumstance that all individuals will one day leave the space in which they were allied with others in a current, strong relationship. That is why death ultimately concerns the survivors more than the deceased."[13]

A constellation can be many things, but, for our purposes, let us push Sloterdijk's argument along an environmental pathway and fill in the content of the abstract alliance with a conception of ecological relation across species. Toward this end, Vinciane Despret provides the paradigm of species extinction. Recounting the effects of the extinction of the passenger pigeon in 1914, Despret argues that what is lost with its extinction is not just *a* being. Rather, the loss is more properly understood as a contraction, a narrowing of world; what is lost, even more fundamentally, is that which makes the world *as* world:

> But what the world has lost is not what people mourn. What the world has lost, and what truly matters, is a part of what invents and maintains it as world. . . . The entire universe thinks and feels itself, and each being matters in the fabric of its sensations. Every sensation of every being of the world is a mode through which the world lives and feels itself, and through which it exists. And every sensation of every being of the world causes all the beings of the world to feel and think themselves differently. When a being is no more, the world narrows all of a sudden, and a part of reality collapses. Each time an existence disappears, it is a piece of the universe of sensations that fades away.[14]

For Despret, extinction implies a reduction of the constitution of the world *as* world and a fading of meaning, being, and sensation. If sensation and meaning are associated with the whole—the constellation, the world, the living, breathing Gaia—then what is lost are the effects of the passenger pigeons upon the sky—the fact that the sun will no longer be untimely eclipsed by vast, dense swarms of them that would darken the sky sometimes for hours, the sensations of wings flapping by the thousands, their play with the wind, and so on.[15] From the inside out, the unique perspective of the passenger pigeon, traversing space freely, feeling airdrops on one's wings, finding thousands of wings around it in the air—all that is lost. As Despret sums this up: "Humanity can mourn the Passenger Pigeon. But it is the world that bursts with its absence."[16]

If we extend Despret's analysis to the threat of extinction and oceanic changes near my childhood home and the North Sea, research indicates a shift in terms of cold-loving (plaice and flounder) and heat-loving (sea bass, shrimp) species.[17] Moreover, what will happen to the crustaceans[18] living in the North Sea and the Oosterschelde, if the pH further dips and their shells dissolve?[19] What if we focus on one of the fifty-two thousand species of crustaceans, for instance, on the sea snail living on the North Sea shores called the common periwinkle (*Littorina littorea*)—in Zeelandic: *krukel*—and imagine its extinction? The common periwinkle lives in the intertidal zone, which is above water level at low tide and underwater at high tide.[20] Should the periwinkle disappear, what would be lost is its connection to the tides, its exposure to air during low tide and its immersion in water during high tide, its ability to experience both the wet and the dry, its liminal position on rocks and kelp along the seashore, and its u-shaped path of grazing algae, not to mention its specific construction of its own microclimate in the sea conducive to building its shell.[21]

On the human side, the *krukel* has its gastronomic appeal—common in Britain, France, Belgium, and part of the Netherlands—and this was also part of my family tradition: collecting, cooking, and eating them. But there are other levels of connection. Should we lose the periwinkle, we may lose the connecting evolutionary bridge to land snails and thus lose their shared evolutionary paths showing divergent paths of adaptation to the elements of earth, water, and air, as "it may be assumed that one of the paths leading to the evolution of terrestrial snails, went by the ancestors of both periwinkles and terrestrial operculate snails."[22]

Overall, should we lose the common periwinkle, we do not only lose this unique being, holding steadily on to rocks while waves crash above, fully committed to water and flux, but we lose, following Despret, its effects on the water and the water's inhabitants, its way of traveling and eating algae, its way of stirring up sedimentation and increasing flow along the shores. Rocks will no longer be covered by dense clusters gathered together, their surface exposed without the whirling and spherical protrusions that now cover them. From the inside out, we lose a being that is both hard and soft, and that can be safely locked up in its own home or be physically disclosed to various elements.[23] We lose its unique ability to attach to rock and be exposed to both air and water, and to dynamically and steadfastly undergo the various surfs and tides. Thus, similar to Despret's analysis of the passenger pigeon, what may be felt in this case is not just the loss of a being, but the central disruption to meaning as the intertidal lived space between rock, water, and air loses its glue, dissipates, and contracts due to lost connections.

From a Narrative of Death and Extinction toward a Narrative of Revitalization

Amid the Sixth Great Extinction and the devastating impacts of climate change, it is hard to escape the narrative of death and loss. And, in many ways, death and loss first have to be truly acknowledged, politically and ethically, before we can move forward. But in order to be able to acknowledge these nonindividuated losses in the social realm of politics and ethics, we need to be able to figure what is being lost. One of the ways of moving forward here, I want to suggest, is to follow Michel Serres's lead in *Biogea*, where he is seeking a new discourse and epistemology that is truly responsive to the forces of life and earth.

Serres's starting point in *Biogea* is that there is (a) a need to first *sense* and grasp the loss that is taking place, for it is from this point that we can understand the causes of our current calamity. However, asserting and examining loss is not enough. Serres's second main point centers on what is to be done toward a possible rebirth of our earth and its diverse species. To accomplish this, Serres provides us with (b) a distinct ontology that views all forms of existence (both organic and nonorganic) as interconnected and communicating. The task he outlines next is that of (c) generating a new semantic realm that *taps into* this communicating ("coding") realm of reality with more receptive, holistic connections.

(a) As Serres is seeking a culprit at the heart of the pollution and extinction that threatens nature, he finds not one in particular, but the murderous capacity of a multitude: "Persons sometimes kill; the collective always kills."[24] It is the collective that is to blame,[25] who names and throws objects before us and considers them rejected and disposable: "trashcan-Earth, polluted air, dead seas . . . soiled by us for us to appropriate them. Destroyed by a collective that's narcissistic in its turn."[26] And in analyzing the various steps in history that have brought us to the point of collapse, Serres points to the "brilliant" scientists in Western history, such as Archimedes, to show how Western thinking,[27] from the beginning, has been preoccupied with competition and warfare.[28]

Additionally, Serres attributes disrespect for earth and life on the current dominant European forms of language, which have put "all the things of the world . . . locked up behind their bars,"[29] removing us from having true contact with the phenomena themselves and ossifying them in their stilted, objectifying approach. According to Serres, our current language and modus operandi are flawed and have covered over the natural forces—both in the sense of earth (*gea*) and life (*bios*)—obscuring reality for what it is and accessing nature in a merely appropriative, anthropocentric, calculative way: "For thousands of years, we have been licking our things with tongues, covering and daubing so as to appropriate things for ourselves. If language boils down to a convention, this convention took place between the speakers without consulting the thing named, become as a result the property of those who covered it in this way with their drawn or voiced productions."[30] For Serres, language has not only covered over but has also made it impossible to *sense* what he calls nature, reality, life: "Thus every inert object, every living thing as well, sleeps under the covers of signs." Nature and reality have become excluded from perception, and "this appropriation covers the world's beauty with ugliness."[31]

(b) Serres is not interested in a nonlinguistic world, however. The force of his critique is largely down to the particular way some dominant languages have come to index nature through linguistics. But before turning toward Serres's radical new language, it is necessary to take a detour through his conception of ontology, which will prove vital in understanding how language functions in Serres's estimation.

The ontological view that Serres provides us of the world and nature is one of complexity, fluidity, chance, interconnection, and communication: "Caused, causing, all things in the world ensue from each other, chained together. Whether fluid or air—even solids communicate—things respire together, they conspire with different breaths, but in a constant and total circulation that's chancy, torn, chaotic and consenting."[32] This interconnection is deep and variable, as Serres's example indicates: "El Niño spreads ocean and atmospheric currents, brush fires, thunderstorms and droughts around the world."[33]

The Biogea, then, has a holistic character, one in which Serres can distinguish certain patterns—"music, waves, codes"[34]—while also emphasizing the role of chance: "Everything, on the contrary, in the unpredictable, via contingent lightning bolts and impacts. Everything via the diagonal, the oblique, the inclines, the random without reason."[35]

A crucial component of Serres's ontology is that living and nonliving things express themselves and do so in reciprocal interaction with each other: for instance, the howling of the wind happens when two different currents of wind—broken up by objects such as trees—mix together. The emergence of expression is, for Serres, born out of commotion, out of turbulence. This "expressive" quality of the wind is, for Serres, no different from the kind of expression that human language offers, in that it is born out of movement, out of embodied affect, and expresses itself in certain kinds of rhythms or patterns.[36] This is a fundamental point in Serres's ontology, namely that all living and nonliving things "receive, transmit, store and process information."[37] Expressive content thus occurs beyond the (traditionally human) linguistic levels: it happens at all inorganic and organic levels.

(c) From this expressive ontology, Serres seeks to engage a language that has "reciprocity,"[38] which means "to be able to understand what the earth is telling us but also effectively communicate for the earth the needs of all the animals and the planet itself."[39] Serres's philosophical mission is to provide new stories that go before and beyond our current language, to tickle our senses to awaken them to the true splendor of the forces of *gea* and *bios*, and to seek a new beginning to our language and thus to our epistemology and to our new being: a rebirth, as it were, to who we may become.

In order to precipitate this rebirth, in Serres's thinking, it will be necessary—like Aldo Leopold's invocation to "think like a mountain"[40] but even more broadly so—to sense and think "like the entire Biogea, the entirety of the Earth and the living species."[41] To think like the Biogea, we have to let go of simply connecting to the Biogea as if it were a background noise to civilization: it has to emerge as the front and center of our lives. "As we recount encounters in the flux spaces of coding that Serres outlines, we provide expressive content to a new semantics."[42]

For Serres, expressive content is not localized in any one arena but can find shape in science, coding, poetry, philosophy, music, sensation, embodiment, dreams, mythologies, and stories. According to Serres, some of these access paths have been walked by previous cultures: for instance, the Druid practice that saw human and tree life deeply interwoven and involved climbing oak trees and deep venturing into the forests. And, adding on to Serres, it is important to note that some contemporary Indigenous people continue to practice lifeways like these. While none of these arenas alone may channel a rebirth, together such various access paths may allow us channels to holistically hear the voices of earth and life.[43]

What unites these various arenas in Serres's thinking is that they are all "soft" places as opposed to the "hard," where Serres, in Treanor's words, associates soft with "culture, concepts, ideas, signs, meaning, and, generally, human accounts of reality," and hard with "the domain of nature, the given, the physical, the world of objects, reality independent of human perception of it."[44] Serres writes: "Without this soft place, spiritually very old, but newly conceived in this way, without the juridical construction of a common good, opposed to our filthy ownership, I don't see how our planet, hard, will survive. Hardness that depends on softness, material belonging that depends on this temporary rented location."[45]

To allow for a transformation that seeks to "efface" the self in order to "let it [the world] ring,"[46] we need to pause and reorient ourselves around that which Serres calls the ultimate eddy: "The meaning of the living and the non-meaning of things converge in the muteness of the world; this meaning and non-meaning plunge there and come out, the ultimate eddy."[47] For Serres, silence plays an important role in turning us around, both in, I want to argue, a literal and a metaphorical sense. Serres asks us to seek a retreat away from the business of the world, and its cacophony of human voices, to efface ourselves and mute our own, anthropocentric language. We may do so, as Serres shows through his autobiographical descriptions, by feeling the rumbling of earthquakes, dwelling in the mountains, and being shaken at sea. In those instances, Serres implores us to turn to the fount of language in the Biogea, where meaning and nonmeaning tumble over each other, and where the inexpressible meets the expressible. We may also access this silence in a more metaphorical way seeking to move away from established languages and the conceptual abyss imposed by the divide between the humanities and the sciences. While critics often see Serres as merely promoting an idea of "deep nature" without necessarily also emphasizing culture and language, Serres is committed to the transformative power of silence in bringing us beyond existing discourses to establish a new, more hospitable, and generous language. Things should not rename hidden behind subjectivist language, nor remain nameless for Serres, but rather should be "reborn in their code proper name."[48]

While I would like to criticize Serres for drawing an opposition between "hard" and "soft" that, at least at first sight, seems to lead us back to problematic dualisms such as nature versus culture, or fact versus value, Serres's intention may be appreciated in its radicality: he thinks that without a new epistemological, linguistic, and social paradigm, not only we, humans, but the entire earth is prone to decay. And, by highlighting the importance of the "common good," Serres also clearly indexes how by tapping into the "universal language" of the Biogea a new language should steer us in our new conceptions: from individuality to commonality, from ownership to temporary tenancy, from separation to interconnection.[49] To exemplify what the grammar of such new languages should entail, Serres highlights his "philosophy of prepositions," which prioritizes random encounters that allow for co-birth and rebirth with other beings[50] and marginalizes focus on subjects and verbs that signify a solitary existence.[51]

Thus, in short, for Serres silence serves as both (1) a negative moment to move us away from our subjectivist, anthropocentric, and one-sided horizons, and (2) a positive moment where silence, by bathing us in deeper truths of the Biogea, promotes and informs a new language.

On the Way to Aquatic Speech Acts: Ingersoll and Glissant

INGERSOLL AND AQUATIC LANGUAGE

If we pay attention to Serres's quest for a language that is responsive to the Biogea, one that is informed by "the codes" emitted by living beings and things, what would a language be that is responsive to the sea, and what guides may such language seek?[52] Who or what may guide the way, and who or what may consequently express its danger, its current vulnerability to extinction, but also its ability to be reborn? Other than its literal way of drowning out noise as one submerses in its water, how may the sea, in both a material and a figurative sense, allow us to gain traction on the silence that may bring forth a new language?

Following Karin Amimoto Ingersoll's book *Waves of Knowing*, we could argue that the sea offers an innovative epistemological paradigm for a language and epistemology that emphasize holism over reductionism and that stimulate us to think, speak, and feel in a more fluid, open, and connected way. In other words, the sea arguably offers what Ingersoll speaks as a "seascape epistemology,"[53] which is grounded on "local ways of knowing, researching, and producing knowledge"[54] as lived and embodied by Indigenous Hawaiians (Kānaka Maoli) rather than as imposed by a colonial reality.[55]

For her, seascape epistemology "is an approach to knowing through a visual, spiritual, intellectual, and embodied literacy of the 'āina (land) and *kai* (sea): birds, the colors of clouds, the flows of the current fish and seaweed, the timing of ocean swells, depths, tides, and celestial bodies all circulating and flowing with rhythms and pulsations. . . . Seascape epistemology embraces an oceanic literacy that can articulate the potential for travel and discovery, for a re-creation and a de-creation."[56]

Ingersoll emphasizes that seascape epistemology does not treat the sea as a thing. Rather, resounding much of Serres's plea for new biogeological sciences that emphasize interconnection rather than separation, Ingersoll argues that seascape epistemology offers "a knowledge about the ocean and the wind as an *interconnected system* that allows for successful navigation through them. It's an approach to life and knowing through passageways."[57] Such an emphasis on passageways, rather than Euclidean geometrical mapping through vectoring,[58] speaks, according to Ingersoll, to the sea's "inability to be mapped."[59]

Ingersoll's focus on epistemology as based on *relationships* to land and sea echoes Leonard's claim about the reclamation of Miami language: namely that such reclamation is ultimately about restoring relationships.[60] Both Ingersoll and Leonard emphasize that an oceanic knowledge (Ingersoll) or the reclamation of language (Leonard) depend on what Leonard references as the "physical, spiritual, and relational contexts"[61] that underpin such knowledge or language.

The advantage of Ingersoll's account over Serres's is that it highlights a particular phenomenology of the sea through a non-Western, Indigenous perspective. And, in contrast to Serres's personal anecdotes of his time in the navy or the male comradery of the pontoon boat, Ingersoll offers a view on a distinctly inclusive and collaborative Hawaiian collectivity living with and off the sea. And, while Ingersoll's account initially seems restrictive, compared to Serres's more global call, it is arguably the case that (re)vitalizing local knowledges and practices is a way toward regenerative (global) futures.

As we ponder the way forward amid climate change and extinction, Ingersoll's focus on the Indigenous act of navigation (*hoʻokele*) at sea brings out "the sea as something that one must connect with in order to navigate and survive within."[62] In contrast with European colonial narratives that relate to the sea "as something to be conquered, survived, and at best discovered," Ingersoll thus provides a way forward to "a malleable understanding of borders and coastlines."[63]

GLISSANT AND THE LANGUAGE OF THE SEA

Another track for an aquatic language may follow the currents of my problematic Dutch colonial past to the Caribbean. The Caribbean islands include the Dutch Caribbean islands, located in the "Lesser Antilles archipelago of the Caribbean Sea,"[64] which were used by the Dutch in the eighteenth century as "depots" for the transatlantic slave trade.[65] To think through a language of the sea that speaks to this archipelago informed by colonialism, Édouard Glissant's *Poetics of Relation*[66] will be particularly productive. While the Dutch treated the Caribbean as a simple navigational link and site of economic rent extraction, Glissant shows us the profound meaning of this sea-informed place as well as the repercussions that the slave trade has had on those who arrived there. The harrowing experience with which Glissant's *Poetics of Relation* begins is that of being cast into the belly of a boat, of seeing fellow humans being thrown overboard as heavy ballast to lighten the boat, and arriving upon a new unknown land, haunted by the mourning of the former land. He writes: "For though this experience made you, original victim floating toward the sea's abysses, an exception, it became something shared and made us, the descendants, one people among others. Peoples do not live on exception. Relation is not made up of things that are foreign but of shared knowledge. This experience of the abyss can now be said to be the best element of exchange."[67] Rather than seeing the experience of the sea's abyss only from the perspective of loss or from the perspective of the singular individual, Glissant demonstrates that a new future may be built upon a collective memory and a shared knowledge. Politically, this may allow for trust and change to emerge out of suffering and loss, and may provide a vision of the possibility of an epistemology that is born out of multiplicity yet built out of shared knowledge relations.

Glissant's embrace of a vision of synthetic possibility as emerging out of the Caribbean stands in contrast to two other influential Caribbean thinkers: Césaire and Fanon. "For Glissant, both Césaire and Fanon are still diverters and not properly producers of a new reality, of a real Caribbean territory and history." While finding himself located in-between those two thinkers, Glissant "neither advocates a reconstruction that points to a past located elsewhere (Africa), nor recommends the rejection and replacement of the here/now with a different, unknown spatiality and temporality. For Glissant, the locus of resistance is located in the present and in the possibilities of decolonisation already contained in the Caribbean, although concealed and understated."[68] Thus, rather than simply yearning for a lost past, or turning to a future-yet-to-come, Glissant finds a synthetic notion of possibility emerging from the here and now of the Caribbean.

Moreover, as Ramírez argues, the poet and thinker Césaire expressed "contempt for the Caribbean landscape: the beach (and the sea), the island and the archipelago. In all three, the poet Césaire suggests the complicity of space in the people's muteness and inert character and thus the landscape itself becomes an ally of the oppressor and not a tool for liberation and resistance."[69] By contrast, Glissant embraces the opportunity of the very locality of the Caribbean and its sea-infused, archipelagic existence.

Additionally, and most prominent for my argument here, Glissant argues that the Caribbean formation of language (which also has had traces of a former Dutch, and Zeelandic past)[70] offers, through its openness, a decentered and multilingual way to think and live. The genius of the Creole language consists, for Glissant, "in always being open, that is, perhaps, never becoming fixed except according to a system of variables that we have to imagine as much as define. Creolization carries along then into the adventure of multilingualism and into the incredible explosion of cultures."[71]

Rather than synthesizing differences into a concentrated unity, the power of the creolization that Glissant addresses lies in its ability to multiply, to be organized nonhierarchically, and to vary time and again. According to Glissant, the so-called "periphery" (the phenomenon of the Caribbean) can come to reorganize the so-called "metropolitan center" and become "exemplary of contemporary language in general."[72]

Thus, aquatic speech acts, such as those emerging in Creole, show that a new language of the sea need not be romanticized or solely reference nature (as is possibly suggested by Serres) or be referenced solely through traditional ways of being, such as the native Hawaiian way-of-living-and-relating (as is articulated in Ingersoll). Rather, with Glissant, we come to recognize that a language of the sea *may evolve geographically, naturally, culturally* out of a variety of stances, out of an *erratic diffraction* of languages, and thus may carry with it horizontal power structures extending into the future, with no one language being ascertained as the "center" of hierarchy. Creolization, as Drabinski clarifies, is "a passage that works *against* conventional models of transition. Diffraction distorts, bends, and chaotically reconfigures."[73] Accordingly, the diffraction of which Glissant speaks may add a helpful caveat insofar as any imagination of a (future) language of the sea should not be monolithic nor hierarchically organized.

To exemplify Glissant's thinking on languages of the sea further, the tradition of tambú as practiced on the Dutch Caribbean island of Curaçao is apt to discuss.[74] With origins in West Africa, tambú includes a drum (tambú) or *barí* (barrel), at least two iron instruments (known collectively as *herú*), vocals and dance.[75] Having originated in the seventeenth and eighteenth centuries, the vocals are spoken in Papiamento, which is comparable to Creole language, in that it is a linguistic synthesis that has evolved by blending various languages. In the case of Papiamento, this entails the blending of African languages and Portuguese with aspects of Spanish, English, and Dutch.[76]

Much like the synthetic possibilities that Glissant indexed, the tradition of tambú stands at a critical distance from events and urges life to go on, but differently, more perceptively, more critically, and with improvisation. Ranging from resistance to critical commentary, tambú signals the power of a musical language that drives life lived on the islands further in a generative direction.

Given its reflective possibilities, it is interesting that many Curaçaoans have acquired negative connotations with tambú parties, possibly due to the fact that the parties associated with tambú are attracting "rebellious" youth, heavy drinking, and sometimes invoke acts of crime. However, for those Curaçaoans living in the Netherlands, such parties are looked upon much more favorably.[77] In fact, given that "tambú had a turbulent past, scrutinized by both the governing Dutch and local Curaçaoans, the parties enabled Curaçaoans in the Netherlands the opportunity not only to rebel against the Netherlands establishment, but to break with local mores on Curaçao as well. As a result, the parties evolved into a strategy of resistance, where cultural expectation and cultural authority could be renegotiated."[78]

Provocatively, tambú parties in the Netherlands afford not only displaced Curaçaoans but many migrants from West and North Africa and the Caribbean as such the opportunity to find what de Jong calls a "space for collective belonging,"[79] where each individual may insert their own identity through dance moves reflecting cultural sensibilities and potencies.[80] Rather than nostalgic longing for a home left behind, they are capable of possessing what Glissant has argued for: a synthetic sense of generating home out of loss and displacement, doing so through creative linguistic fusions and a nonhierarchical sense of music and dance.

Languages of the Sea

As we circle back to our current predicament—oceanic extinction and the central disruption to meaning as the world narrows and absence echoes through the cracks of what constitutes the world as world—Serres's proposition to turn to silence and invent a new linguistic "code" to reattune ourselves more symbiotically to the Biogea finds helpful pointers in the works of Ingersoll and Glissant. While Ingersoll postulates a native Hawaiian oceanic literacy that embraces holism over reductionism, Glissant offers the motif of relation as a way forward to think through loss, language, and culture. In my view, Serres would be receptive to both Ingersoll's and Glissant's ideas, insofar as he argues, with Ingersoll, that language should be part of an interconnected way of addressing the Biogea;[81] and, he argues, seemingly along the lines of Glissant, that "Babel is an unintegrable multiplicity, a sort of intermittent aggregate, not closed upon its unity. Together we are this strange object, immersed in the clamor. At times constructible, here and there, and yet not totally constructible. We are this tatter of languages fringed with murmuring."[82]

As I return to the issue of loss with reference to the sea-born islands of Zeeland, a complex, paradoxical situation presents itself. On the one hand, due to the construction of the "Deltawerken"—an elaborate system of dams, barriers, and dikes that connected the islands to each other and the mainland—Zeeland's population has benefited from increased safety, prosperity, healthcare, and so forth. Also, due to increased individualization of its population and the fraying of local municipal bonds (originally infused by religious differences and rivalry between municipalities), collaboration across municipalities has increased as well as cohesion with the Netherlands and Belgium.[83]

On the other hand, decisions regarding the ongoing sea risks that threaten Zeeland, which have to do with rising sea levels and the risk of floods, have increasingly made the population of Zeeland less resilient: as the population progressively lives more removed from the sea, and as a brain drain removed its sea-knowledgeable citizens from its rural areas to other locations in the Netherlands, water management became increasingly centrally coordinated from elsewhere and accordingly the population became increasingly removed from decision-making processes. Along with the issue of human resilience is the issue of the ecosystem. The dams, locks, and barriers that have been part of the Deltawerken have had a large ecological effect on various forms of marine life in Zeeland's waters, although it's difficult to disentangle the specific effects of dams and dikes from other influences such as climate change–related higher water temperatures and the increased presence of seals and porpoises.[84] If we take a look at the estuary of the Oosterschelde, once called the "incubator of the North Sea," a powerful Marine Research report covering benthic fish and epibenthos in the Oosterschelde in the period 1970–2018 concludes that "both biomass and densities show a sharp decline from around 1986. . . . This decrease largely coincides with the construction of the storm surge barrier and the compartment dams."[85] One Zeeland skipper dramatically declared: "The water is simply dead."[86] Thus, while many factors have been involved leading to shifts and decreases in (certain forms of) marine life, we can conclude that Zeeland's sea-and-rural landscape has become homogenized and emptied out, and that a sense of "home"—a deep connection to the shores, transitions, and the interfaces to the open—seems lost. How can this sense of loss and estrangement from water transform into a renewed sense of belonging, a newfound resilience?

If it is the case, as Wittgenstein argues, that "to imagine a language is to imagine a form of life,"[87] it is the task for philosophy to think through possibilities of a new language—or better said: new languages—languages that are both informed by the loss of world *as* world but also trusting that imaginative forms of life and culture may emerge or be sustained. And, as Schneider-Mayerson and Bellamy argue in their *Ecotopian Lexicon*, a critical analysis of language "does not stop at critique of what exists today; it argues for what could or even should be. To think of language in this way is to implicate the daily choices we make as individuals and communities—to utter one word instead of all others is to shape the direction of our living language, consciously or not. Insofar as every choice shapes the cognitive frames we inhabit, our future is established not only through dramatic historical events but also through gradual accretion: moment by moment, act by act, word by word."[88]

To forge ourselves collectively forward, the model of the "seagoing pact" as Serres relates it may serve us well. Notably, this is a different kind of collective than the one addressed earlier, which was an objectifying, possessive "we." The seagoing pact, instead, is one that co-emerges with the elements, in symbiosis. Much like the pontoon boat in the Garonne, here "the collectivity, if sundered, immediately exposes itself to the destruction of its fragile niche."[89] Similarly, the success or failure of our own endeavors to navigate the troubled waters of the Anthropocene depend upon the formation of such a pact, ideally formed in solidarity.

Concluding Thoughts

> A being dedicated to water is a being in flux. He dies every minute; something of his substance is constantly falling away.
>
> —Gaston Bachelard, *Water and Dreams*

While usually the lithosphere is seen "as the key slate onto which accounts of the Anthropocene are written—deciphered by present-day stratigraphers and to be read, presumably, by some distant future decoder of our fossilized remains,"[90] this chapter focuses on the sea and our relationship to the sea to show both the local and global transformations that the element of water, in the form of the social-material interface of sea and our seascapes, has undergone. In the age of rising sea levels, oceanic extinction, unpredicted flooding, and more, the Anthropocene makes itself powerfully felt in water. Accordingly, this chapter, following Neimanis, seeks "to pay more attention to the hydrosphere as the (again, oft-overlooked) fascia that lubricates and connects the Earth's lithosphere to its biosphere and atmosphere."[91]

However, while this chapter pointed to the harm and loss that is being felt as part of the Anthropocene narrative lived on the sea and its shores, it also sought to reclaim the idea of the sea and its shores as liminal spaces that offer counterpoint to our potentials. Specifically, by rethinking oceanic languages that defy hierarchy, create solidarity, and that respond to the vicissitudes of the real, the liminality of the sea may again be felt and open to a different way of living, thinking, and speaking alongside the sea. Thus, away from the Anthropocene and the key words of extinction, this chapter seeks to move beyond the flattening of potentialities and time, toward both deeper historical and futural orientations for our relationship with the sea.

If it is the case, following Neimanis, that water is both "a substance, but it is also an idea," and that water "has a materiality" as much as it "has a history,"[92] then it is worthwhile to pursue this same kind of trajectory with regard to the element that is discussed next: fire. As I will try to show in the next chapter, fire offers another access point to grasp our sense of "home" in the world, and, like water, has its own materiality while being part of a complex natural-social interaction that humans have had with the world. As in the case of water, we experience our relationship with fire as shifting so radically that we feel a sense of "loss."

However, unlike water, our relationship with fire is particularly paradoxical, as we commonly associate it with not only life, warmth, and energy but also with death, danger, and destruction. Thus, although we face similar issues with fire as currently discussed in this water chapter, our approach must consider the unique challenges that fire confronts us with. Some of those challenges have evolutionarily been with us, but, as the next chapter will show, some of the shifts that have taken place in the elemental sphere of fire have unfolded with the rise of industrial fire. Thus, the next chapter will seek to follow the material and conceptual schema of fire, and will do so starting with the myth of Prometheus.

Chapter 2

Fire

Pyrogenic Creation and Destruction

Contemplating the Meaning of Fire, Affect, and Loss in the Pyrocene

Thunderbolt steers all things.

—Heraclitus, frag. 22.B64 Diels-Kranz

The fire that has burned in humanity's hearth from the beginning, the fire with which we have remade the world, is a profoundly double-edged symbol both of our Promethean power to control the earth ... and of the frustratingly unexpected limits we repeatedly encounter in our exercise of that power.

—William Cronon, foreword to *Fire: A Brief History*

Our entire world is the *cinder* (*Asche*) of innumerable living beings; and what is living is so little in relation to the whole, it must be that, once already, *everything* was transformed into life and it will continue to be so.

—Friedrich Nietzsche, *Nachgelassene Fragmente* (1881)

This chapter turns to the element of fire as another access point to grasp our sense of "elemental home" in the world. Similar to what we saw when we looked at water, fire is part of a complex natural-social constellation that mediates and has mediated our human sense of being-in-the-world, as fire is co-originary and coimplicated with human evolution. This central role is attested to in the numerous reflections in early Greek thought—both in Greek epic and in Greek philosophy—speaking both to fire's life-bringing force as well as its destructive qualities. If we are trying to distill and differentiate the essential characteristics of fire, we could say that it is an element that is more concrete and direct in its effects than the abstractions induced by water and is most often associated with the notion of (sudden) change.[1] As Bachelard writes: "If all that changes slowly may be explained by life, all that changes quickly is explained by fire. Fire is the ultra-living element."[2]

But as in the case of water, the way fire appears to us is not unchanging, and, in fact, we can say that our relationship with it as an element has shifted so radically that it is increasingly marked by a sense of "loss." This sense of loss is not abstract to me. To clarify what I mean in a close and concrete way, let us take the example of the Pacific coast of the United States, which had been my home for many years and has been ablaze with deadly megafires in recent years, leaving behind a devastating trace of lost lives, homes, and businesses. If anything for me has announced the arrival of the Anthropocene (or, perhaps better said, the Capitalocene[3]) then it was this: as the air became unbreathable and plants, animals, and humans went up in flames, I realized how revered *anthropos*[4] has, with all due capitalist energy, radically turned the tables and made parts of its world—and the atmosphere—increasingly unlivable and unbreathable. What, I wondered, *can* or *should* be our response to this drama beyond the initial fight-and-flight reaction? And what might philosophy have to offer in this regard? Where might we find the resources for installing a new approach that can steer us toward a new epoch, with more livable, sustainable,[5] and breathable conditions for all?

To answer these questions, this chapter will seek theoretical guidance in the myth of Prometheus and, specifically, the interpretation of this myth through Bernard Stiegler's *Technics and Time*. For Stiegler, the myth of Prometheus presents the human as originally without qualities and it is the gifts of Prometheus that compensate for this inherent lack.[6] The gifts of fire and technics offer us an opportunity to invent and *be*, but they may be dangerous and (self) destructive as well. My central argument is that the Promethean duplicitous gift—of fire and *technē* (which means, in ancient Greek, art, craft, technique, or skill)—to humanity has led to the current tragedy of the Anthropocene, a tragedy understood at temporal and ontological levels as the elemental space of a fire-made world comingles with our own being. Nonetheless, Stiegler's emphasis on the radical possibility of another becoming that is possible in our prosthetic being may offer impetus to imagine a future beyond the Anthropocene, but only if fire and technical skills come to be seen in a different light and solicit different affects.

To imagine such a future—our own posthuman existence[7] as part of the presumed new epoch of the Pyrocene[8]—I propose to follow the meaning of fire and technics both on a local, Californian scale and on a global scale. At the local, Californian scale, I focus on the enduring fire-adaptable existence of California's giant sequoias and the pyro-diverse practices of the California Indigenous Miwok in order to critique dominant forms of property regimes rooted in settler colonial logics that are generative of the affects of loss. This critique gives way to a call for new forms of relation to a landscape on fire. And to address the global scale, I will emphasize the need for a mosaical form of affect and habit to take hold, a form that should pivotally be constituted by, in line with the myth of Prometheus, shame and justice in order to change our political-economic regimes and foster a broader community in solidarity with each other.

The Myth of Prometheus and Epimetheus and the Duplicity of Prometheus's Gifts

From its early theorization, fire is thematized both as a natural entity and as a social entity. Gaston Bachelard argues that "fire is more a *social reality* than a *natural reality*"[9] given its function in our childhood, where prohibitions about fire precede our actual physical handling of it. That fire is so strongly connected to our way of being and becoming finds early articulation in Greek epic. In the myth of Prometheus, fire is closely connected to the technologically savvy yet burdensome way in which humans are said to live their lives.

The myth has various versions. To take the version of Hesiod's *Theogony*, we find fire to be already known among humans but taken away by Zeus after Prometheus deceives the god during a sacrificial offering. Undeterred, Prometheus steals fire back from Zeus in order to give it back to humans:

> Thus, Zeus, angry, whose wisdom never wears out.
> From then on he always remembered this trick
> And wouldn't give the power of weariless fire
> To the ashwood mortals who live on the earth.
> But that fine son of Iapetos outwitted him
> And stole the far-seen gleam of weariless fire
> In a hollow fennel stalk, and so bit deeply the heart
> Of Zeus, the high lord of thunder, who was angry
> When he saw the distant gleam of fire among men,
> And straight off he gave them trouble to pay for the fire.[10]

Prometheus's theft of fire brings humans difficulty: due to Zeus's punishment, life (*bios*) is no longer easy. Instead, humans are obliged to work and "to handle instruments."[11] Controlling fire comes with a hefty responsibility and price. She who controls fire has power: the power to create—to cook, to build an environment conducive to living, to gather people around a central hearth—but also the power to destroy—to scorch and burn, to cleanse and fumigate, to turn what lives to ashes.

The crucial value of fire, as well as its connection with *technē*, emerges in another version of the Prometheus myth, the one recounted in Plato's *Protagoras*. There, humans, due to the forgetfulness of Prometheus's brother Epimetheus, have no qualities at all—all qualities to be distributed[12] have been doled out to the other animals (e.g., as compensation for their size, some animals receive the ability to make a winged escape, etc.[13]). Close to the day that humans should come forth from the earth, humans, due to Epimetheus's forgetfulness to assign them specific qualities and thereby provide them with a distinct nature or fate, are left with a void. To compensate for this, Prometheus chooses as preservation for humans two attributes: skill (*sophia*) and fire (*pyr*) (321c).

Stiegler, in *Technics and Time* (vol. 1), emphasizes Epimetheus's forgetfulness. The gift of fire and what Stiegler calls "technics" are, in his analysis, inextricably bound to this act of forgetting—of "appearing through disappearing."[14] At the heart of human existence stands a lack of being and essential qualities: "The qualities of animals make up a sort of nature, in any case a positive gift of the gods, a predestination. The gift made to humanity is not positive: it is there to compensate. Humanity is without qualities, without predestination."[15] Humans thus are gifted with *technē* and are therefore "prosthetic," not merely accidentally so, but "prosthetic in their very being."[16] Stiegler continues, "A pros-thesis is what is placed in front, that is, what is outside, outside what it is placed in front of. However, if what is outside constitutes the very being of what it lies outside of, then this being is *outside itself.* The being of humankind is to be outside itself."[17] In Stiegler's perspective, the story of human origin is that of *non*-origin. We are grounded in a "de-fault of origin or the origin as de-fault."[18] Humans need to "invent, realize, produce qualities,"[19] without any guarantee that these qualities will become their qualities. In fact, they may become part of the qualities of technics or they may become dangerous and self-destructive: "Technics, art, facticity can harbor madness: the prosthesis is a danger, that of artifacts, and artifacts can destroy what gathers within an effective and active being-together."[20] But the trace of Epimetheus's forgetting is not beyond us. We *forget* about the prosthetics we use—from pens to glasses to shoes—and are thereby forgetful of our own non-origin, of our own technical prosthetic nature.[21]

The Gift of Fire and the Mutual Evolution of Fire and Humanity

> Among all phenomena, [fire] is really the only one to which there can be so definitely attributed the opposing values of good and evil. It shines in Paradise. It burns in Hell. It is gentleness and torture. It is cookery and it is apocalypse.
>
> —Gaston Bachelard, *The Psychoanalysis of Fire*

What happens if we read Stiegler's account of the danger of *technē* in conjunction with the ambiguous power of fire, a gift that runs parallel to the acquisition of *technē*? If we follow the work of a leading authority on the history of fire, Stephen Pyne, we can then see how "fire and humanity pushed and pulled each other around the globe. They advanced together—spreading like flaming fronts, spotting into favorable sites, probing into marshes, flaring amid thickets, smoldering amid peat, crackling through scrub, all as the fuels of environmental opportunity and the climate of culture allowed."[22]

The evolution of our species and the evolution of fire are mutually dependent, and their evolution informed and changed the material, geographic conditions of their encounter. As fire began to be used on the landscape, the landscape increasingly became engineered "to concentrate more subsistence resources in a smaller and smaller area," and consequently became more "systematically intense."[23] As for the human species' own body, fire's use in cooking, especially its ability to disassemble raw food, allowed for the human digestive process to become partially "externalized," making the process of eating and extracting nutrition from it far more concentrated and efficient.[24] Thus, as digestion changed due to cooking and our bowels shortened, the material interface that is mostly associated with our sapience, the brain, expanded: "In the archeological record the surge in brain size coincides with hearths and the remains of meals."[25] Additionally, cooking allowed for increased socialization, affording occasions of eating together around common meals (of what is called in the academic literature "commensality"[26]), sharing cooked food.[27]

Given the role that fire has played in adapting "our habits, diet, and body to the characteristics of fire," humans could be called *pyrophytes*—based on the ancient Greek *pyros* (fire) and *phytos* (plant)—a term used for plants and trees that have adapted to tolerate fire, as James Scott suggests in his book *Against the Grain*.[28] Signaling fire's importance for our evolution as well as our future, Scott argues that "[if] the litmus test of domestication for a plant or animal is that it cannot propagate itself without our assistance, then, by the same token, we have adapted so massively to fire that our species would have no future without it. . . . It has in a real sense domesticated us."[29]

However, as fire domesticated us and made us into true *pyrophytes*, we should be mindful of the power of fire. Fire is not *simply* a tool—it is, as Scott reminds us, "at best, a 'semi-domesticate,' appearing unbidden and, if not guarded carefully, escaping its shackles to become dangerously feral."[30] Similarly, Stiegler argues that "fire is not, however, the power *of* mortals, it is not their property; it is much more a domestic power that, when escaping the technical mastery of domesticity, reveals its wild violence, disclosing the powerlessness of mortals, only appearing in their hand yet, again, through disappearing."[31] Still, fire and technics are the *only* ways by which human existence can live—can *be*—by living prosthetically and dangerously. As Seitz has it in more ontological terms: "We would not *be* were it not for fuel, leading us to an understanding of the human as the evolutionary and historical effect rather than the operator of power."[32]

Within the perspective of industrialization and the Anthropocene, both the feral power of fire and humans' ability to increasingly manipulate fire through technics in the form of industrial fire seem to have risen in prominence and scale. *Industrial fire* substitutes the controlled burning of renewable materials by the controlled combustion of ancient biomass extracted from beneath the ground.[33] Where natural elements such as flame, vegetation, and air had ruled before, now a technological setting defined by "combustion, fuel and machinery"[34] coevolved, drafting biomass "from the geologic rather than the biologic realm."[35] It uses second-order technology (heated wires and electrical arts) and burns within enclosed chambers.[36] Thus, while industrialization is mostly understood as a "social, economic, and perhaps political process that redefines the relationship of people to one another," it refers to a different *kind or process* of fire when defined in terms of fire history: "the burning of fossil biomass."[37]

Industrial fire has had many consequences: it expanded fire's realm, increased the number of fuels available,[38] drew combustion closer to culture, and has made humans "designers of novel ecosystems that cannot exist without us."[39] It is exactly here that we encounter fire again in a very different manifestation: namely as feral fire. For instance, these days, the megafire—defined as a "fire[s] that burns at least 100,000 acres"—erupts more often, displacing or killing people, animals, and plants, and reshaping the landscapes and ecosystems affected.[40] It is precisely these megafires that have deeply impacted the West Coast of the United States over the past few years and that will likely continue to be part of California's future.

If it is the case that the increased prevalence of such megafires and wildfires is related to industrial fire and, thus, human-induced climate change, then we can argue that we have fallen victim to fire as "a profoundly double-edged symbol both of our Promethean power to control the earth ... and of the frustratingly unexpected limits we repeatedly encounter in our exercise of that power."[41] The human proposition to "tame" fire as industrial fire (which extends fire's range, power, and quantity) seems to find punishment for its *hybris* in the "revenge" of the divine Promethean gift of fire, whose heart holds wild violence.

However, if fire has domesticated us and has made us into true pyrophytes, then might there be an option for us, as a fire-adaptable species par excellence, to reimagine our attitude toward fire and toward our fire-engulfed predicament? This leads us to the issue of affect, and rethinking affect in light of fire and our current ecological predicament. What affects can or could fire solicit, and how might we prepare ourselves best for what may be called the new era of the Pyrocene?

Affect, Fire, and the Future

> All things are an exchange for fire and fire for all things, as goods for gold and gold for goods.
>
> —Heraclitus, frag. 22.B90 Diels-Kranz

The discourse following the alarming recent wildfires in California indicates a surge of feelings, such as anger, anxiety, sadness, and resignation, all of which are understandable given the fires' range and devastating effects. The affective charge of fire is described in Struzik's book *Firestorm: How Wildfire Will Shape Our Future* in terms of fire as a "beast" or "wild animal"—"unpredictable" or independent of and unaffected by human actions. The consequent human affect is discussed in terms of "defeat," "desertion," "scared," "unsightly," and "apocalyptic."[42]

What heightens these negative affects and the ensuing sense of disorientation is a marked sense of human responsibility—given that climate change and its consequent environmental losses are due to human action—and a sense of powerlessness in the face of the global factors influencing our losses, such as multinational corporations, global economic systems, and policy choices by governments.[43] As Albrecht writes: "In the Anthropocene there is no longer mystery attached to a great deal of disaster and misfortune since, to a very large extent, there is an element of self-imposed vulnerability to what are euphemistically called 'natural disasters.'"[44]

However, while Albrecht analyzes this sense of disorientation to discuss a new form of mourning prevalent in the Anthropocene, I want to access the problems of fire in the Anthropocene through a different affective lens. My question is: How can our affects toward industrial fire and wildfires transform beyond simply becoming adaptable and resilient, in order to truly prepare us for a new era beyond the human-centered epoch of the Anthropocene? How might affects toward fire be productive in moving us *toward* a new era of living creatively together (provocatively called the Pyrocene, full of new opportunities, new potencies, and new forms of habitation and life)?

One key component in rethinking affect in preparation for such a new era is contemplating the ontological and physical status of fire. As we have seen, for both the Greek mythical tradition as described by Hesiod and the philosophical tradition as described by Plato's *Protagoras*, fire is a divine force provided to humans through illicit actions or as compensation for a radical absence at the core of their being, and the ownership of fire comes at the hefty price of divine revenge and extreme danger to humanity. However, if we go deeper into its ontological and physical significance with the Presocratic thinker Heraclitus, we find fire involved as a stable power underpinning the everlasting change and cycle of all things. Not only does fire, for Heraclitus, "steer all things" (22B4) but "all things are an exchange for fire, and fire for all things" (22B90), indicating that fire is a fundamental mover of change—a stable flame that keeps the cycle of life and death going precisely in and through its changes.

If we follow this track of thinking of fire as the ontological mover of change and as the very physical manifestation of stability-in-change, then the corresponding affect it may give rise to proves productive. It is true that we sometimes feel fire as a completely deleterious force (as indicated by the previous descriptions of apocalypse and terror) that transforms everything into an unrecognizable, uninhabitable space and leaves our home and our lifeworld shattered in pieces. However, if we follow the Heraclitean trajectory, then we may observe that many fires also leave behind something recognizable, even beyond or amid the devastation and the uncanny they bring about: for instance, certain aspects of a burnt landscape can, seemingly at random, be completely unaffected, while other aspects may be recognizable *even as ruins* (e.g., tree stumps, ruins of garages, burnt car frames). If fire allows for the possibility of such constancy amid change, then this offers some room for rethinking a productive space of affect beyond simply feeling devastating loss in the face of fire.[45]

Of course, what complicates the reimagination of affect toward fire beyond the Anthropocene is the often-*hidden* component of that very other kind of fire—industrial fire—that is the culprit of much of our current predicament and that is far too often sheltered from our direct phenomenological experience. However, I want to argue that the feeling of shock-and-recognition in the wake of wildfires may offer us a possibly affective productive space for bringing the hidden element of industrial fire into our imagination and into our affective space. If Pyne is correct in saying that "the competition for combustion—hidden from most people by the machinery of modern industry—must surface as the value-laden choice it has always been,"[46] then it may be through the altered, "value-laden" space of the affects provoked by recent or currently raging wildfires that we may find the resources for a different affective regime regarding industrial fire as well. In other words, in my view fire's ontological and physical status, indicating constancy amid change, offers a potentially productive space for affect beyond simple mourning. Rather than simply focusing upon loss, I would like to argue for a mosaical space of affect promoted by trust. I choose trust rather than hope, given the more enduring, participatory nature of trust,[47] which contrasts with the more fleeting, and often deceptive, nature of hope.[48] I will expand on my reasoning for focusing on trust rather than hope in chapter 5.

Native American Practices, Redwoods, and a New Pyrophytic Affective Regime

How can we move toward this new space of affect using trust in the continuously regenerative nature of fire as the soil out of which this mosaic of affect may arise?

My first suggestion turns to the local California level, and seeks guidance in the local fire regimes that have proven productive and creative. In California, there is a long history of pyrophytic practices. For instance, the Sierra Miwok have used fire to instigate productive transformative changes in a landscape, which have also had beneficial effects for the natural world: they enhanced "the diversity, productivity, and availability of the wild resource base by complementing and working with ongoing natural ecological processes."[49] What resulted from these fires is not only "an anthropogenic mosaic of productive habits"[50] but "the creation and enhancement of environmental mosaics—complex quiltlike environments with multifaceted habitats."[51]

What we may learn from these Native American practices for our own pyrophytic future is the opportunity to reimagine the connection with fire *creatively*, as a life-inducing force that can support *many* forms of life as mosaics—rather than just the monoculture of the human species. However, given that "a staggering 6 to 16 percent of the state" would be on fire in previous late prehistoric or early historic ages, and that a "distinct haze would have hung in many places in California during the summer and fall months,"[52] we also have ample warning against romanticizing Native American practices and are incentivized to handle new fire regimes—and smoke—carefully and responsibly in light of air quality and air pollution.

Second, we may follow the trace of another local pyrophyte: the giant sequoia trees (*Sequoiadendron giganteum*), which have lived in the

Sierra Nevada and Yosemite Valley and whose existence and symbolic imagery may serve to recalibrate our affects toward fire for the future. In the case of the giant sequoia, we find a tree that stands out in terms of both size and age.[53] Sequoia trees are well adapted to fire, as fire allows them to prepare seedbeds and cycle nutrients, and it allows for a mosaic of age classes and vegetation types in the forest.[54] Compared to fungal and bacterial action, fire offers a faster and more complete process of decomposition, which allows "minerals and energy to recycle faster within the ecosystem's operation."[55]

Based on their pyrophytic existence, we might discern a few qualities that are of metaphorical import to reimagine our own posthuman existence as part of the Pyrocene. In the first place, the general ability of giant sequoias to embrace fire to live and propagate is a helpful reminder for rethinking our own affect toward fire for the future. Second, sequoias' thick bark and resilience to fire offers a helpful image for long-term human resilience toward fire. I am not thinking here of short-term solutions, such as fire-resilient buildings or other forms of resilience that sustain the status quo, but rather *sustainable, long-term forms of resilience* that rethink our interactions with fire and that draw upon broader, long-term temporal regimes that truly foster resilience for the planet.[56]

Relatedly, and third, given sequoias' connection to deep time,[57] their enduring existence should give us pause to rethink adaptability in the face of change and the need to ponder our own 24/7 regimes that merely excrete affect as based on the present. Fourth, given the ability of sequoias to form underground communities that clonally reproduce through massive, underground lignotubers,[58] we find an illuminating image of a *powerful affective community regime* that informs and transforms symbiotic connections in the face of threats, such as logging.

Beyond emulating the controlled burning practices that may be productive for certain parts of California, a recalibration of the broader economic and political regime—which is grounded upon some of the same affects that made a flourishing symbiosis between fire, Native Americans, and environmental context possible—is needed. Such a recalibration of the political regime has to address broad questions of economic growth and capital accumulation of property, as well as specific questions regarding real estate development in the forest-wildlife interface.[59]

If it is the case that fire has not only changed physical landscapes but also informed and transformed our bodies, culture, and social and economic institutions and thereby our existence at large, then we need to think through the existential repercussions of the current fire regime. The case of California's transformation is telling of such existential repercussions.

In the wake of a series of wildfires, PG&E, the American investor-owned utility company with publicly traded stock, had to declare bankruptcy. In addition to the legal consequences that the company has faced in prior years regarding the San Bruno Gas explosion in 2010, they have most recently been held liable for the deadliest wildfire in California history: the Camp Fire that raged in 2018, which left eighty-six people dead, fourteen thousand homes burned, fifty-two thousand people displaced, and caused about $16.5 billion in damages. Given the enormous liability claims, PG&E had to file for Chapter 11 in January 2019. In a conciliatory yet empty gesture, PG&E replaced all members of the board and committed itself to proactive damage avoidance by spending money to cut down trees near power lines. Public criticism has been voiced advocating for a government takeover or a forced subdivision of PG&E into small regional operations.

Many of these disasters involving PG&E have invoked the public's ire, but the fault lies not only with PG&E and its infrastructure; it also involves a complex range of factors, including climate change and increased fuel load. Nevertheless, the legal doctrine of "inverse condemnation" holds PG&E "responsible for wildfire damage caused by their equipment—whether the companies acted negligently or not."[60]

Both public outrage and an outdated legal system are preventing more transformative and constructive legal and political rethinking. Without denying PG&E's involvement in some of the unfolding dramas of wildfires in California, it is high time to think through the meaning of PG&E's bankruptcy on a broader level. What ramifications does PG&E's bankruptcy have for the concepts of "liberty" and "responsibility" in the age of climate change? Is a liability suit able to proffer recompense to affected parties at such a scale and frequency? What does such appeal to liability say about the affect of trust and the possibility for transformation? Since PG&E represents the "industrial fire" model, based as it is on fossil fuels, while at the same time experiencing the dire consequences of this model in the form of raging wildfires and now undergoing bankruptcy, we may ask: In what ways does the collapse of the Californian industrial fire model due to its own consequences—that is, climate change and ensuing megafires in California—transform the framing of the Californian landscape as part of the "American West" or the "California Dream," each with their attendant colonial aspirations of quickly gaining wealth or fame,[61] which have produced in no small part the current political-economic regime as we have it?

If the settler colonial California Dream focuses on individualism and on the issue of accumulating private property quickly, the recent wildfires puncture this ideal. If recent megafires are, broadly speaking, caused by factors related to human-induced climate change and settler colonial ideas of fire suppression, and if multinational companies are largely responsible for such climate change and perpetuate the disturbed fire load balance, then the existential effects of megafires show the limits of unbridled capitalism and its means of conflict management, which supposedly have at their core the human individual and its freedom but, in fact, serve the social, collective power of corporations and their accumulation of profit.[62] In the face of the damage done, should such large and powerful corporate institutions (which in some sense now constitute "the public"[63]) lack responsibility? Or should the so-called "public" utility companies, despite being underfunded and subject to abstruse legal liability rules, continue to find themselves accountable?

This suggestion—that is, tackling the broader economic infrastructure of our society and the primary contributors to climate change rather than local utilities—should go hand in hand with a revision of how we relate to property and to the natural resources that we hold in common with all other living beings. Ownership is not just a relationship between a person and a thing—it is "a set of relationships between the owner of something and everyone else's claims to that same thing."[64] Moreover, as the much-discussed provocative "statement of progressive property" indicates, property implicates "plural and incommensurable values," and the pursuit of such values requires "virtue, particularly humility, and attentiveness to the effects of claiming and exercising property rights on others, including future generations, and on the natural environment and the non-human world."[65]

Thus, as megafires burn properties and entire forests on the Pacific coast, they affect not only the so-called owners but also the general structural way we relate to land and property. As we think of the scale and the impact of those fires, we must also consider another relationship with the environment and the land. Following past Native American practices, we can argue that alternative relationships to property may offer a more productive vantage point. More specifically, we should look to Native American property rights regimes and land use to better manage the ongoing risks of wildfires.

For Native American peoples, "the idea that human use *ensures* an abundance of plant and animal life appears to have been an ancient one."[66] Land and culture are thus integrally connected for Native Americans, especially since "the very bones of our ancestors are present in the earth and help make the soil that grows our food."[67] Even if it is *not* the case, as the romanticized image of Native practices has it, that Native American peoples had no private property,[68] the way Native American tribes in California approached property rights—as part of an evolving system of responsibility to plant and animal life—should still give us pause. If it was the case that the various geophysical features of the land and water gave rise to specific tribal regimes in California, then the task is to again align our property rights and land use with the needs of the current "social, economic, political, and ecological conditions."[69] The task is thus to recreate functioning property regimes "that meet local needs . . . and evolve to meet future conditions,"[70] of both human and nonhuman life.

Such a broader perspective resonates also with current scientific studies into California forests, which support the idea that, in order to combat megafires, we need to start managing forests not just on "a relatively small spatial scale (e.g., 20–100 acres)," but "at the watershed scale (20,000–50,000 acres)": by combining mechanical thinning, prescribed fire, and naturally ignited wildfire, one could "restore/reduce fuels on a significant proportion of a watershed such that there is limited potential for large wildfires with extreme patches of high severity effects (all trees are killed)."[71]

The problem with many current resource-specific policies is that they are "so focused on individual concerns that they may be missing the fact that there are 'endangered landscapes' that are threatened by changing climate and fire."[72] Following the idea of "endangered landscapes" rather than individual, short-term concerns, I want to similarly plead for a renewal of efforts to reconsider our energy and fire policies in California.

Only a political regime that is open to such broad issues and questions, such as the meaning of an "endangered landscape"; how to have an alternate economy; or how fire can become less polluting and less influential in promoting climate change can be successful in moving us toward the Pyrocene. The cinders of past fires that are housed within our own present point toward that future. At the local Californian level, successful collective action toward a more sustainable future can emerge only when we move beyond issues of strict legal liability (i.e., a "legal" superstructure of trust) and again develop authentic, localized trust in engaging our land, fires, and each other.[73]

Concluding Thoughts

> For fire will advance and judge and convict all things.
> —Heraclitus, frag. 22.B66 Diels-Kranz

If it is the case that fire is a necessary part of the evolution of human, pyrophytic existence, and if it is the case that fire can bring about regeneration and is the underlying mover of change, then we have to admit that the current fires that have been undergirding industrialization and that have wreaked so much havoc on our planet—both indirectly as industrial fire or directly through climate change and consequent megafires—are putting to the test our *trust* in the regenerative and life-affording power of fire. In this light, Prometheus's gifts of fire and technics have to be reassessed both in terms of the locale out of which we operate, as well as the general political-economic climate and habits that have made these fires possible. In this respect, even Stephen Pyne's deep and thoughtful diagnoses of our current fire regimes, which, in his view, boil down to a "fossil-fuel civilization and the world it shapes," lack the broad vision addressing the root cause. In fact, Pyne offers two rather instrumental and limited solutions: "One is to protect ourselves from bad fires, the kind that burn into towns, savage municipal watersheds, disrupt ecosystems. The other is to promote more good fire, which can enhance ecological goods and services, reduce fuel loads, and generally dampen the prospects for bad fire and horrific smoke episodes."[74]

On the local Californian level, the enduring existence of the giant sequoia points at the possibility of long-term regimes grounded in deep time, creatively adapting to fire in seeking new opportunities and strengthening life through forming powerful communal bonds. Additionally, on the local level, the recollection of the past pyrogenic practices of the Miwok indicate the possibility of a reinvented pyrophytic regime that embraces fire as a co-creative mosaic force, potentially unlocking and empowering the potencies of life for a diverse range of beings—not just humans.

However, such local regimes need to be supplemented with a more global approach. When we look at fire from a global perspective in our current age, "fire combusts more than what the biosphere grows,"[75] indicating that we need to stimulate the biosphere's growth and restrict fire "to the cycles of what can be grown."[76] Additionally, given such need for the restriction of the fire load, we need to create "sources of power other than controlled combustion."[77] Such efforts—that is, encouraging biosphere growth and creating new technical fire regimes—can only happen, in my view, when our political-economic regimes, affects, and habits are changed on a global scale. Only then can we become the regenerative pyrophytes that embrace, with new trust, the forthcoming era of the Pyrocene. As Roy Scranton articulates: "Humanity's survival through the collapse of carbon-fueled capitalism and into the new world of the Anthropocene will hinge on our ability to let our old way of life die while protecting, sustaining, and reworking our collective stores of cultural technology."[78] Similar to fire's ability to instigate death *and* regeneration, "learning to die as a civilization means letting go of this particular way of life and its ideas of identity, freedom, success, and progress,"[79] and unlocking new forms of political-economic regimes, habituation, and affect.

It is precisely at this point, as we contemplate our global-political sphere, that we may reinvoke the ending of the myth of Prometheus for further suggestions. For, in the version of the myth in Plato's *Protagoras*, humans, after having received the gifts of fire and skill, receive a final gift. As the myth has it, fire and *technē* allow humans to procure food, but they are still threatened in their existence since they live "scattered," lacking the means to live peacefully together, therefore making them vulnerable to attacks by wild animals. For that reason, Zeus sends Hermes to bestow on humans the gifts of "shame and justice (*aidō kai dikē*)" so that there may be "regulation of cities and friendly ties (*philia*) to draw them together" (*Protagoras* 322c). This indicates that humans do not innately form a peaceful community: they need to be *gifted externally* with the feelings and values of shame and justice to ensure mutual respect for each other and their community.

How may we turn our attitude toward fire around, creating a more sustainable life for all—not just for ourselves, but for all other parts of our joint ecosystem? The answer Plato's myth provides is to *feel* our own lack through the affect of shame (*aidōs*), recognizing what Stiegler calls the default at the core of our being: the finitude and mortality that is our way of life.[80] It is also to feel and habituate ourselves—through a sense of justice—as part of a broader community of a wider political landscape that needs to contemplate what resources are available and with whom and how to share them. Paradoxically, only through these senses of respect and justice, and by accessing the political skills that all point at our de-fault, can we *come together* instead of being polarized and driven apart.[81]

How can we *begin* anew, feel the weight of our mortality, and (re)install the feeling and meaning of justice as we enter the Pyrocene? The starting point is trust in the enduring power of fire. In the novel *Frankenstein: or, The Modern Prometheus*, the protagonist Dr. Frankenstein abandoned trust in his own creation and thereby allowed all of the havoc to occur; the monstrosity at the heart of the novel is not to be associated with his creation, but instead with Dr. Frankenstein, the Modern Prometheus, himself.[82] Have we, modern prometheuses in the twenty-first century, similarly given up trust in our own pyrophytic existence and its ensuing pyrotechnical, industrial fire monsters? Whether we like it or not, our lifestyle has been changing, following the wake of industrial fire and its ensuing tragedies. The example of Dr. Frankenstein may give us pause: only by turning ourselves—and our current lifestyles—into cinders[83] can a new space of affect—a mosaical space permeated by trust toward fire—emerge.

The need for the creation of a new lifestyle bringing about new habits and affects is not only necessary when it comes to our relationship with fire: it is also pertinent in relationship with the element of air, to which the next chapter is devoted. For, similar to fire, the air we breathe has co-evolved with human history and culture; and, over time, due to industrialization, colonization, and migration, the issue of access to clean and healthy air has become a site of contestation. Moreover, on top of anthropogenic climate change affecting our air and producing inequities in the air breathed, the recent Covid-19 pandemic has highlighted the precarious nature of who or who is not becoming subject to shared bad air. Thus, as in the case of water and fire, we experience that our relationship with air has shifted so radically as that a sense of "loss" has come to characterize it.

While there are similarities insofar as we experience fire and air in terms of loss, each element also has its own meaning and materiality. To access the particularities of air, I will discuss in the next chapter the meaning of atopic allergies, which will allow me to grasp the diachronic formation and influence of air at the intersection of body, place, culture, economy, and ecology. In particular, I will seek to cast light on the incremental slow changes to air that have informed allergic and asthma-infused lifestyles leading to diminution and loss.

Chapter 3

Air

The Breath of Decaying Constellations
A Phenomenology of Loss, Illness, Allergies, and Bad Air

> For man, like everything else, is a pupil of the air.
>
> —Johan Gottfried Herder, *Outlines of a Philosophy of the History of Man*

> Air . . . from Johannesburg to Tehran, to Delhi to Jakarta, isn't about aesthetics, or even possible climate change at some point in the future; it's about life and death now.
>
> —Timothy Doyle and Melissa Risely, *Crucible for Survival*

> The near becomes one's own, through air. If breathing estranges me from the other, this gesture also signifies a sharing with the world that surrounds me and with the community that inhabits it. Food and even speech can be assimilated, partially become mine. It is not the same for air. I can breathe in my own way, but the air will never simply be mine.
>
> —Luce Irigaray, "From *The Forgetting of Air* to *To Be Two*"

To delve into the specifics of air—and its connection to life—necessitates special attention to oxygen. While air only secondarily consists of oxygen

(78 percent nitrogen, 21 percent oxygen, and 0.03 percent carbon dioxide[1]) it is crucial to life given that "oxygen is a reactive gas—that's why it starts fires—so when some organisms figured out how to harness it, they suddenly had access to a major new source of energy."[2]

Here, in this elemental causal interplay, we can see a subtle connection to fire, the element of our previous chapter. Air begets fire, science tells us. Air is an ontogenetic principle at the material level. But this dynamic has a deeper relation. For the Presocratic philosopher Anaximenes, the Greek term *aer* (1) includes not only mist, as his predecessors had it, but also a *broad* spectrum of visible appearances (water, clouds, clear air, etc.) and thus is closer to our concept of air; and (2) appeals to both its *invisible*[3] and visible aspects. Air as informing clouds and fire can be made perceptible, but it is, for Anaximenes, in its most "even" state imperceptible.[4] The fact that air can originate many kinds of substances speaks to both its invisible (unifying) and visible (diversifying) force.

Explaining how this variety of appearances is possible, Anaximenes appeals to the quantitative process of rarefaction and condensation. When the element he called "air" becomes finer (rarefied or thinned), Anaximenes argues it becomes fire, and through thickening (condensation) it becomes water, earth, stone, and everything else. As Daniel Graham clarifies: "Air is part of a series of changes. Fire turns to air, air to wind, wind to cloud, cloud to water, water to earth and earth to stone. Matter can travel this path by being condensed, or the reverse path from stones to fire by being successively more rarefied."[5] Given this dynamic, elemental interplay, Graham stipulates that Anaximenes might be read as "a forerunner of process philosophy."[6] Graham argues: "By changing the density of the matter we change its essential properties to make it something essentially different. Air perishes and wind comes to be; wind perishes and clouds come to be, and so on. Air is not in principle different from the other elements, and it does not remain through all transformations as a continuing substratum."[7]

Our air is thus an ever-changing substratum, a product of history. And in our present, the air we breathe has never been so thoroughly scrutinized or hotly contested as in recent times during the Covid-19 pandemic.[8] As the virus spread, leaving in its wake death, loss, suffering, fear, and isolation, the breathing spaces of our lives emerged as both unavoidable places needed for survival as much as dangerous coexisting places of infection. While the pandemic and consequent lockdowns jolted our lives in synchronic fashion, propounding catastrophic suffering and the deaths of millions, it also brought to the surface long-standing, diachronic inequities[9] that have long marked access to "good air" or exposure to "bad air," terms that will be unpacked in what follows.

Thus, loss involving air, initially synchronically experienced as part of the "event" of Covid-19, is broader and deeper than the moment or even the few years of the pandemic. What is truly needed is an examination of the diachronic fault lines that range far and deep, and that have fractured and prefigured our breathing spaces over a much longer period of time than the pandemic.

It is exactly in theorizing those diachronic traces and in philosophizing the intertwinement of body, illness, home, and air that this chapter seeks to find traction. It sees its aim precisely in thinking beyond catastrophic loss and instead moves toward slow, ephemeral loss in the spaces of air. This chapter does so by turning to a prevalent, seemingly innocuous, but possibly damaging form of illness whose playing field is the intersection of body, place, economy, ecology, and air: "atopic" illness, with a special focus on allergic rhinitis and asthma. Atopy is generally defined as "the genetic tendency to develop the classic allergic diseases—atopic dermatitis, allergic rhinitis (hay fever), and asthma."[10] What is particularly fascinating about this atopic "cluster" is the fact that it often involves a form of place-based illness, even if, paradoxically, the very name of the cluster indicates, literally, the privative nature of place and home (*a-topos*).

What may be gleaned philosophically from this form of illness is that it offers a *portal* to elemental loss as different bodies come into being, in step with the coming to be of air as a medium in constant change. For following Anaximenes, we can strip air of its transcendent associations and illuminate its role as a co-constituting material medium. My analysis will proceed by first discussing the meaning of illness from a Heideggerian perspective, rethinking how illness in the form of allergic disease confronts us with the benefits and detriments of the medium of air, posing questions to our sense of finding a "home" in the material milieu. To grasp how air is not merely a "natural" medium but is also socially engineered, I turn next to Peter Sloterdijk's account of the construction and generation of air as part of the sphere-building done by humanity. Anaximenes's philosophy will augment Sloterdijk's account by providing us with a processual philosophy that unpacks (1) the broader natural, material, and ontogenetic principles at stake in air; and (2) the impacts of air not just on individuals, but on the broader contours and climates of our lives.

With this theoretical scaffolding in place, it is necessary to think through our historically present medium. Considering migration patterns, social inequities, and climate change, the following questions emerge: In what way have allergic and asthmatic patterns developed along the fault lines of social inequity? More specifically, how can it be that, despite increased affluence in certain parts of the world, there has also been a divergence in asthmatic patterns along the lines of social inequity and—across the board perhaps—a remarkably *negative gain* in what we might call the embodied breathing spaces of our life? Who is made subject to "bad air," and who has the privilege of being able to "air-purify" and "air-condition" their breathing spaces? How might climate change, and the Anthropocene more widely, further exacerbate the difference in the way allergies and "bad air" are experienced across various strata of society?

The Revelation of Illness as Portal into the Swinging Pendulum between Home and Homelessness

My way of thinking through the meaning of illness is informed by various contemporary phenomenologists of illness who prioritize grasping illness as it is lived and experienced in the first person.[11] Fredrik Svenaeus, a contemporary phenomenologist of medicine, offers an interpretation of the way illness interrupts our daily flow; he appeals to Heidegger's *Being and Time* to clarify how our sense of home and being-in-the-world is shifting due to illness.

While Svenaeus's account is helpful to initially thematize the notion of home, my account will also critique and move beyond his position to argue that some forms of illness (such as atopic allergies)—rather than elucidating a state of disturbing homelessness that needs to be brought back to "normal home," as Svenaeus argues—offer a key portal to grasping our fundamental oscillation in a zone of the airy elemental in-between.

Svenaeus argues that illness inserts a level of otherness and alienation in relation to our sense of home. Diseases, as he articulates, "remain *a threat to the homelike being-in-the-world* of Dasein in their radical and dreadful otherness."[12] What worsens the notion of alienation is that one's own intimate body is being othered, on top of which medicalization adds another layer of otherness. However, Svenaeus also sees hope for contemporary medicine: "Just as the bridge helps the Rhine disclose itself, medical practice can help the nature of our bodies to make itself at home in the culture of our being-in-the-world."[13]

What is powerful in Svenaeus's articulation of illness is the credible narrative regarding the palpable threat that illness inserts in our life. Especially when applied to terminal or chronic illnesses, such a narrative proves its value given the unsettling nature of such diseases. However, Svenaeus's account misses the mark in a number of respects.[14] Most importantly, his reading of Heidegger overlooks the fact that, for Heidegger, the experience of *Unheimlichkeit*—the unsettling uncanniness or homelessness of being—is in fact *central* to who we are. It is not the exception but is the central point of our existence. As Heidegger states in his *Introduction to Metaphysics*: "Dasein is the happening of homelessness itself" (*die geschehende Unheimlichkeit selbst*).[15] Also, as Heidegger postulates in *Being and Time*, "uncanniness is the basic kind of being-in-the-world, even though in an everyday way it has been covered up."[16]

Svenaeus's turn to Heidegger is productive in indexing how illness may offer us insights into our condition of homelessness; however, Svenaeus inserts a mistaken notion of "primordial being-at-home," thereby overlooking the fact that the experience of homelessness, for Heidegger, is liberating us from a "stifling"[17] sense of home and opens up to a more fundamental way of being.

If my reading of Heidegger is correct, then we need a more complex phenomenological account of illness. Rather than articulating, as Svenaeus does, that illness drives us out of our homelike situation and into a state of homelessness that needs to be countered, we could argue, following Heidegger's text, that illness opens up an ontological portal into a sense of recalibration of what we call home, a recalibration that is not necessarily only problematic but is also productive in terms of accessing the fundamentals of the human condition. However, this still seems facile and obvious, as we could argue that we arrive at the conclusion that illness—insofar as it is a confrontation with one's finitude—allows for the anxious experience of being-toward-death and thus a moment of realizing the uncanny and the opportunity to come into one's own—that is, into authenticity.

More than this turn to Heidegger's Messianic moment of vision, I wonder what would happen if we take a slightly different existential point of departure: ephemeral illnesses that are not just associated with death but predominantly with an altered sense of living. What if we take, for instance, the case of living with atopic allergies? What happens to our sense of home and homelessness? If we follow some of the accounts that have been given, then we find (1) a sense of *altered* living, (2) a sense of *living on*, and (3) a powerful (objective and subjective) recognition of the *elemental context* within which we dwell.

In many cases of such ephemeral accounts of illness, we need to insert an alternative account of the experience of home and homelessness. In the case of ephemeral illnesses, namely, there is no "hovering" in either home or homelessness. Rather, in an altered sense of living that is yet living on, in which the environment and the lived body co-emerge not only in hospitable but also harmful ways, such forms of illness allow for an oscillation in the zone of the in-between, following the swing of a pendulum from a sense of home to homelessness and back. Ephemeral illnesses arguably allow us to recognize the precarious in-between and the broader milieu, where life lives on, but in a diminished fashion, questioning the meaning of home and homelessness in altered bodies and environments.

Moreover, if it is the case that many such ephemeral illnesses emerge at the intersection of biology, environment, economics, and culture, then this account of the implication of illness for our sense of home and homelessness acquires further complexity. In other words, if many ephemeral illnesses are related to factors that stand at the "core" of what we call our elemental (natural and cultural) "home," then what does this imply for our sense of home and homelessness as experienced with and through illness?

Thus, I want to argue, versus Heidegger's focus on finitude, that illness affords something else than a moment of vision that enables the opportunity to be "individualized down to itself in its uncanniness."[18] Rather, illness may reveal another dimension of our lives, especially in the form of ephemeral atopic allergic illness where cycles of attrition slowly erode one's existence. These cycles make visible the core of airy elemental becoming, a historical interaction between air as exterior and air as interior, an interaction that opens up a liminal third space that is the matrix of the affective legibility between the two prior components that produce our breathing-in-the-world as a specific moment in space and time. Allergic illness highlights this elemental mediation, by indexing the discomfort and suffering that a breakdown in this airy interaction space may bring, recalibrating our bodies and our sense of well-being, just as much as another cycle, one that bolsters this affective space of legibility, might create new possibilities for breath. Thus, in sum, atopic allergies offer us a portal into (1) a milieu that has both positive and negative social impacts (versus the more "negative" impact of Heidegger's "the They"[19]); (2) a milieu that is deeply material (both biological and social);

(3) a milieu that connects not only *human* beings but all beings alike; and (4) a milieu that affects not only the individual's temporal immediacy but also the temporal horizon of a range of beings.

The Constitution and Generation of Air: Peter Sloterdijk and the Importance of Reenvisioning Air as the Potential Space of Illness

To articulate the liminal space of our airy elemental medium more broadly, we may do well to appeal to Peter Sloterdijk, who explicitly redirects the Heideggerian project in a fundamental direction from (presumed) solipsism to coexistence, and from finitude and the quest for weight and burden to the lightness and airiness of bubbles and foams. For Heidegger, true notions of place, locale, and home seem to depend on the disclosure of Being; however, Sloterdijk repositions the account of place on the level of co-creation and co-evolution with human coexistence. For Sloterdijk, the concept of "foams" offers an alternative to grasping society either on the basis of a contract theory or on the basis of holism. Foams, instead, do justice both to the unique spheres of our individual lives *and* to our intimate coexistence with each other. Foams thus access our social, political life as an "aggregate of microspheres (couples, households, businesses, associations) of different formats that, like the individual bubbles in a mountain of foam, border on one another and are layered over and under one another, yet without truly being accessible or effectively separable from one another."[20]

In his exposition of such shared spaces, Sloterdijk turns explicitly to air and air-conditioning. It is in this light that Sloterdijk recalibrates the meaning of the term "homelessness" after Heidegger:

> If Martin Heidegger often spoke in his essays after 1945 of "homelessness" as the existential watchword of humans in the age of enframing (*Ge-stell*), this referred not only to the lost naïveté of residing in country houses and the transition to existence in urban living machines. At a deeper level, the term "homeless" refers to the expatriation of humans from their natural air shell and their move to air-conditioned spaces; in an even more radical reading, the discussion of homelessness symbolizes the exodus from all possible niches of security in latency.[21]

Accordingly, Sloterdijk argues that the "technological answer" to Heidegger's being-in-the-world is the insight that "human being-in-the-world is always and without exception a modification of being-in-the-air."[22] As the air—and more generally the atmosphere—becomes a subject of explication in the twentieth century, it demands, as Sloterdijk writes, a "corresponding emancipation. It calls for and achieves the active reshaping of the element."[23] As we thematize air, we encounter what Sloterdijk calls an *airquake*:

> Airquake: as air, climate and atmospheric conditions become explicit, the primal advantage of those who exist over the primary medium of existence is challenged and exposed as naïve. Whenever in their history humans have been able to step into the open or under a roof in any given climate, relying on an unquestioning assumption of breathability with reference to the air around them—excepting miasmic zones—they made use, as one sees in retrospect, of a privilege of naïveté that was irretrievably lost with the advent of the twentieth century. Anyone living after this caesura and operating in a cultural zone synchronized with modernity is condemned to veritable climactic concern and atmospheric design, whether in rudimentary or elaborated forms.[24]

Sloterdijk's point requires emphasis. The uncanny or the homelessness that is the basic condition of our existence, according to Heidegger, is for us in the twentieth and twenty-first centuries marked by air warfare, air-conditioning, and general climatic concerns less an issue of a theoretical, ontological ground structure (*Existenziale*) as Heidegger would have it, and more so an issue of being driven out of a "natural" assumed airy background to, as Sloterdijk words it, the explicitly theorized "homeless" state of living in increasingly explicit *mediated, and engineered air*. Moreover, the air that has been engineered has often been at the detriment of our well-being, certainly with the rise of "modernity" (as the toxic gases used in World War I prove).[25]

With that, we find again another access point to the theorization of the elemental airy medium. While I would not want to go so far as Sloterdijk to argue that we have been driven out toward homelessness per se into purely "artificial air," what I do want to argue is that, in the twentieth and twenty-first centuries, we would do well to consider how the liminal space of air—which I, unlike Sloterdijk, will not necessarily call the space of homelessness but rather a medium that defies essentializing notions of home or homelessness given the air's ontogenetic principles—has materialized increasingly in the form of both natural and artificial air transformations, underpinning our lives, health, and illnesses.

What I want to highlight is (1) the broader ecological air of which we are part; (2) the idea that air itself is changeable and self-forming; (3) the importance of recognizing the consequences of bad air across the globe in the form of ephemeral illnesses; and, finally, (4) the need for an ethical-political assessment of whose bodies are made subject to increasingly problematic "bad air."

Sloterdijk's theoretical account of air is rather "thin" when it concerns the co-constitution of life and air, certainly in light of the fact that air, as Irigaray emphasizes, speaks to the cultivation of life and of its relationality to the environment.[26] Sloterdijk's account mostly pertains to human life without considering the broader facets of air—the way that air is an element with both human and more-than-human dimensions. Additionally, Sloterdijk focuses on very specific forms of human life in the Global North that are luxuriously "pampered" with air-conditioning qualities and care by the state; in this, he fails to consider others who are less well off. Sloterdijk's account of air runs the risk of playing into the hands of libertarian defenders of individual rights without considering the broader political-economic factors that underpin the unequal division of "good" air. Thus, a broader examination of breathing, environment, and air is needed to consider the notion of the inequity of good air versus bad air that is crucial to how we live our illnesses.

Anaximenes on Air:
Reenvisioning the Generation and Dynamics of Air

By turning to Anaximenes, we find access to a philosophical pathway that considers the ontogenesis, distribution, density, and rarity of air. His account also speaks to the effects and impact of air on the generation and corruption of other bodies. This account thereby complements Sloterdijk's account by showing the broader natural and ontogenetic principles at stake in air and the impacts of air not just on individuals but on the broader contours and climates of our lives.

Anaximenes highlights the importance of air as (a) an ontogenetic principle, and (b) he grasps both the particularity and universality of air—that is, air is what I breathe as much as it is an overall principle of life.

(a) Anaximenes argues that air is the principle from which the things that are (and have been and will be) come into being—either directly or through its products:

> Anaximenes . . . said that the principle is unlimited air [*aera apeiron*], out of which come to be things that are coming to be [*ta ginomena*], things that have come to be [*ta gegonota*], and things that will be [*ta esomena*], and gods and divine beings. . . . The form [*eidos*] of air is the following: when it is most even [*homoiōtatos*], it is invisible [*adēlon*], but it is revealed by the cold and the hot and the wet, and movement. It is always being moved [*kineisthai*], for all the things that undergo change would not change unless it was moving.[27]

In philosophizing air, Anaximenes argues that *air* is an ontogenetic principle: It originates all beings—past, present, and future—and those beings usually said to originate life and the world as we know it—that is, the gods.[28] With that, Anaximenes prioritizes the importance of this material element over the mythological, divine dimension of our lives, thereby arguably transforming the meaning of "transcendence" to what is also dependent upon and informed by a materiality that makes all beings possible. Moreover, as Anaximenes thinks through the ontogenesis of the world, the first "change" out of air consists in the emergence of the earth (DK13 A6), after which the heavenly bodies (sun, moon, etc.) arise out of the earth. When we speak of climate and season, this is, according to Anaximenes, in turn caused by the influence of the sun on the air and the according density or rareness of the air.[29]

We thus have here an early climatological account of the way that our world with its temporal flows and patterns is dependent upon the broader, reciprocal architecture of the world as originated by, and mediated through, air. Air is key for Anaximenes insofar as it "defines the one, undifferentiated state before the cosmos existed."[30] Furthermore, as Graham clearly stipulates, air has "special properties associated with life, which can account for the orderliness of the world as well as for animal and human intelligence."[31] However, this does *not* imply that air stays "the same" throughout all consequent manifestations. Rather, what results might be called "products or offspring of air."[32]

Contemporary science has confirmed air's importance for earth and all its inhabitants. While various kinds of atmospheres have been in place since the earth's formation,[33] only with the "Great Oxidation Event," which took place in the early Proterozoic period (2,500–2,542 million years ago), did air, and life, truly emerge. However, while Anaximenes asserts that air originated life, modern scientists would contest that: while oxidation was undoubtedly crucial to the proliferation of life, it is the case that living organisms in the form of cyanobacteria originally *produced* oxygen and, thus, gave rise to the kinds of air and forms of life we know today. Thus, almost paradoxically, "life itself was responsible for creating the air that we breathe."[34] And it is particular with the transformation of cyanobacteria into multicellular beings that their impact on the world became larger—especially given their new ability to move and become attached to surfaces by creating mats, which infused the earth with oxygen.

A metabolism driven by oxygen (aerobic metabolism) is more efficient than anaerobic metabolism.[35] Thus, "by breathing oxygen, organisms could become much more active, and much larger. Moving beyond the simple multicellularity developed by cyanobacteria, some organisms became far more intricate. They became plants and animals, from sponges and worms to fish and, ultimately, humans."[36] Extrapolating from these scientific insights, it is important to underline that life produced air as much as it became dependent upon it, and that life only could develop into the complexity of vegetal and animal life due to the efficient metabolism oxygen provided. Thus, while modern scientific insights pose some challenges to Anaximenes's ideas, they maintain his main line of insight, namely that air is a natural and ontogenetic principle for multiple forms of life.

(b) Secondly, what is remarkable about Anaximenes's thoughts on air is that he emphasizes air's commonality, flexibility, and particularity as it grounds, informs, and connects our own bodies. For instance, sensations of coldness or warmth as associated with our breath disclose air: "For he declares that matter which is contracted and condensed is cold, whereas what is fine and 'loose' . . . is hot. As a result he claimed that it is not said unreasonably that a person releases both hot and cold from his mouth. For the breath becomes cold when compressed and condensed by the lips, and when the mouth is relaxed, the escaping breath becomes warm through the rareness."[37] Anaximenes's phenomenology of air draws upon our inhalation and exhalation and on the fact that our breath can feel cold or warm, depending on whether we purse our lips (when the air is compressed and cools through a process scientists call "adiabatic expansion") or relax our muscles, in which case the air exhaled feels like your own body temperature. Since air acquires our own unique body temperature or is mediated through our own movements, this example shows the transit space between individual and material space—elemental mediation is not only a general but also a specific organizing principle for our own embodiment.

That breath and air are also connected, for Anaximenes, on a larger cosmological level is indicated in this excerpt: "Just as our soul [*psychē*], being air, holds us [*sygkratei*] together, so do breath and air surround [*periechei*] the whole *kosmos*; for air and breath are said synonymously."[38] On the relation between soul and air, McKirahan insightfully writes that this idea follows "a well attested prephilosophical view that the air we breathe is our soul and vital principle, that which distinguishes the living from the nonliving and from the dead."[39] As McKirahan continues, "Because air plays the same role in the universe as it does in humans, and it makes humans alive, it seems to follow that the universe is alive. . . . Air gives life to its offspring, including the entire *kosmos*."[40]

Should we translate Anaximenes's insights to our current times and particularly to an account of illness in relation to the social-natural constellation of air, then what stands out, first of all, is Anaximenes's ability to address the architecture of climate and air, and the notion that air is an ontogenetic principle for multiple forms of life. Moreover, Anaximenes's philosophy enables a view of the body that connects the particular and the universal: as I breathe, my body mediates the air in both its particularity and simultaneously connects to its universal aspects. For our account of illness, this is important, given that we seek to analyze air as a material medium (both biological and social), connecting the individual's existence to the temporal horizon of a range of beings. Finally, as Anaximenes analyzes air, he reports on its visible and invisible aspects, thereby enabling views of air that think beyond the singular event and that postulate a broader architecture and meaning of air.

The Modalities of the Medium of Air: Mitman, Berlant, and Nietzsche on the Generation and Distribution of Bad Air

Anaximenes's account stresses the ontogenesis crucial to air and speaks to the effects and impact of air on the generation and corruption of other bodies. Moreover, Anaximenes addresses the architecture of air and the way in which singular bodies communicate with air in its universal aspects. This, in turn, for my analysis, opens the door to thinking through the social-material spaces of air—how do we *live*, socially and culturally, with air? To whom is good air distributed, and who is made subject to poor air quality? For sure, certain so-called natural geographical locations impact air quality—based on locations such as valleys and mountains, for instance—but these geographical locations acquire social complexity as we think about the built infrastructure that informs them (highways, industry, pollution, homes, parks, etc.).[41] How does our own breathing, and what we might call *the ontological right to breathing good air*, stand in relationship to the inequities and the problematic distribution of good air? Is it possible for us to guarantee good air equally to all people? And is there a reciprocal duty to breathe bad air, if those in the Global North outsource their bad air to the Global South, carbon taxes notwithstanding?

If we follow the rise of allergy research, for instance, in Gregg Mitman's book *Breathing Space*, which focuses on the United States, the spaces where we breathe "have been shaped, not only by the ecology of animals, insects, plants, and man-made allergens, but also by the unequal distribution of wealth and healthcare in American society."[42] Mitman demonstrates this thesis through articulate sociological and historical research and through a powerful autobiographical point. He compares and contrasts his own childhood struggles with asthma and allergies with that of the asthmatic childhood struggles of his brother-in-law. The contrast between himself, a middle-class boy growing up in the suburbs, and his brother-in-law, a low-income boy growing up in the inner city,[43] grappling with the so-called "same" illness but in very different circumstances, highlights that allergy and asthmatic disease and their effects are not only the products of our body's inner sensitivity or simply a response to the allergens of a place, but they also intersect in a complex way with the broader social-political and economic forces that underpin our lives. Thus, while allergy is in many ways a disease of place and biology, it is also in many ways a *social* disease.[44] Perhaps it is better to say that atopic disease is a disease of both biogeography *and* social place, which then results in the fact that, as Mitman writes, "the problems a poor, asthmatic child in the inner city faces are far different from those of a middle-class, asthmatic child in the suburbs."[45]

Mitman's book is itself an elaboration of the thesis that "if place shaped illness, illness also shaped place."[46] He provides a rich reading of the colonial history of hay fever treatment in the United States, which involved the construction and consequent popularity of hay fever resorts for the white middle and upper classes in the 1880s, such as Newport or Mackinac.[47] He also relates Pirquet's coining of the term "allergy" in 1906, and the rise of the emergence of allergies as the land became increasingly colonized.[48] Mitman's account shows how, with the settler colonial spirit going west and railroads being built, the ragweed that was causing much of the allergies accompanied every step of human development seeking precisely escape *from* ragweed.[49] For that reason, paradoxically, "ecological havens," such as Tucson and Denver, which were initially greatly attractive to asthmatics and allergy sufferers because of their clean air and low allergens, became "ecological hells," especially for a vulnerable population that had a large number of asthmatics to begin with.[50] This was due to the arrival of railroads and accompanying growth of ragweed; the arrival of nonnative grasses and allergenic trees, such as mulberry and olive; and the building of factories and their consequent dust, smoke, and pollution.

This story of the coevolution of migration, place, and allergy demonstrates that relocation was no longer seen as the medical answer to allergies; rather, also due to the rise of biomedical knowledge, the body itself became the space of medicine's hope and profit. As Mitman potently writes: "Allergic bodies not only opened up new vistas on the frontiers of biomedicine, but they also brought into sharp relief changing land-use patterns that destroyed the healing properties of place and reinforced the need for a new space of hope within the body's immunological landscape."[51] In extension of Sloterdijk's idea on the co-creation of the spheres within which we emerge and dwell, Mitman here articulates that much of the engineering of the breathing space within which we live does not just depend on so-called "external" environmental factors but also on manipulating the internal space of the body, thereby opening up medicine to a "lucrative transnational market in pharmaceutical research and treatment of allergic disease."[52] Additionally, with increased scrutiny on the home and its allergenic factors such as dust mites, a sprawling industry has emerged: "manufacturers of air conditioners, portable air filters, special vacuum cleaners, and allergy-proof covers have been eager to sell a breathing space made pure through technology."[53]

Overall, Mitman's argument is built around the co-emergence of breathing space, bodies, illness, and the social-economic and environmental elements that underpin air. His argument returns us to the breathing place where ephemeral illness emerges in the airy intersection of nature and culture, to the liminal spaces that, through our bodies, track historical, cultural, and institutional changes. The breathing space theorized here is, modifying Sloterdijk, not just an expulsion from natural air to artificial air, but an acknowledgment of the (historical and emerging) *interaction* between so-called natural air and so-called artificial air, where our bodies live through and become who they are by way of the air of which we are part, with air constantly evolving holding particles that may or may not be allergenic or harmful, and where "good" air and "bad" air are not shared equally across populations or continents. More specifically, Mitman's account shows that our bodies' illnesses trace the historical paths that our civilization, migration patterns, and "air-conditioning patterns" have traversed. Moreover, allergies express a distinct vulnerability, a disjunction, in our ideally "trusting" relationship to the environment of air.

While many of us these days suffer from "bad air," it is predominantly the marginalized that suffer most in such disasters, as they have no means to escape the outdoor air or purchase expensive air purifiers to keep their air clean. Still, without denying the personal drama of such big disasters affecting the air, the broader question that the issue of asthmatic distress and bad air evokes is that of the structural injustice that affects many more in their day-to-day existence—a fact of "bad air" and asthmatic distress that is not usually seen or that rarely makes the headlines.[54]

To demonstrate, in their research of the quality of life among the homeless living on the streets in Delhi, Walters and Gaillard speak of the "silent disasters" of ordinary urban life. As their research shows, "the most marginalized are particularly vulnerable not only to large-scale events but also to small-scale, high-frequency hazards which easily impair their fragile livelihood and hence their ability to sustain their daily needs."[55] In Delhi alone, "it is estimated that every year 10,000 people die prematurely as a result of air pollution and that respiratory illnesses from poor air quality number in the hundreds of thousands."[56] Thus, "while everyday hazards may have a low impact on a city they can be the cause of premature death and serious injury for many urban inhabitants, cumulatively killing or injuring more people than a large-scale low-frequency event."[57]

The lives of those exposed to such bad air on a daily basis may be part of the ordinary yet devastating phenomenon of what cultural theorist Lauren Berlant has called "slow death." As Berlant points out, "slow death, or the structurally motivated attrition of persons notably because of their membership in certain populations, is neither a state of exception nor the opposite, mere banality, but a domain of revelation where an upsetting scene of living that has been muffled in ordinary consciousness is revealed to be interwoven with ordinary life after all, like ants revealed scurrying under a thoughtlessly lifted rock."[58] Berlant's analysis of slow death is done in the context of examining obesity in the United States, and the "attrition" she speaks of in the preceding quote speaks to the fact that current economic and political regimes gradually reduce the strength or effectiveness of certain groups of people due to sustained pressure. What is particularly potent in Berlant's analysis is her focus on how *sustained pressure, context, and time* structurally inform our lives. While much of our attention to conditions of suffering is usually drawn toward the immediate and the crisis, what is "scurrying underneath the rocks" and out of sight is the slowly accumulated weight of pressures that make up the context and material components of our lives. What Berlant highlights is the importance of addressing the accumulative sense of an environment, which surreptitiously informs our lives through patterns that may either "build us up" or allow us to "live on" however poorly, enervated, and interwoven with decay, stress, and morbidity.

Berlant's focus on the enervating forces that interweave decay in our lives evokes Nietzsche's climatological and cultural concerns with the decay associated with bad air. Nietzsche is, as a cultural diagnostician, always looking for the broader forces that underpin bad air. He diagnoses the nineteenth century as a culture that oozes decay out of its pores—since it is built out of nihilistic, weakening tendencies, continuing to embrace what Nietzsche calls "falsified ideals," such as the ascetic ideal and leveling down the potencies of human beings to that of mere averageness: "Whoever still has a nose to smell with as well as eyes and ears, can detect almost everywhere he goes these days something like the air of the madhouse and hospital—I speak, as is appropriate, of man's cultural domains, of every kind of 'Europe' that still exists on this earth."[59] Air, for Nietzsche, is thus found more broadly in a culture's constellations and in its abilities to generate healthy and creative opportunities or weak, death-bound ones.

While one easily could take issue with Nietzsche's problematic association of cultural air as being associated with the "smell" of hospitals or madhouses, a key point I want to highlight here is Nietzsche's understanding of "bad air" as emerging from a *contextual, cultural place*—a place of structural values that may inform our physiology and our ideology either positively or negatively, conveying health and hopefulness for the future or, conversely, ideas born out of frustration and decay that will bring us down. Furthermore, if we recast Nietzsche's critique for our own time, even if it does not *reek* in the Global North, then does this undo the "bad air" the Global North produces by allocating its factories elsewhere? How do clear natural air and ethical poor air intersect? What does cultural hypocrisy mean these days in times of bad air? Where does it *reek* most?

Thus, Nietzsche's understanding of "bad air" further complements Berlant's account of slow death by bringing perspicuity to the structural, political-ideological foundations of our lives and thereby elucidates how some structures may bring about refreshing air, that is, what Nietzsche calls "good, thin, clear, free, dry air, the air in the mountains, in which all animal existence becomes more spiritual and takes wings."[60] Conversely, other structures may bring about bad air such as are found in "the enormous hypocrisy in ideals, spirit's strongest liquor, and therefore, also, the disgusting, foul-smelling, mendacious, pseudo-alcoholic air everywhere."[61] The false crutches of hypocritical ideals according to Nietzsche serve as a way to temporarily soothe and numb our suffering, but they are betrayed by their foul smell, which expresses the weakening effects on our being.

Concluding Thoughts

Allergic illness offers a portal into the element of air and shows both the ecological constellation of the elemental as well as its historical and artificial transformations, tracking migration, infrastructure, class structures, and more. Allergic illness taps into the notion of liminality, offering oscillation between the breath of our individual bodies and the larger elemental constellation of which we are part, and makes us realize that air is not simply neutral or static or purely life-giving but dynamic; it has both positive and negative effects. Air is deeply material and is shared across different forms of life. It connects us to all living beings dependent upon the air and productive of it, and it is not only reflective of past historical transformations but intimately connected to possible futures lying ahead.

If bad air is not a local phenomenon, but instead drifts from one place to another, we may pose the following question: Rather than "building out of space on top of itself"—engineering and protecting good air for the select few while keeping the inequities in place—what other possibilities for mediating air, with a different underlying form of politics, may be possible? How may we address the fact that bad air is lived and examined not just in this individual life but also synchronously across segments of society and diachronically across various generations? As Stephen Graham writes: "The colonization of (air-conditioned) vertical space is now largely an elite programme—a three-dimensional rising up of the powerful and wealthy bound up with the neoliberal and revanchist reengineering of entire cityscapes largely for their needs. As elites literally rise up into gated, air-conditioned, vertical communities and tall, climate-controlled workplace towers, so they work to escape both the din of urban life and the pressing heat and pollution of the hotter urban surface."[62] Can we imagine other structures or political interventions that allow for different societal-collective individuations other than the imaginary and reality of the "colonization of (air-conditioned) vertical space" by the current elites? How can we make visible the often-invisible division of poor air? What kind of political sensitivity does this require? I propose two pragmatic warnings that speak to the need for a new political and ecological sensitivity:

(1) The formation of a new kind of political sensitivity should warn against current practices that take the installation of individual AC units for granted. This is only a short-term solution, which ultimately locks us long term into what Buraniyi calls "the air conditioning trap":[63] "Warmer temperatures lead to more air conditioning; more air conditioning leads to warmer temperatures. The problem posed by air conditioning resembles, in miniature, the problem we face in tackling the climate crisis. The solutions that we reach for most easily only bind us closer to the original problem."[64]

AC units work "by breathing in warm air, passing it across a cold surface, and exhaling cool, dry air."[65] In the United States, they became popular after World War II as a selling point for generic buildings that could be built in "any" climate. With the globalization of AC units, traditional and far more sustainable methods of cooling buildings, such as "window screens[;] facades[;] and brise-soleils," were replaced and became obsolete.[66] Moreover, design techniques that reconsidered reducing heat—such as those that balance "the sizes of openings, the area of the wall, the thermal properties, and shading, the orientation"[67]—were increasingly ignored due to the pressure of development companies.

In sum, it is high time to reconsider the use of individual AC units and to rethink the implications of buildings and industrial tendencies for air: How do they affect the air's quality long term? How can we rework the air more sustainably, with less negative effects long term, and reimplement time-proven sustainable techniques for reducing heat in homes?

(2) Additionally, we need to gain the political and ecological sensitivity that the construction of our breathing space has always been ongoing and is always shared—what constitutes "good air" for some is actually bad or even poisonous air for others. With the help of contemporary science, we can trace the importance of the oxygenated air that we breathe currently.

As scientific studies show, and as mentioned earlier in the chapter, while various kinds of atmospheres have been in place since earth's formation,[68] only with the "Great Oxidation Event," which took place in the early Proterozoic period (2,500–2,542 million years ago), did air, and life as we currently know it, truly emerge. However, what is often forgotten is that while this event allowed for the creation of multicellular life and mitochondria, this came at the expense of "many types of primeval bacteria,"[69] which relied on what scientists presume were the most prevalent gases at the time: carbon dioxide and methane. With the great oxidation event, "almost every species of life on Earth died," which, as Peter Steeves writes, is "a sad reminder that air is always shared."[70] Reflecting back upon the great oxidation event thus offers us insights into deep time, revealing continuous changes of our atmospheres either set in motion through so-called natural means (e.g., in the case of oxygenation, the production of oxygen through cyanobacteria) or through human-imposed changes such as industrialization. What the great oxidation event can teach us, in relationship to our current air crisis of pollution, warm air, and allergenics is this: an atmosphere, and thus air, is always shared.

From the earlier catastrophes of shared air to our current crises centering around air pollution, allergenics, and Covid-19, we are reminded that true "care" in the case of our breathing space means a care that reinserts itself in this material space of the in-between, recognizing the precarious milieu—both on the level of the individual and on the level of its social and natural milieu—out of which life, illness, and death emerge. Thus, renewed attention is needed to elemental loss and the way that we live our illnesses through the element of air. Nothing but our conspiring, co-breathing selves are at stake. As architect Alexander Pope asks: "Can a set of ontological rights—such as breathing—actually challenge or even displace economic hegemony?" The answer I would give is an unwavering yes. If nothing but the "key ontological preconditions of human existence"[71] are at stake, then we must seek opportunities to reorganize the construction of our breathing space, for instance, by rethinking the infrastructure and building regulations for our homes and cities.

As we turn in the next chapter to earth, it is important to note that, similar to air, our relationship with earth is also complex, historically changing, and in need of further examination and reformulation. Though we view earth as starkly different from air—especially since we generally view the former as heavy and powerful and fundamental, while we view the latter as weightless, swift, and dynamic—they possess similarities that may assist us in analyzing our relationship with each of the elements. For, in both cases, we encounter a relationship to the open, where we find a sense of ecological belonging yet one that is also ever evolving, tracing histories as well as providing futures. However, in times of climate change both of these elements seem to leave us with a sense of loss. While I have articulated in this chapter the incremental slow changes to air that have informed our allergic and asthma-infused lifestyles leading to diminution and loss, it is less clear what the equivalent would be on the level of the element of earth. It will be my thesis in the next chapter that the increased prevalence of earthquakes has much to do with climate change, industrialization, and human technologies such as fracking, thereby showing yet another aspect of emergent elemental loss, right at the bottom of our feet.

Chapter 4

Earth

Silent Tremors

Earthquakes and the Question of Balance and (Dis)Orientation

The spasmodic earth comes to unite ... with my shaky body. The world finally comes to me, resembles me, all in distress ... [we] liv[e] in a permanent earthquake.

—Michel Serres, *The Natural Contract*

For what can anyone believe quite safe if the world itself is shaken, and its most solid parts totter to their fall? Where, indeed, can our fears have limit if the one thing immovably fixed, which upholds all other things in dependence on it, begins to rock, and the earth lose its chief characteristic, stability? What refuge can our weak bodies find?

—Seneca the Younger, *Natural Questions*

Small, beautifully formed and locked in the skull, the vestibular organs continuously bombard the brain with messages.... They tell of accelerations, how the head is rotating and translating and its orientation in space. The messages never stop and cannot be turned off. Even when we are completely motionless, they signal the relentless pull of gravity. Perhaps because of their constant monologue, the vestibular sensation is different to the other senses. There is no overt, readily recognizable, localisable, conscious sensation from these organs. They provide a silent sense.

—Brian L. Day and Richard C. Fitzpatrick,
"The Vestibular System"

It is difficult to underestimate the foundational nature of earth. It is the element on which we learn to crawl and walk, and where we stand, move, fall, and get up. It is on earth's ground that we farm and find shelter, and it is the element where our bodies ultimately return after their deaths. Beyond the soil, we also call our entire planet "Earth."[1] Thus, earth seems to easily escape simple limits and parameters—it is "confoundingly complex," as Macauley has it, or "wild bewildering," in the words of Edgar Allan Poe.[2]

Amid the difficulties in containing the wide field of meanings of the term "earth," this chapter will examine earth as *elemental constellation*. This methodology—discussed in previous chapters—furnishes us with a structure to think through earth both through the microlevel of our engagements with it, as well as through our overall (ontological-causal and social-semantic) framed engagement (i.e., the macrolevel of our engagements with earth). More specifically, I will use the notion of elemental constellation to think through our dynamic interactions with the *moving* earth, and in particular the *disorienting* shifts that align with the instability of earthquakes. Earthquakes are shifts in the elemental constellation of earth that confront us with the broader question that this book is asking: In the era of anthropogenic climate change, what are the meanings of loss, grief, and mourning beyond that of individualized loss and individualized life?

Thinking through the notions of the various constituents of elemental constellations, the following question emerges when we make earthquakes our central focus: To what degree are the losses we experience in earthquakes natural losses, social losses, or a combination of the two? And exactly what is lost as the ground shifts, literally, and we find ourselves tumbled, shaken, and recalibrated? Moreover, being-in-the-world has always been a question of movement dependent upon our connection to the earth. So, if our own interactions with the earth have led to increased and changed movements of the earth (e.g., increased earthquakes due to fracking or climate change), then how are we—or how ought we to be—handling the earth's increased instability and our co-emerging disorientation? These are questions that can be answered by unpacking the affective-philosophical concept of orientation.

If it is the case that "the dizzy man cries the terror of earthquake wherever he goes, feeling that for him all order of the universe is at the end,"[3] then it is this chapter's task to simultaneously confront us with the dynamics of a world in motion (indexed by the instability of earthquakes) and grasp our co-emergent search for order and balance. While we often take balance for granted, it is anything but: our daily existence of sitting "upright" and moving forward depends on us scanning the horizon and having a sense of what's up and what's down, detecting gravity, being able to connect what we see to how we move, and "knowing where our body is in space."[4] As Svec puts it: "Each step we take is a miracle of balance as our bodies compensate for hundreds of tiny changes in weight distribution and body position."[5]

Exploring our sense of balance and orientation is fruitful—especially now—because anthropogenic climate change is threatening to "wake up the slumbering giant"—that is, the earth.[6] Accordingly, we must consider the possibilities to deal with coming disorientations and unpack how the hitherto silent structuring concept of orientation has played out in the background of our elemental realities and has been constructed at both a conceptual and affective level over time. From this genealogical vantage point (i.e., the concept of orientation), we begin to see that the discourse regarding the Anthropocene provides a kind of return to a deterministic, fate-based lens, steering us toward complete disorientation—a flight into the contingent.

Similar to how gluteal muscles and pelvic bone transformation allowed earlier hominids a biped traversal of the earth by changing their center of gravity,[7] I argue that there are benefits to thinking through the complex challenges lying ahead of us so that we can adjust our own affective, embodied apparatus to enable a recalibrated, effective, ethical, and socially informed center of gravity. As we walk through a world that trembles, the challenge is to transform our embodied sense of orientation—or rather disorientation—along with the changes in the landscape. We must not merely mirror the changes in the landscape but, more importantly, anticipate the challenges ahead to make the posthuman dispositionally adaptable to the changes ahead of us. Since our own orientation tracks elemental qualities, the co-affective space that is earth-body and stability-orientation need to stand front and center in our deliberations. This follows Michel Serres's call to "caress and follow the fissure's trembling"[8] without losing all senses of orientation.

In this chapter, I will structure my account of earth and earthquakes in a genealogical-historical fashion, starting with early Greek cosmologies and ending with theories of plate tectonics. As I will show, the question of earthquakes is prominently present in Greek cosmologies, despite the question of human orientation emerging later. This early theory affords us a preliminary glance at the meaning of abstracting the forces of the earth and trying to come to terms with frightening and destructive shaking. Greek mythological storytelling steers us away from seeing the world's shaking in terms of mere destructive chaos and instead categorizes the violent upheavals of the natural world by highlighting the notion of divine fate. As I will argue, such a fate-based perspective has returned in our current age in the form of the mythos of the Anthropocene with its doom-based scenario. Notwithstanding natural scientific insights ruling in the background, the dismissal of human agency and communal effort combined with a reliance on determinism has strong similarities with Greek mythos.

Narrating the Earth as the Origin of Stability and Creation: Hesiod's and Homer's Perspective

In this section, we turn to Greek mythology and philosophy to reconceptualize earth as a living being. The first subsection on Greek epic seeks to grasp the elemental constellation of earth through mythological storytelling oriented around Gaia and Poseidon. My genealogical reading of the mythologies of earthquakes serves as both a clarifying look into the abstract models that we, as humans, have drawn to make sense of a moving earth and a strategic scaffold for my own argument that defies the fate-oriented mythos at the heart of the Anthropocene. The second subsection on Aristotle's theory of the earth and earthquakes seeks to analogize earth and its movements to our own human bodies. In sharp contrast to the mythological fate-based accounts, Aristotle provides an account of earth as a natural body that stands in relationship to other natural elements.

Hesiod and Homer on the Stabilizing Origin of Earth and the Divine Interruptions of Earthquakes

In a world where little is under human control, the divine forces associated with Gaia and Poseidon—the earth and the earthshaker—demonstrate the need to outline order and stability in the world. This is punctuated by the temporary instability we experience as earthquakes, a result of divine infighting.

In Greek epic, figures of earth appear prominently in creation myths. In Hesiod, earth is portrayed in the form of a deity, Gaia, who is the first to appear after chaos:

> In the beginning there was only Chaos, the Abyss,
> But then Gaia, the Earth, came into being,
> Her broad bosom the ever-firm foundation (*asphales*) of all,
> And Tartaros, dim in the underground depths . . .[9]

Gaia offers the first solid "ground" away from crevices and ruptures and gives rise to an ordered universe. She is also described as a creative force, giving birth to many other beings and elements, including heaven and the sea:

> Earth's first child was Ouranos, starry Heaven,
> Just her size, a perfect fit on all sides.
> And a firm foundation for the blessed gods.
> And she bore the Mountains in long ranges, haunted
> By the nymphs who live in the deep mountain dells.
> Then she gave birth to the barren, raging Sea . . .[10]

Evidently, Gaia is a dynamic entity whose life-creating force stands at the foundation of the Greek cosmos. Hesiod's *Theogony* thus presents us with the figure of earth as a solid ground, a firm foundation, and a source of fertility.

Hesiod's cosmology also includes other figures that speak to the turbulent side of our living world, where thunder, fire, storms, and earthshaking occur. Whereas Zeus represents thunder and lightning that rule the skies, Poseidon represents earthquakes and tsunamis—he is the "earth-holding" (*gaiēochos*)[11] and "booming earthshaker" (*epiktupos ennosigaios*).[12]

Interestingly, for Homer, earth itself is not "ruled" by any particular god or goddess; however, that does not mean that earth itself does not resonate with "divine echoes": "The mother-goddess is in Homer forgotten or ignored, but the earth is constantly represented as a divine, life-giving power. There are no mountain-gods, but a mountain is the mother of the wild beasts, it shakes, it feeds springs, it quivers in the foliage of its forests."[13] Homer views earth like other natural experiences: "from within, at the source of its operation, in intensive moments when what stands out is the pervasive effectiveness of one vital principle."[14] And, like Hesiod, Homer designates Poseidon as "earthshaker" (*ennosigaios*; l. 173) and "earth-holding" (*gaiēochos*; l. 174) in addition to being the ruler of the sea. In the *Iliad*, Poseidon presents himself as being on an equal footing with his brothers, Zeus and Hades, and he explains their territorial divisions in the following way:

> . . . Since we are three brothers born by Rheia to Kronos,
> Zeus, and I, and the third is Hades, lord of the dead men.
> All was divided among us three ways, each given his domain.
> I when the lots were shaken drew the grey sea to live in
> forever; Hades drew the lot of the mists and the darkness,
> and Zeus was allotted the wide sky, in the cloud and the bright air.
> But earth (*gaia*) and high Olympos are common to all
>   (*ksunē pantōn*).[15]

Thus, as Poseidon's pronouncement confirms, earth itself is omitted from the "division" of the elements between the brothers—it is not ruled by one particular god or goddess. Earth is seen as a *common* terrain—one shared by all divinities. Zeus can strike the earth with thunder and lightning. Hades can interact with the earth by holding its former occupants. And Poseidon can interact with the earth by causing earthquakes. As this division shows, the Greek myths viewed the elements and the world through an architectonic lens, figuring out the various "building" components that structure our living world as one coherent whole. The neat architectonic division of the components (i.e., elements) of the sea, underworld, and sky stands in contrast to the "common living space" of earth, which is thereby the common "living room" within which the gods perform and battle for dominance.[16]

When we turn to Homer's discussion of Poseidon, we find that Poseidon's actions upon the earth and sea in the form of earthquakes and tsunamis are described as nothing but powerful. As Burkert notes with respect to the early Greeks, Poseidon is for them "an embodiment of *elemental force*; sea storm and earthquake are the most violent forms of energy directly encountered by man, while the horse was the strongest energy which man could then control."[17] In a world in which little is predictable or under human control (e.g., illness and crop failures),

Poseidon's shaking presents the summum of an uncontrollable, contingent force. Accordingly, for Homer, the only meaningful reaction is to recognize it—that is, to "take account of it."[18] In this case, taking account of such violence means to pay careful witness to it and to vividly detail such violence as affecting vast parts of our living world, including the lives of the dead. It also means to describe such violence as meaningful within the Greek pantheon, thereby showcasing that contingency can be grasped through the interplay between divine stability (primal) and instability (temporary, secondary, hidden, and able of stirring fright in gods and humans alike). Thus, in book 20 of the *Iliad*, we find the following scene:

> From high above the father of gods and men made thunder
> terribly, while Poseidon from deep under them shuddered
> all the illimitable earth, the sheer heads of the mountains.
> And all the feet of Ida with her many waters were shaken
> and all her crests, and the city of Troy, the ships of the Achaians.
> Aïdoneus, lord of the dead below, was in terror
> and sprang from his throne and screamed aloud, for fear that above him
> he who circles the land, Poseidon, might break the earth open
> and the houses of the dead lie open to men and immortals,
> ghastly and mouldering, so the very gods shudder before them;
> such was the crash that sounded as the gods came driving together in wrath.[19]

While other divinities such as Athena and Apollo provide illumination and technological skills to humans, the bare force of Poseidon is distinctively natural and does not entail such insight nor skill,[20] indexing the limited rational power that humans must contain this kind of forceful contingency in an otherwise stable world. Moreover, since Poseidon mostly operates secretly and does not challenge his brother openly, this elemental force is not only illogical but also elusive.[21] Furthermore, Poseidon's force overpowers both nature and artificial beings. His force extends to nature (e.g., in the form of mountains and waters) and to emblems of human culture (e.g., ships and cities). Finally, his force is a threat, which frightens even the gods, and poses a threat to the organized separation between the dead (in the underworld) and the living.

Thus, the descriptions of Gaia and Poseidon in the texts of Hesiod and Homer provide insights into the meaning and importance of the creation of earth as a stabilizing origin, which can temporarily be

88 | Beyond Elemental Loss

disturbed by the divine, elemental force represented by Poseidon. Poseidon emphasizes that the earth belongs to all the gods in common and that no single god in particular can hegemonically determine the affairs taking place there; Poseidon's own actions reach beyond the nature-culture division and threaten even the fundamental distinction between the dead and the living. Poseidon's actions are more-than-human (i.e., divine) and escape logic, observation, and premonition. While Poseidon is never in a position to take over Zeus's realm nor to block the ultimate goals outlined in Homer's *Odyssey* (e.g., Odysseus's homecoming is merely delayed by Poseidon's storms), his actions have significant effect as they *interfere and disrupt*—human or divine—plans and power struggles, as well as the organized division of the world.[22]

Overall, these accounts of earth and earthshaking express three points regarding balance. First, for the early Greek world, the earth, as foundation, provides order to the *kosmos*, and while other divine forces may temporarily disturb this equilibrium, the question and meaning of balance is dependent upon the divine world. The postulation of a divine earthly being (e.g., Gaia) and the divine personification of the earthshaker (e.g., Poseidon) enable the Greek world to access contingency through an interplay between divine stability (primal) and instability (temporary, hidden). Second, the central cause for instability is divine interaction with some possible instabilities as punishment for immoral human actions. Third, humans remain at the mercy of divine stabilizing—or rather destabilizing—forces; still, humans are made more intelligible by grasping their fate as lying in the hands of divine agencies whose forces are architectonically divided up between them. In sum, the mythological access to earthquakes is achieved through proposing a divine, architectonic order with disturbances of balance diagnosed as divine, temporary interruptions. Our own embodied orientation to the world is dependent upon this divine framework, thereby making the question of human orientation conditional upon the fate of the world.

Accounting for Earth and the Causes of Earthquakes in Aristotle: Rethinking the Movements of Earth in Analogy with Our Own Human Bodies

Of the early Greek philosophers, the Presocratics had a wide range of ideas on the notion of earth and the cause of earthquakes. Ultimately, it was Aristotle who proposed the most influential and complex theory of the earth and earthquakes, which would persist into medieval philosophy.[23] While earthquakes were initially thematized as fate-based, external divine irruptions, Aristotle's shift to the idea of earth as a composite natural body with dynamic relationships with other elements (such as wind), allows for a view of earth as a *dynamic inter-elemental space of causation* that is no longer fate or divine based.

Aristotle accesses the question of earthquakes through a philosophical and natural-scientific lens. He zooms in on the dynamic interaction between wind—or, more precisely, "dry exhalation" (*pneuma*)—and earth (*gea*). While some of the particulars of the theory are antiquated, the upshot of the Aristotelian account is that it makes inner-elemental pressure—a kind of elemental interaction that unites the stuff of the world with the stuff of an individuated being—the driving force of earthquakes.

To see this upshot, let us look more closely at the particulars of Aristotle's theory of interaction. For Aristotle, "atmospheric events" (e.g., wind, thunder, lightning) and how they connect to "subterranean events" play a special role in earthquakes occurring.[24] He argues that earthquakes (*seismos*) and earth tremors (*kinēseis gēs*, Meteorologica II.7, 365a14) are caused by the trapping of dry exhalation in the earth (*Meteorologica* II.8, 365b21–366a5). Oeser explains the difference between moist and dry exhalation, articulating how dry exhalation (in his translation, dry and smoky vapor) is involved in earthquakes: "The moist vapours form the metals under the earth, clouds, rain, snow and hail in the atmosphere and finally the phenomenon of the halo in space. The dry and smoky vapours cause earthquakes under the earth, wind, thunder, lightning, comets in the atmosphere, siderical comets, the northern lights and the galaxy in space."[25] Since earthquakes are dependent on dry exhalation, they occur, according to Aristotle, more in spring and autumn and during rains and droughts because dry exhalation is brought forth the most during these times (*Meteorologica* II.8, 366b1–14).

The crucial point in Aristotle's argument for us, however, comes from this kind of cosmic scalar reckoning. Aristotle is a scalar thinker, and to grasp the force and inner dynamic of pressure-building relating to earthquakes, Aristotle makes a telling turn to our own bodies to explain the movements of the earth: "For we must suppose that the wind in the earth has effects similar to those of the wind in our bodies whose force when it is pent up inside us can cause tremors and throbbings, some earthquakes being like a tremor (*tromōn*), some like a throbbing (*sphygmōn*)" (*Meteorologica* II.8, 366b15–18).

Aristotle views the earth as a macro-version of our own body. More specifically, he grasps earthquakes as movements of the earth's body, similar to the movements caused by illnesses (*pathē*) that can affect the human body. He continues to explain the pent-up force in the earth to the case of tetanus, which provokes similar strong movements due to trapped exhalation: "Tetanus and spasms are movements caused by exhalation (*pneuma*) and are so strong that the combined strength and efforts of a number of men is unable to master the movements of their victims. And if we may compare great things with small, we must suppose that the same sort of things happens to the earth" (*Meteorologica* II.8, 366b26–30). Earthquakes manifest *pathos*, indexing a disturbed, diseased balance of the earth in the form of excess wind.[26] In contrast to previous accounts of earth and earthquakes deeming the earth as a divine entity prone to the interference of gods such as Poseidon, Aristotle views earth from a scientific-natural perspective, deeming earth everlasting, immobile, and at rest in the middle of the *kosmos*.[27] Earth, like our own bodies, is part of the elemental world. It is engaged in dynamic elemental interactions and susceptible to *pathos*. The earth is seen as a fundamental place of health and balance, but its conditions shift and provoke temporary turbulences. Earthquakes can thus be understood as elemental imbalances or "diseases."

There are important shortcomings to this understanding of *pathos* as incidental change—not only in light of contemporary understandings of earthquakes that speak to an understanding of earth as an infinitely dynamic and unstable ground, but also in light of Aristotle's general categorical characterization of *pathos* as an incidental, external affect that does not truly speak to nature's inner essence and order as it is. As I have tried to argue elsewhere, Aristotle's philosophy of keeping substance and *pathos* separated by arduous "border control" is subject to categorical contamination, which means that *pathos* and substance are always co-implied by each other.[28]

Nonetheless, for the sake of this genealogical account of grasping the various building blocks of the constellation of earth and earthquakes, Aristotle's account yields a productive turn toward grasping earthquakes and instability—namely, in allowing close alignment between the movements of the earth and our own internal orientation. Moreover, the Aristotelian framework of approaching quakes and instability in terms of equilibrium will offer further epistemic access to a rethinking of our own orientation—or rather disorientation—in an increasingly shakier world. If one leverages Aristotle's account, one can see how it provides a crucial opening to ask about the interrelationship between (external) stability and (internal) orientation. Posed in question form, is it the case that our own sense of embodied disorientation may allow us a more fine-tuned sense of the meaning of elemental shifts such as earthquakes? And, once we grasp the world of shaking in more rational terms—both in terms of the earth and our body—does that mean we are afforded a clearer path to discerning the role of human agency as it interacts with the elemental?

To answer these questions about orientation and human agency, it is imperative to rethink earth and stability—or rather instability—from the perspective of interiority—that is, the idea that earthly instability is not only an issue of externality (whether it be divine or natural) but also an issue that co-involves the subjects *needing and seeking* orientation. In other words: this raises the question of *internally emergent (dis)orientation*, which, to some degree, Voltaire and Kant prepare as they analyze the 1755 Lisbon earthquake. This is yet another important building block to my proposed idea of the elemental constellation of earth, which seeks to do justice both to the externally and internally emergent features of our earthly world.

Interpreting the Lisbon Earthquake of 1755: Voltaire, Kant, and the Question of Internal (Dis)Orientation

The 1755 earthquake in Lisbon has become known as a "seminal event" in European history.[29] It took place on November 1, All Saints Day, with many people gathered in churches for mass. It was a large earthquake (estimated by current seismologists to have been about 7.7 on the Richter scale[30]) accompanied and followed by tsunamis and fires that brought further destruction to anything that was still left standing. It is estimated that at least sixty thousand people died in Lisbon alone.[31] Moreover, the quake and tsunamis were not limited to one place or one time: "The earthquake extended across the whole of the Iberian Peninsula and the seas surrounding it. . . . All Europe and parts of North Africa felt the aftermath of the shock. . . . In Lisbon itself intermittent shocks continued for 10 years."[32]

While this earthquake was a large and tragic event, it evoked, as Besterman argues, "moral repercussions" that "exceeded by far its physical and even its personal consequences," and it led to a "permanent transformation in every thinking man's philosophy."[33] Much of this is due to

Voltaire's pointed, angry, and compassionate writing about the earthquake, which also influenced Kant. The 1755 earthquake came to inform the philosophies of Voltaire and Kant, as they conceived it as a sign of the remarkable extent of natural power and as an indication of the material powerlessness that humans possess as they confront natural disasters.

While Greek cosmologists such as Hesiod and Homer viewed earthquakes as acts of gods (due to internal divine feuding or in response to human action), Voltaire and Kant continue Aristotle's line of thought that diagnoses the question of earthquakes in terms of the logic of natural bodies. However, Voltaire and Kant added *moral, social, and metaphysical* perspectives to the question of earthquakes, thereby showing that philosophy's learning process regarding earthquakes is not simply one of following, or updating the mythological or natural explanations, but also a process that entails epistemological and dispositional shifts (i.e., questions of [dis]orientations) in its own philosophical orientation. While committed to grasping the natural causes of the Lisbon earthquake, Voltaire and Kant each in their own way show the importance of looking inward upon the human being's rational and moral orientation toward the world's shaky grounds, thereby making internal orientation and the search for a metaphysical and moral compass part and parcel of the discussion on earthquakes.

Voltaire on Earth and Earthquakes: Shaking Off Divine Purposiveness

> This is indeed a cruel piece of natural philosophy! We shall find it difficult to discover how the laws of movement operate in such fearful disasters *in the best of all possible worlds*—where a hundred thousand ants, our neighbours, are crushed in a second on our ant-heaps, half, dying undoubtedly in inexpressible agonies, beneath débris from which it was impossible to extricate them, families all over Europe reduced to beggary, and the fortunes of a hundred merchants—Swiss, like yourself—swallowed up in the ruins of Lisbon. What a game of chance human life is! What will the preachers say—especially if the Palace of the Inquisition is left standing! I flatter myself that those reverend fathers, the Inquisitors, will have been crushed just like other people. That ought to teach men not to persecute men: for, while a few sanctimonious humbugs are burning a few fanatics, the earth opens and swallows up all alike. I believe it is our mountains which save us from earthquakes.
>
> —Voltaire, *A Letter on the Lisbon Earthquake*
> (to M. Tronchin de Lyons), November 24, 1755

For Voltaire, the suffering at the heart of the Lisbon earthquake stands as a final condemnation on the main-standing influential ideas of his time. In contrast to Leibniz, Voltaire sees the Lisbon earthquake as evidence that the world we live in is definitely not the "best possible world." The power of the earthquake prompts Voltaire to view human communities similar to how we view ant heaps—fragile and vulnerable congregations that stand at the mercy of larger forces. Thus, there is no saving power in God. If anything, it is the "mountains which save us from earthquakes" rather than the power of a presumed God. This provokes Voltaire to reject the world and its actions as simply being the product of an all-knowing and all-powerful being, as such a being cannot be squared with provoking such evil events:

> Are you so sure the eternal cause
> That knows all things, and for itself creates,
> Could not have placed us in this dreary clime
> Without volcanoes seething 'neath our feet?[34]

While some "preachers" blame the inhabitants of Lisbon and their immoral behaviors for prompting divine punishment, Voltaire points out the inconsistency of this argument—not only because innocent children have died, but also because supposedly equally morally indulgent cities such as Paris are still "dancing" while Lisbon burns:

> Will you say, in seeing this mass of victims:
> "God is revenged, their death is the price for their crimes?"
> What crime, what error did these children,
> Crushed and bloody on their mothers' breasts, commit?
> Did Lisbon, which is no more, have more vices
> Than London and Paris immersed in their pleasures?
> Lisbon is destroyed, and they dance in Paris![35]

Instead, for Voltaire, life is "a game of chance." However, as much as he acknowledges the inherently violent and contingent character of nature as he sees it, he also blames humanity for needlessly bringing *additional* suffering into the world. Voltaire condemns internal feuds and the fanatic persecution of people: "Men do themselves more harm on their little mole-hill than nature does. More men are slaughtered in the wars of our own creation than are swallowed up by earthquakes."[36]

The end of the "Poem on the Lisbon Disaster" ends with the faint possibility of hope:

All will' be well one day—so runs our hope (*espérance*).
All now is well, is but an idle dream (*illusion*).

However, in a manuscript from his own library that was originally not published, Voltaire later questioned his own appeal to hope, wondering "what a frail [*sic*] hope."[37]

In sum, Voltaire's interpretation of the Lisbon earthquake provides us with the following ideas: (1) a condemnation of the thought that the world as we know it is perfect and completely under the power of an all-good and all-powerful God; (2) the earthquake shows the nature of chance; (3) humans compound suffering through their own fights and conflicts; and (4) whether we ought to have hope for the future remains a question.

In contrast to earlier (classical) accounts of earth and earthquakes that viewed earthquakes as acts of God, Voltaire sees the Lisbon earthquake as evidence of the irreconcilable nature of suffering and destruction with an all-good and all-powerful God. Voltaire moves the idea of ground away from the divine toward natural irrationality, leaving us without a clear path toward a meaningful future. Hope is contested, indicating that human orientation toward the world and our own future is in doubt. Rather than condemning natural forces, Voltaire thinks that humans should take an introspective look at compounding sources for destruction and violence. Voltaire thereby moves the question of external natural violence ("the earth") toward our inner, human landscape ("our dispositions toward orientation") directing us toward nihilism and suggesting the need for a clearer, more peaceful compass to orient us.

For my own account of earth as elemental constellation, Voltaire's essays offer significant reason to turn the question of external (in)stability into one of inner (dis)orientation, while adding a doubtful, nihilistic question mark to the issue of hope amid elemental loss.

Elevating the Human Mind: Kant's Reorientation of the Human Ground in the Wake of the Lisbon Earthquake

In three early (precritical) essays written in 1756, Kant writes about the Lisbon earthquake. For him, the Lisbon earthquake was an opportunity to analyze both the causes of earthquakes, in terms of natural science, and the ways that the human mind relates and responds to natural events. Kant turns to Newton and his calculations and measurements to provide scientific reassuring; even so, Kant admits that the Lisbon earthquake itself is unique and without comparable precedent.[38] As he writes, "We have another world beneath our feet, with which we are at present but little acquainted."[39] Still, he urges us to be patient and "wait until she [(i.e., nature)] reveals her secrets in distinct activities."[40]

While his scientific analysis is outdated, what is worth examining is his general approach to grasping the causes and effects of earthquakes and his analysis of the human mind. He argues that we are prone to viewing earthquakes as emblems of natural disorder, while we know that they, like other natural disasters, "invite man's contemplation, and are planted in nature by God as a proper consequence of fixed laws no less than other accustomed causes of discomfort which are thought to be more natural merely because they are more familiar."[41] In other words, just because large earthquakes are rare does not mean that they do not follow the laws of nature. Driven by fear, people think "without reflection or understanding" that the Earth has gone off course, assuming the cause to be far away rather than close to us.[42] However, rather than inciting fear, which is for Kant "the weakest motive" for piety, earthquakes, in the words of Watkins, should, for Kant, inspire "careful thought about how best to control their effects (by engaging in, for example, appropriate urban planning)."[43] In this context, Kant analyzes the location, building materials, and height of buildings in earthquake zones,[44] thereby encouraging the inhabitants of Lisbon to appeal to "common sense" as they rebuild the city away from the zones where "earthquakes must naturally occur."[45] Thus, even while Kant may have misunderstood the specific scientific dynamics of earthquakes, he presciently moves his understanding of it toward the need for *social-urban responsibility*. Praising the benefits of the low height of buildings in Peru—built with just mortar and reed—Kant comments that "man must learn to adapt to nature, but he wants nature to adapt to him."[46]

Moreover, as he thinks through the drama of the Lisbon earthquake, Kant writes that the imagination can only acquire access to a sliver of the actual drama, thereby foreshadowing his later account of the sublime:

> All the terrible things the imagination can conceive have to be taken together to understand even to a small extent the horror people must experience when the Earth moves under their feet, when everything around them crashes to the ground,

when a body of water moved in its foundations completes their misfortune through flooding, when the fear of death, the despair at having lost all one's earthly goods, and finally the sight of other people in misery must dishearten even the most courageous.[47]

In their interpretations of Kant's essays on earthquakes, both Watkins and Jones highlight the fact that earthquakes, in Kant's view, should induce humility with respect to the larger context of nature within which humanity is placed. In other words, Kant urges us to recognize that we are not the sole "object of God's actions"—we are part of a bigger whole.[48] As Jones reads the essays, she finds Kant highlighting

> the need for humility in place of hubris: If the earthquake's effects are almost beyond measure, man's mistake, Kant says, is to think God intended him to be the sole measure of nature, as if God had only human beings in mind when setting up the rules that govern the natural world. On the contrary, human beings are only part of nature and we should learn to accommodate ourselves to it, taking into account nature as a whole instead of judging it solely in relation to our own desires.[49]

Kant thus advises us to practice *epistemological and ontological humility*—we need to recognize the limits of our own standing and our own knowledge. Rather than claiming control over nature and wishing everything to go according to our own needs, we need to accept our own finitude and the complexity of nature, which brings both pleasure and pain.[50]

Still, as *moral* subjects, we also rise above—we "transcend the earthly realm"[51]—since there is a "far nobler aim" for us in the world: "Man is not born to build everlasting dwellings on this stage of vanity . . . his entire life has a far nobler aim."[52] In fact, Kant references the "infinitely higher aims that far surpass all the resources of nature."[53] This leads Kant to emphasize the importance of just and reasonable governance, which may "prevent the threatened destruction."[54] This indexes the importance of distinguishing between "man's material existence and his moral vocation."[55]

Kant's ideas on the dynamically sublime in the *Critique of Judgment* show the importance of this distinction as well, but rather than appealing to humanity's moral superiority, here Kant juxtaposes the power of nature with the inner power of human *imagination*—a power that is not tied to natural concerns but can instead rise above nature's might due to the infinity of its nonsensible standard: "Though the irresistibility of nature's might makes us, considered as natural beings, recognize our physical impotence, it reveals in us at the same time an ability to judge ourselves independently of nature, and reveals in us a superiority over nature that is the basis of self-preservation quite different in kind from the one that can be assailed and endangered by nature outside us."[56] Thus, Kant postulates the sublimity of our mind in relationship to nature, and in investigating the feelings evoked by the dynamically sublime, he speaks of a mix of pleasure and pain and that "the liking for the sublime contains not so much a positive pleasure as rather admiration and respect, and should be called a negative pleasure."[57]

Overall, Kant's project in rethinking earthquakes from the early essays through mentioning them in the *Critique of Judgment* involves, above all else, (1) recognition of the power of nature manifest in earthquakes and a consequent human ontological or epistemic humility (or respect); (2) recognition of the power of human thinking to anticipate such dangers as associated with earthquakes, thereby invoking the need for proper government and appropriate urban planning; and (3) appreciation for "infinitely higher ideas" associated with the human mind—that is, the human ability to think and imagine infinity, which for sensibility is an abyss.

From Instability to (Dis)Orientation and Human Agency: The Lessons to Be Learned from Voltaire and Kant

In overview, thinking through both Voltaire and Kant, we can ascertain that, for Voltaire, the Lisbon earthquake proves that our world is outside of the control of an all-good and all-powerful god. With a nod toward nihilism, he questions the grounds of our existence, interrogating hope and blaming humans for adding unnecessary suffering. Kant's perspective is far more hopeful as, for him, (a) there exists the hope that the forces that rule earthquakes can ultimately be scientifically grasped; (b) good governance means anticipating danger and providing proper building codes; and (c) earthquakes, despite their might, can be juxtaposed with the infinite range and power of the human mind, which either rises above nature through its capacity for moral judgment (as is argued in the "Earthquake" essays) or through its capacity for imagination (as is apparent in the *Critique of Judgment*).

In assessing Voltaire and Kant's approaches to earthquakes, we can establish that they continue Aristotle's line of thought by pinpointing the cause of earthquakes to natural origins. Additionally, they take Aristotle's metaphoric comparison between a diseased earth and an ill human to the next level. Namely, they urge us to investigate the precise role of human agency in preventing or complicating natural/social disasters and thereby pose the crucial question regarding our moral, metaphysical, and rational (dis)orientation when it comes to shaking grounds: What may we hope for in times of elemental loss, and what, if anything, should be our role in preventing further harm as we plan buildings and erect a governmental system?

Said differently, Voltaire and Kant push the project of philosophizing earthquakes in the direction of reflection on the internal human orientation toward the world. As we assess the power and might of nature and confront our own material powerlessness, we come to recognize the need for humans to plan, act, and imagine in a way that's fitting to our capacities, thereby moving the *external ground further away from us while reorienting the internal dispositional plane*. While Irigaray, in this context, has argued that Kant wanted to put nature "under the control of the human spirit" while adding a "transcendental ceiling" to human ground,[58] the more relevant issue emerging from Kant and Voltaire's interpretations of earthquakes is the *quest to open up space for questioning human inner orientation*: not in separation from the world, but alongside its disorienting shaking we should rethink human vulnerability and propose to engage the power, imagination, and anticipation of the human mind. Voltaire and Kant ask us for a new orientation toward seeking ground and equilibrium since the world as it shakes may not provide one. If the elemental is not static and will remain subject to external imbalances, and if Voltaire and Kant ask us to rethink our own relationship to shaking grounds, then the question of stability acquires a new meaning; *it becomes a question of human orientation*.

Rethinking Human Orientation beyond the Anthropocene: Plate Tectonics, Social Inequities, Climate Change, and Fracking

This third section turns to our current moment in time, when our natural-scientific understanding of earthquakes has undergone a major shift due to the emergence of the theory of plate tectonics and fault lines. I will review the theory of plate tectonics with a special eye toward grasping our increased sense of disorientation toward shaky grounds, particularly as emerging in an age of climate change and elemental loss. While the theory of plate tectonics demonstrates in principle a "neutral" notion of a planet in motion—a world that is very much continuing to change and regenerate and shake along its fault lines—in combination with the unmistakable doom sketched out by the Anthropocene, the result seems to be a net sense of loss: loss in terms of agency and futures. In other words, much of the power of the question held out by Enlightenment thinkers such as Voltaire and Kant—namely the question of holding ourselves, our building structures, and the world accountable for the *social suffering* that may be prevented by us or that is compounding natural earthquakes—seems lost. Thus, this section asks the key question: How can we reinsert the question of human agency and responsibility beyond the return to the fate-based myth that the Anthropocene imposes? How might we transform our sense of elemental loss into an issue of elemental change?

The Earth Sciences and Plate Tectonics: The Slow Gathering of Evidence to Prove Instability and Moving Plates

Our current understanding of the earth and its dynamics is to a large extent informed by research done by the earth sciences in the twentieth century. The contemporary theory within which earthquakes are grasped is that of plate tectonics,[59] the idea that continents, embedded in plates, are constantly moving at a rate of about one to four inches per year.[60] More specifically, the theory of plate tectonics consists of the core idea that "the Earth's solid outer crust, the lithosphere, is separated into plates that move over the asthenosphere, the molten upper portion of the mantle. Oceanic and continental plates come together, spread apart, and interact at boundaries all over the planet."[61] It is thus at the intersection of plate boundaries, "where the plates meet or divide," that we find "most geologic activity,"[62] such as mountains, earthquakes, and volcanoes. Interestingly, such boundaries can either move into each other ("convergent"), move away from each other ("divergent"), or "move sideways in relation to each other" ("transforming").[63] The scientific explanation for plate tectonics is "convection currents in the earth's mantle,"[64] with the purpose of shedding "excess radiogenic heat produced in the mantle."[65]

Evidently, earthquakes are but one manifestation of forms of change happening in the earth. Others may include "mountains rising and eroding, oceans expanding and shrinking, volcanoes erupting."[66] The overall picture therefore that has been developing is that of the earth's surface as being "in a constant state of change."⁶⁷ The event of an earthquake is thus part of a larger story. While earthquakes may occur anywhere,⁶⁸ they most frequently occur at the intersection of tectonic plates: "The boundaries between plates contain systems of deep cracks, called faults. Most earthquakes occur along these faults. Within a fault, rock masses on either side of the break are pushed by geologic forces in opposite directions. Friction, however, holds the rocks in place, causing stresses to build. Finally, the mounting pressure overcomes the friction and a sudden movement occurs along the fault, releasing a large amount of energy. This is an earthquake."⁶⁹ Accordingly, the pressure that builds up at fault lines may find expression in earthquakes.

What is crucial to the story of plate tectonics is that much of it is *invisible* due to the fact that "most of the evidence for plate tectonics is covered by 2.5 miles (4 kilometers) of ocean water."⁷⁰ The story of continental drift may be exemplified by geological records of the continental plates, but "data from the oceans provide the primary confirmation of the theory."⁷¹ This invisibility stands in contrast to the remarkable features at the heart of the story of tectonic plates shifting:

> rigid crustal slabs sliding thousands of miles across the mantle of the earth at rates that are too slow to be observed without the aid of sophisticated instruments; sea floor spreading ridges with submarine hot springs under thousands of feet of ocean water; deep ocean trenches where the oceanic plates of the earth literally fall into the mantle; neat orthogonal ridge/transform patterns, and a magnetic field that reverses at just the right rate to be recorded by cooling lavas at the spreading ridges.⁷²

As Sandwell observes, much of the work took such a long time (i.e., forty years to prove the initial hypothesis) because it had been difficult at the time to "develop a planetary-scale model" looking at the earth from a far distance.⁷³

Sandwell's point is illuminating, as it shows that a comprehensive theory of the earth's dynamical forces could only be grasped from a bird's-eye view, viewing the earth as a planet rather than as our localized embodied home. Only by abstracting from the places where we currently live to hypothesize their connections to the larger continental forces, including the seafloor, was it possible to rethink the meaning of the fault lines that divide and run through our world.⁷⁴ Moreover, the abstract spatialization of earth as a planet has provided us with a different sense of earthly temporality, since in witnessing the current continental plates and their outline, we may access a far deeper temporal past of which our current present is only a small sliver. Finally, in witnessing these various forces, we can also imagine different geological futures. In the case of California, for instance, the forces that underpin the San Andreas Fault and connected faults "are slowly tearing California apart, so that much of what is California today will be transformed into a collection of islands that are destined to be rafted northward across the Pacific."[75] This image of a futural Californian archipelago[76] serves to emphasize the dynamics undergirding our present and the instability of our so-called geological place.

In the twentieth and twenty-first centuries, this idea of a dynamic earth has gained traction in our everyday epistemologies and practical lives. We know of these forces, we grasp their scientific causes, and even though our imaginations long for a stable world, in the Global North many areas prone to earthquakes, such as California, are prescribing building codes to comply with earthquake safety and/or retrofitting buildings and bridges to make them compliant. This indexes that earthquakes, once shelved as incidental fluctuating happenings (*pathē*) in an otherwise stable earth ("substance"), have become a central theoretical part of our understanding of the affective-substantial workings of earth.

However, even while the Global North has acted "locally" in conformity with the knowledge provided by twentieth-century earth sciences, our current engagement with earthquake dynamics shows three important shortcomings: (1) failures of social justice, namely tendencies to close our eyes for the dysfunctional building regimes in states and countries left in shambles in the wake of colonialization; (2) failures to grasp the gravity of the effects of climate change in the form of increased frequency of earthquakes; and, finally, (3) failures to anticipate and reckon with the broader physical and social problems following the discovery and implementation of techniques such as fracking, which create multiple problems in terms of quaking and pollution.

In the following subsection, I will address these three issues and attempt to prove how plate tectonics in itself offers a compelling and far-reaching theory. Admittedly, however, plate tectonics is in and of itself a necessary but insufficient condition to grasp the complexity of earthquakes and earthquake loss. In other words, a natural-scientific abstract understanding of earthquakes in the form of tectonic plate shifts cannot sufficiently gain traction alone on the reality of earthquake loss. Hence, social-political theorizing needs to be an added component of our argument on elemental constellations; this is needed to do justice to the complexity of the issues at the heart of the earth's elemental shifts.

Complicating Plate Tectonics: Dysfunctional Building Regimes, Climate Change, and Fracking

The first point complicating plate tectonics is the very fact that the so-called "natural" fault lines of our existence have increasingly expanded to include those of the social-economic order. We find in this yet another regime: this time of a social-affective kind that needs to be drawn into the understanding of earthquakes. In this regard, French philosopher Michel Serres continues the Kantian line of argument regarding earthquakes, addressing the blame humanity has to take on for not properly addressing the toll earthquakes can take. As Serres compares the death toll of the 1989 Loma Prieta earthquake in the San Francisco Bay Area—resulting in sixty-three deaths—to the Haiti earthquake of 2010—resulting between one hundred thousand and three hundred thousand deaths—he writes: "Human, collective, political, economic, social conditions—poverty for example—prevail, and by far, over the purely physical cause. Voltaire and the Enlightenment were mistaken: only society can be accused."[77] Although Serres overlooks this convergence with Kant, he actually, along Kantian lines, drives home the important point that earthquakes confront humans with not only the material-ontological forces of our world but also with our semantic-cultural forces.[78] Especially now, in this time of exploding world populations increasingly living in dense, unsafely built urban centers, Serres's point deserves underlining: the fault lines of our existence have both a natural-ontological and social-economic character.

Accordingly, the death toll and the suffering entailed by the 2010 Haiti earthquake[79] can only be grasped when seen as part of a broader political economic history—not just a devastating moment or "isolated event." Only by looking back in time can we understand the disorienting shambles in which this country is still finding itself, long after the 2010 "natural" quake took place. The 2010 earthquake was a crisis, but one that had gradually—over centuries—been building in a country left impoverished by its French occupants: Haiti, a country that on top of all the past suffering had to pay a hefty "prize" or heart-wrenching "reparation" to its former French occupiers for its independence.[80] The result was a country that did not have "political stability,"[81] could not invest in capable structures and agencies of government, could not invest in education, and could not enforce building codes.

This means that the death toll of the 2010 earthquake unfortunately is not a singular catastrophic incident, but something that had been in the making for centuries. It is part of a gradual, step-by-step process of "slow death" (as cultural theoretician Lauren Berlant has described it in the context of other forms of politically motivated gradual diminution of life).[82] The earthquake and its aftermath—one hundred thousand to three hundred thousand deaths, millions homeless, political riots, and a cholera epidemic—are unfortunately *only* extreme signs[83] of the far broader and deeper constellation of elemental loss.

⁓

The second point complicating plate tectonics is our failure to grasp the gravity of the effects of climate change in the form of the increased frequency of earthquakes. This is especially true if we follow the outlines of Bill McGuire's argument in *Waking the Giant: How a Changing Climate Triggers Earthquakes, Tsunamis, and Volcanos*.[84] McGuire analyzes the temperature increases at the end of the last Ice Age and concludes that they caused many changes, including geological hazards such as earthquakes.[85] Similarly, he warns that over time—in addition to droughts, floods, and other harmful environmental conditions—the temperature changes associated with current climate change may lead to landslides and earthquakes comparable to the changes that took place after the last Ice Age.[86] Accordingly, small climactic changes could set off much larger changes in the earth's surface. In other words, it will take merely "a little nudge" to awaken the "sleeping giant" (i.e., the "broadly benign earth"): "As a seismologist colleague of mine is fond of saying, if a fault is primed and ready to rupture, all that is needed is the pressure of a handshake to set it off. If systems are critically poised, then the environmental changes associated with rapid and accelerating climate breakdown could easily do the job."[87]

To explain the connection between climate change and earthquakes, McGuire and other scientists point to a scientific mechanism called *isostatic uplift*, the process of the earth lifting up as it experiences less pressure.[88] Namely, as climate change causes glaciers and large ice sheets to melt, the crust of the earth experiences less pressure and thus experiences an uplift—it bounces back: "Depending on the rate of the isostatic uplift due to melting glaciers and the composition of the underlying strata, these stresses can be released as landslides, ductile formation and also as earthquakes."[89] Evidence that this process is already underway can be found in a number of studies performed by earth scientists, noting that the number of earthquakes in earthquake-prone zones has already dramatically risen.[90]

∽

Finally, the third point complicating plate tectonics is the rising prominence of technological forces interacting with the earth. New technologies have added onto elemental loss, specifically by causing new and additional kinds of earthquakes. Particularly, gas drilling and fracking are new means of causing earthquakes.

Fracking is the hydraulic fracturing of shales to allow gas to "flow through the rock mass and be extracted through production wells."[91] Fracking consists of a drilling process "that injects millions of gallons of water, sand and chemicals under high pressure into a well, cracking the rock to release natural gas and oil."[92] It is precisely the process of *disposing* of the drilling wastewater (thousands of feet below the surface) that causes earthquakes.[93] In other words, "Fracking intentionally causes small earthquakes (magnitudes smaller than 1) to enhance permeability, but it has also been linked to larger earthquakes."[94] For example, in the Dallas–Fort Worth area, since building fracking wells in 2008, "there have been more than fifty earthquakes."

Another example prominent to the situation in the Netherlands has been the Groningen field, a gas field operated jointly by the Dutch government, De Nederlandse Aardolie Maatschappij (NAM), and Exxon-Mobil/Shell.[95] Since the 1960s this gas field has been an important source for domestic energy use. While initially hailed for its benefits (e.g., its gas being "relatively clean" compared to coal), its downsides have ultimately outweighed its benefits: "Decades of extraction have reduced pressure on the gas-bearing rocks below the surface, causing them to contract. That has led the ground to sink by about a foot, and earthquakes have rumbled. More than a thousand tremors have been recorded since the mid-1980s."[96] In the aftermath of the quakes, inhabitants have been traumatized, many homes have been uninhabitable or have needed reinforcement, and property values have radically declined. Moreover, the Kafkaesque unfolding of administering subsidies for reinforcing homes or rebuilding them more generally has been a topic in a protracted, painful political debate.[97]

As the examples of fracking in Texas and gas drilling in the Netherlands show, much more than "tectonic shifts" are at the heart of earthquake hazards. If we are to take seriously the threats associated with instability and general disorientation, the anthropogenic hazards of fracking and drilling that come on top of "natural" quakes need to be considered.

Thus, if we consider all three areas of concern discussed here (i.e., the social injustices prevailing through earthquakes, the danger posed by climate change for "waking up the giant," and the dangers of fracking and drilling for gas), then Michel Serres's visionary insight clearly comes to the fore. He argues in *The Natural Contract* that the former background conditions of our lives—"nature"—have returned with a vengeance to haunt us by stepping into the foreground.[98] Humans, through their own competitive wars and obsession with fossil fuel extraction, have compounded the causes and effects of shifting grounds, and they have added larger pressures in certain places while other pressures are lifted to wake up "the giant" earth beneath our feet.

This leads to the following questions: How may we find a new sense of orientation, a new sense of health and balance, in our engagement with a "sickened" earth? How can we reach balance in our engagement with the earth's dynamic forces to reorient ourselves in a more sustainable, equitable way?

Shifts in the Elemental and the Search for an Ethics of Balance

> How one walks through the world, the endless small adjustments of balance, is affected by the shifting weights of beautiful things.
>
> —Elaine Scarry, "On Beauty and Being Just"

Following Michel Serres, if we seek a new language to address the material-physical and social-cultural aspects of earthquakes in our lives,[99] and if we seek to find a new balance engaging with the earth's dynamic forces, then our vocabulary needs to approximate this material-physical world more closely. That is, we need to rethink our impoverished language that cannot get at the interactions key to the fault lines of our existence.

To think about such new vocabulary, our own sense of embodied orientation needs to be examined, as this is where a possible new spatial and temporal orientation toward the world may be inserted. How do we stand affectively and physically toward tectonic shifts, and how have we become habituated to respond to shifts in the elemental?

Similar to responses in shifts to the elemental constellation of fire, our response has predominantly been in the register of the legalistic-economic. When homes are damaged, insurance claims are filed, companies are sued for extraction claims, and governments are charged to support earthquake claims that private companies cannot underwrite because of risk.

However, comparable to my argument in the fire chapter, here the quest is to think beyond the legalistic-economic register. For what may be at stake, certainly in the case of earthquakes, is the need to forge a new "contract" with the earth—one that is not simply legalistic or economic but also cognizant of its dynamic expression. What if we follow Kant's and Voltaire's claims of the late 1700s to rethink the ontological and moral humility that earthquakes inspire? Moreover, what if we follow their insights into the realm of inner orientation such that we seek to take hold of the opportunity to transform loss into change alongside the trembling of the world and ourselves? The final section of this chapter aims to bring much-needed attention to the ethics of balance.

What I propose here is renewed attention to an ethics of balance—an ethics that sees our existence as emerging along the lines of an earthly dynamic flux and tries to gain equilibrium in adjusting to external and internal moments of shaking. It is Aristotle who proposed such ethics on the personal level. In his *Nicomachean Ethics*, he tried to seek a sense of ethical perfection precisely by seeking balance in responding to the needs of a dynamic, contingent world. Translating this out from his personal virtue ethics to a wider world in need of ethical balance, his ideas can (1) provide traction to the idea of finding balance in a changing world while (2) abandoning the idea that this is up to each individual—instead postulating that seeking balance these days is a *communal* act, entailing broader dispositional changes to emerge from our joint predicament.[100]

In order to enable this, we may take a clue from *Homo sapiens'* evolutionary development—from walking on all fours to walking upright, which entailed a reorientation of our visual field, a different way of engaging our proprioception, and changes to our inner balance organs in the inner ear. If *Homo sapiens* were able to adapt, physically and dispositionally, to a changing world, then what changes might be ahead for us, as we broach the issues of the Anthropocene? If it is the case that our physical orientation is informed 50 percent by body cues, 25 percent by gravity cues, and 25 percent by vision cues,[101] indicating that orientation is far less an issue of simply *one* organ (the vestibular) but is part of a much wider compass entailing our vision and proprioception, then the necessary ethical reorientation of balance that I am arguing for will consist less in a rethinking of special human attributes in need of being fine-tuned (comparable to the crystals in the inner ear for instance) and more in a holistic, fully embodied, dispositional sense of reorientation.

Moreover, because of evolution, our "new" centers of gravity that have allowed *Homo sapiens* to stand for hours were made possible by our hips. We have a precarious balance enabled by gluteal and pelvic bone transformation. What used to propel apes forward now stabilizes humans.[102] What this means is that our stability—from moving as quadrupeds over the ground versus on two legs—entails crucial embodied changes enabling a changed center of gravity. Amid a world in crisis and gravitational forces acting up, this means nothing less than rethinking our own centers of gravity. As we walk through a world that trembles, the challenge is to transform our embodied sense of centrality along with the changes in the landscape—not merely to mirror them, but more so to anticipate the challenges ahead and to make the posthuman dispositionally adaptable to the changes ahead of us. Whether we walk on the shaking ground or embrace the trees for further stability, the center of gravity is adaptable but will depend on motoric and anatomical changes.

It is imperative that such a reorienting response considers the various textures of agency involved in (re)building elemental constellations of loss to turn them into constellations of change. Certain countries, predominantly in the Global North, are far more responsible for climate change and thus need to make drastic changes toward further preventing or exacerbating climate change, while other countries, predominantly in the Global South, find themselves seeking a new equilibrium in terms of *adapting* and *preparing* for climate change's effects.

The complexity of climate scenarios[103] adds another unknown into the various narratives of seeking a new orientation of balance and equilibrium. Will the search for a new equilibrium be based on the highest predictions of carbon dioxide emissions, a medium range, or the lowest possible? And what other non–carbon dioxide factors do we need to take into account to think through the various plotlines unfolding from here and now? Both the abstractions as offered through these scenarios in combination with the complexity of contingent particulars carve out multiple options for futures yet unknown.

Concluding Thoughts

As we seek stability and guidance amid these various scenarios, perhaps a few final images can guide us. The first is that of the tightrope walker. While the tightrope walker seems to be associated with childish fantasies and the circus, the skill, courage, and agency of the tightrope walker speaks to the imagination of finding balance amid uncertainty. Dependent upon inclination and rope, surrounded by wind and pulled by gravity, there is art, skill, and enjoyment in finding, holding, and keeping one's balance amid the elements: "Working under the greatest possible constraints, on a stage no more than an inch wide, the high-wire walker's job is to create a sensation of limitless freedom."[104] Beyond sensationalism, the tightrope walker elevates the struggle for finding balance, "the quest for immobility,"[105] into an art, an art of embracing danger while finding freedom of movement. The dangerous crossover into an era that promises creativity rather than fate, the crossover into an era that transforms elemental loss into elemental change, demands nothing but the art of finding balance amid danger. As Paul Auster, speculating about the art of Philippe Petit, argues: "High-wire walking is not an art of death, but an art of life—and life lived to the very extreme of life. Which is to say, life that does not hide from death but stares it directly in the face."[106] Nietzsche's Zarathustra would nod in approval: "You have made danger your vocation; there is nothing contemptible in that."[107]

Perhaps another example that can guide us toward finding a sense of balance is dance, particularly its ability to artistically choreograph the refinement of movements across bodies in search for balance. For instance, the modern ensemble ballet *The Promised Land*, choreographed by Dwight Rhoden and premiered in San Francisco in 2022,[108] is a piece that speaks to notions of loss and suffering invoked by the Covid-19 pandemic, and simultaneously addresses the human tendency to recover and find fulfillment and happiness. The strength of this ballet is the ability to show, through partner and ensemble work, the unraveling of life as frenetically moving bodies fall to the ground and group constellations dissipate. Still, in remarkable acts of holding and catching each other—either in partnerships, groups, or as an ensemble—the dancers' movements also show that, through careful anticipation, responsiveness, and skillful maneuvering, we may empower each other and move forward. Addressing the core of this contemporary piece, Rhoden speaks of resilience and comments: "We're nothing without each other."[109] Such communal holding, as the piece shows, is anything but facile—it is a careful act of balancing collectively in a disorienting world.[110]

With those two images in place, we may be able to move forward to the last, and concluding, chapter of this book, which seeks to think through the notion of how elemental loss may be transformed into elemental change. Following Rhoden's artistic masterpiece *The Promised Land*, the transformative key enabling a shift from loss and climate fatalism to change and agency lies in collective support and communal rebuilding, particularly, I argue, rebuilding the affective interface of trust. For it is this affective interface of trust through which we relate—with each other, collectively, and with our infrastructure and our institutions—to the elemental.

Chapter 5

Elemental Trust

Transforming Elemental Loss into Elemental Change

The more you face the absurdity of paradox in your losses—the need for both continuity and change—the more likely you will find meaning and purpose to move forward again with your life.

—Pauline Boss, *The Myth of Closure*

The thought of desire and of the Thing, which is not a thought of "lack" but of default, that is, of the *pharmakon*, is a thought that remains yet to come: it is the question par excellence of a century—ours—that has not begun well. It is the question of that *which does not exist*, but which, inspiring trust, ties together relations of fidelity in this *economy of the infinite* that is the only economy of true value, that is, an economy which is not just sustainable but in principle *"to the infinite"*—and which makes life worth living beyond the calculating fiduciary system which *ratio* (reason) has become in *all* its forms.

—Bernard Stiegler, *What Makes Life Worth Living*

Trust those who let go—the wisest among us—trust those who descend, who leave behind, who can but don't, trust the detached, trust those who give way, trust the poor and those who live apart.

—Michel Serres, *Variations on the Body*

The previous chapters have laid out a landscape of elemental loss—that is, the experience of loss in conjunction with oceanic extinction and our impoverished relationship with our seashores and oceans (chapter 1); our interface with fire, with industrial fire leaving in its wake a trace of devastation entailing losses of homes, property, and lives (chapter 2); "slow death" as the airy shared spaces of our world become contaminated with allergens, pollutants, smog, and more (chapter 3); and, finally, the upheavals of an increasingly shaky earth causing a sense of imbalance and disorientation (chapter 4). These experiences of loss are not "equally" carried across the globe but, due to systemic inequalities, are carried mostly by those who have had the least involvement in setting in place the drama that has unfolded, that of anthropogenic climate change.

The losses that are tangible in our elemental constellations have been accompanied by, in the first place, a loss of trust in the elemental (social-ecological) constellations that provide us a sense of orientation, and, second, a loss of trust in our *relationship* to these elemental constellations, affecting the interface—that space where the elemental as such and our ability to know and feel it intertwine as a locus of response and decision. If it is the case that trust, when operative, is invisible,[1] and if it is the case that trust, when functioning, offers a sense of security,[2] then anthropogenic climate change has confronted us with a marked sense of insecurity and disorientation in this interface: we witness a changed elemental landscape we hardly recognize, and we are at a loss how to interpret and interact with it.

If Glenn Albrecht is correct to highlight that the loss felt due to our current climate predicament has to do with two fundamental principles—powerlessness and disorientation[3]—then the question this book takes on for its final chapter is whether this powerlessness and disorientation is inevitable. This means that this chapter will need to ask: Is the question of elemental loss to inevitably *remain* the question of elemental loss, or can it make place for another future, one that opens up instead to a sense of elemental change, one where our dynamic interactions with the elemental regain a sense of agency and reorientation? And when I speak here of a moment of reorientation, I am not hinting at an individual Heideggerian moment of vision, but rather of a collectively altered affective habitus toward the elemental. Thus, if psychologist Pauline Boss is correct to argue that even the most difficult forms of ambiguous loss, even as they linger without finding closure, *can be endured and make way for change*,[4] then I am asking whether, scaling up, there might be a way to transform the fate-based myth of the Anthropocene—that begins and ends with loss—into a different kind of scenario that enables a decisive interaction that builds out to other possible, and more trusting, elemental futures?[5]

Here, in this chapter, I will postulate the thesis that a sense of elemental loss can be transformed into a sense of elemental change, if we regain trust in rebuilding our own relationship with the elemental, which depends on both (a) regaining trust in each other, (b) regaining trust in the—scientific, technological, and economic—institutions dealing with the elemental (e.g., our handling of fire), and (c) rebuilding trust in the material force of the elemental (e.g., the material force of fire).[6]

Before I begin explaining what I mean by elemental trust, I want to distinguish trust from hope. While hope, in times of climate change, has been conceived in positive terms, enabling "psychological and physical health"[7] and encouraging "pro-environmental behavior," hope can also be short-lived and illusory. That hope can be short-lived and illusory was the predominant view for the ancient Greeks. For instance, Hesiod's account of hope in his *Works and Days* warns against "a man out of work, a man with empty hopes and no livelihood,"[8] as he explains that the dreams of such a man are vacuous if they lack the means of support—that is, the "work." Lacking the means and built on empty figments of the imagination, hope can be an obstacle to a person's truly preparing for and achieving things necessary and, instead, lead to deception and harm. This warning against the emptiness of hope runs parallel with Aristotle's idea in the *Nicomachean Ethics* that hope can be based on empty belief or ignorance, and it is thus to be carefully distinguished from another form of hope that can inform fear and thereby courage.[9] Translating this in terms of our current ecological crisis: some social scientists warn against a form of hope they call "false," since it is premised on the belief that ecological problems will resolve "without the need for human intervention":[10] this follows Hesiod's idea that hope can only be constructive when premised on the right kind of means or "work."

Given both the short-lived and illusory nature of hope, the focus of this chapter will be trust. In contrast to hope, trust has a longer temporal arc and can undergird a society in powerful and often invisible ways. In discussing trust, some authors explicitly reference the temporal arc of trust, arguing that trust "can only be stabilized over time,"[11] while others highlight the fact that trust, versus hope, has a more practical—and thereby enduring—direction. For instance, Marín-Ávila argues that "while hope entails a gaze or a direction of interest that is predominantly emotional or axiological, in trust this direction of interest is practical."[12]

Trust not only has a longer arc and a practical direction, but, additionally, as I argue in this chapter, trust also extends beyond individualized affect and can function as a cultural, affective interface, connecting people to each other, to institutions, and thereby reconnecting us to the elemental worlds we no longer feel to be our home. If it is worthwhile to envision an age that prepares us for a transformation from elemental loss into one of elemental change, then we need a long-term and in-depth vision of our—institutional and social—affective relationships that connect us to the elemental and that can undergird such change. In my view, trust can perform this work.

In the first section of this chapter, I will explore trust's preliminary definitions and its role in society, harkening back to both historical thinkers on trust as well as contemporary sources. I end that section by discussing how, ideally, trust functions as the underpinning for social and ethical life, and how, in modern society, distrust seems to have replaced trust. In the second section, I discuss two possibilities for rebuilding trust: (1) Ostrom's model of collective action—working on the side of human agents—and (2) Serres's philosophical model of embodied elemental trust—indexing trust in the ontological layers of responsiveness to the elemental—supplemented by Daniel Wildcat's appeal to Indigenous practices that open up to a world of familial trust.

Defining Trust with Bernstein, Godfrey, and Hegel

Common Definitions and Defining Trust with Bernstein

The *Oxford English Dictionary* defines trust as the "firm belief in the reliability, truth, or ability of someone or something; confidence or faith in a person or thing, or in an attribute of a person or thing."[13] Tracing its etymology, the term also conveys, via the Middle High German *getrüste*, which means the notion of company and troop, something like accompaniment, and, connected to its etymological meaning in Old Dutch, means something like "consolation."[14] Philosophically, trust can be said to be "a many splendoured thing, referring to a variety of attitudes, feelings, relationships, and activities."[15]

Most commonly we use trust in an interpersonal way, addressing the way we trust each other in intimate relationships, at our workplace, and in various institutional frameworks. Jay Bernstein in "Trust: On the Real but Almost Unnoticed, Ever-Changing Foundation of Ethical Life," argues that trust is "the ethical foundation of everyday life." Following Annette Baier, Bernstein's focus is on the interpersonal dimension of trust: "Trust is trust in others before whom we are unconditionally vulnerable that they will not take advantage of our vulnerability."[16] Bernstein argues that trust is mostly *invisible* given what he calls the "exorbitance" of the fact that trust is founded in vulnerability: "Trust turns out to be most effective or most fully actual when it remains unnoticed: trust ideally occurs as the invisibility of trust. Hence, the ethical foundation of everyday life is a set of attitudes, presuppositions, and practices which we typically fail to emphatically notice until they become absent."[17] If we follow this line of reasoning, then any talk of trust *begins* only when trust has disappeared—that is, when trust has been violated and/or when distrust has emerged. While there is daily risk in the vulnerability established by trust, this trust does not come to the surface unless betrayed. Bernstein further clarifies: "The space between the exorbitance of the danger and everyday obliviousness to the danger is the actuality of trust as the condition for everyday interpersonal engagement in the world."[18]

While Bernstein in his examinations talks about how trust has been lost "at the very juncture where actual moral life has collapsed,"[19] my own account takes on a different approach—it addresses the very slow and gradual changes that have been affecting our elemental constellations, so much so that they have left a sense of loss in their wake. For my account of elemental loss, this means that, vis-à-vis, Bernstein, I am aware of the need to speak of a juncture in regard to our sense of trust, but that (1) I do not address this in terms of a collapse of moral society but rather in terms of our perceived sense of loss happening to our elemental constellations, and that (2) I see this change less in terms of an *event* but rather as a slowly built-up cascade of incremental changes. These changes to the elemental flux space, however, have transformed the *conditions of the possibility of the elements*. That is, these slow, incremental, infinitesimal changes have affected the possibilities of the elemental and its ontogenetic power and expression. As the underlying conditions of the elemental are undergoing change in a way that we are now observing at the scale of anthropogenic climate change, we can witness, for instance, that the fluctuations in elemental expression—for instance, changes in the currents of the ocean—that have always been "normal" in a certain area—variance within a distribution pattern—are now varied in a way that breaks with established expectancies. It should be noted that this conception is not arguing for a former stable elemental that has given way to changes in our current era, since the elemental has always been a space of flux. However, I argue that incremental changes have changed the very conditions of the possibility of the elements, providing a different elemental expression (in terms of both range and quality) than we are habituated to. This also means that (3) I see the task of philosophizing trust in an age of anthropogenic climate change as one that not only has to begin with theorizing the disappearance of the (former) invisible nature of trust but also as one that has to imagine a method for instilling future forms of trust as the elemental remains a space of flux going forward. Such future imaginations of building trust are crucial as they allow transformations to our epistemic and affective habitus that are needed in light of continued changes to the elemental.

Since, for Bernstein, trust is dependent upon a deep sense of vulnerability, he turns to the analysis of trauma in Susan Brison. For Brison, trauma is to be understood as "loss of trust," and specifically "loss of trust in the world reveals the self to be in some respect existentially helpless before others, that is, existentially vulnerable not only physically but metaphysically."[20] Thus, we emerge as "second persons," persons that are always dependent upon other social persons. Our existential vulnerability exists in our deep dependence upon others to acknowledge us and keep us feeling safe and "at home." This is what Judith Butler, in the context of mourning, has also indexed—namely, that we are deeply and fundamentally constituted by others—we are always relational beings.[21]

If we relate this back to the question of loss of trust in the elemental, then an interesting question could emerge: As we seem to have lost our "bearing" in the elemental world, then does this in fact indicate that our elemental trust has been violated? But what does this exactly mean? Can Bernstein's definition of trust apply, when he defines that trust is "trust in others before whom we are unconditionally vulnerable that they will not take advantage of our vulnerability"?

The trust that is at stake in the elemental will include vulnerability, but it *cannot* include the idea that the elemental cannot "take advantage of our vulnerability," for this (1) would mistakenly assume the elemental in terms of intentional personhood, and (2) mistakes the elemental for an only presumed beneficial force, which it surely is not. Trust in the elemental cannot mean unequivocal trust in the fact that the elemental will *always everywhere* benefit us, since the elemental is precisely composed full of ambiguity and dynamic changes. For instance, in their engagement with the sea, sailors may trust the sea as they embark on their travels, trusting each other and their seafaring skills, but they do not naïvely trust the sea such that they think it will always keep them safe. Rather, what's at stake is a more nuanced sense of trusting the sea, so that it is grasped as both potentially calm and wild, and life-giving and life-taking. In other words, to trust the sea is to grasp the sea in its inner complex dynamisms, as well as in its complex interaction with air streams, storms, currents, temperatures, gravitational forces, shores, and so on. Thus, when we speak of "trust" in the elemental, and the current "loss of trust" in the elemental, this cannot imply that we are suddenly confronted with a ruptured sense of vulnerability. Rather, what this means is that the vulnerability we are currently experiencing—in contrast to the vulnerability we experienced in the past—is of a *different kind, or scale, or both*. I want to propose that both are the case.

If we return to the example of how trauma unveils the vulnerability we always already had, which stipulates our co-relational sense of being, then perhaps this also uncovers a clue for how to grasp the emergent loss of trust as our elemental worlds have shifted. That is, as slow, incremental changes shifted the elemental constellations of which we are part, and thereby transformed the conditions for elemental ontogenesis and expression, the affect we *always* navigate to some extent in the realm of the elemental has qualitatively shifted—from trust in change to an affect of loss in the face of change. This sense of loss has become more acute as we have also experienced the qualitative force of that changing: from incremental changes in the expression of the elemental to the more drastic and qualitatively unexpected changes characteristic of the current climate crisis upheaval. It is difficult to put our finger exactly on *what and how our trust has been shifted*; however, as Baier argues, such fundamental confusion in the "what and how" of trust's dissipation is common to trust, since trust, being similar to an atmosphere, is spread out. Baier claims that trust "comes in webs, not in single strands, and disrupting one strand often rips apart whole webs."[22] Thus, as trust dissipates, the atmosphere of security within which we have operated similarly is felt to collapse as a *whole structure*—both qualitatively and quantitively—not as a missing strand.

To grasp how trust can have such a foundational sense of being, it is important to link the more interpersonal notes on trust, proposed by Bernstein, to a broader and more general sense of trust that is key to our way of life. Specifically, I will turn here to the account of Joseph Godfrey, whose account of trust—in terms of openness and enhancement—sets up the larger question of trusting impersonal things or beings, such as the broader network with which we connect to the elemental.

Godfrey on the Common Core of Trust, and Trust as Openness to Benevolence

Godfrey in *Trust of People, Words, and God* speaks of a family-resemblance approach to trust. Godfrey argues that trust has many meanings, but he also aims to categorize it clearly, discerning four dimensions and what he calls a "common core."[23] As for its four dimensions, he proposes reliance-trusting, I-thou trusting, security-trusting, and openness-trusting.[24] Reliance-trusting is put in the most formulaic and instrumental of terms—it is understood schematically as "X trusts Y with Z, and has in view the outcome O, because of basis or reason R." I-thou trusting, following Buber and Marcel, is understood as intersubjective or relational trust.[25] Unlike reliance-trusting, I-thou trusting is more general and it is no longer seen in the context of instrumentality; however, it does include the interpersonal. Security trust is defined as "a sense of being basically secure, at home, upheld in my basic self . . . a sense that I belong, am accepted, am ok."[26] Finally, Godfrey defines openness-trusting as a dispositional form of trusting, equal to a "readiness to be affected," entailing a ground for trusting rather than the focused forms of trusting that reliance-trusting and security-trusting represent.[27]

The common core that Godfrey discerns is the following. He argues that trusting across all four dimensions is an activity—"it is something that is *done*"—rather than a belief.[28] While he thinks trusting implies certain beliefs, he also draws the border further by acting on those beliefs.[29] Moreover, Godfrey argues that, at its core, trusting is receptive, in that it has to do with a disposition of receptivity, of giving ourselves over to something or someone we trust. Finally, trusting has to do with something we deem "good," in that we intend something good to come out of our trusting. Thus, gathering all these lines together, he concludes that "to trust is to be receptive to enhancement."[30]

While Godfrey's definition of trust offers his particular take on defining trust and ultimately stands in light of his goal to define trust in a benevolent God, his way of assessing and evaluating the various meanings of trust and selecting a "common core" that grounds trust is helpful for my project, particularly in gaining oversight on the various philosophical notions of trust. Moreover, since Godfrey does not make distinctions in his concept of trust in whether trust extends to persons or to impersonal things such as institutions or things, his definition can helpfully resonate with the outlines of my own project, rethinking trust regarding elemental constellations. This is particularly helpful since other theorists, such as Bernstein, distinguish between reliability and trust, arguing that failures of reliance result in surprise or disappointment, whereas trust, when broken, speaks to deep moral betrayal.[31] However, following Godfrey, I want to argue that trust can have broader parameters; especially in the case of the elemental, which includes trust in both natural and social interactions with the elemental, I argue that we are not simply affected as if normal predictable patterns are broken, but we are affected in a way in which our world, our home, is shaken.

A third aspect of Godfrey's approach is valuable, namely in that he differentiates between "foundational" senses of trust—an openness to the world—and more focused forms of trust; this is relevant insofar as my proposed sense of elemental trust aims to cross various tiers—from a more foundational sense to the specifics dealing with particular elements. Fourth, what is key about Godfrey's definition of trust is his emphasis on participation and receptivity. He thereby acknowledges what I have called elsewhere the "middle-voiced" dimension of trust, or "the genitive" grammar of trust. Since trust goes beyond the object-subject relationship, the trust we have in people, ideas, and other things goes beyond naming them in the accusative—the genitive or the middle voice would be more apt to name "the participatory nonpossessive nature of trust that transforms those involved."[32] Finally, the definition of trust that Godfrey offers—namely "to trust is to be receptive to enhancement"—clarifies that trust includes a *normative* stance, insofar as his focus on "enhancement" indexes a particular good or norm that trust is seeking to invoke and achieve. This invocation of the normative dimension of trust finds echoes in various other authors, appealing to the "normative parameters"[33] invoked in trust. Given our current perceived sense of loss of trust that is ruling our engagement with the elemental world, this chapter thus needs to (a) rethink our participatory middle-voiced involvement with the elemental and each other, and (b) rethink the normative dimensions that ought to guide the emergence of our trusting relationship with the elemental.

To gain further clarity on the participatory middle-voiced nature of trust, I will turn next to discuss Hegel's account of trust. Hegel, like

Bernstein, argues that trust, when functioning, is invisible, and he argues that it informs and ties together our social and ethical life. Even if my account of the elemental does not want to reinstitute an idealized sense of institutional "trust" owed to an ideally benevolent political state (e.g., Hegel) or an authoritative sense of trust in a benevolent higher being (e.g., Godfrey), Hegel's account can carve a path forward toward rethinking trust as an effectively social, affective interface capable of rebuilding our relationships with the elemental in a dynamic, dialogical fashion, thereby offering further *social and institutional particulars* of Godfrey's notion of trust as "openness to enhancement." Admittedly, I will not propose that we need to return to Hegel and his notion of a benevolent nation-state to reimagine trust. Rather, I want to think *with Hegel against Hegel* to simultaneously show the foundational nature of trust for our sense of being and home, while also reimagining what trust, post-Hegel, could look like in a world that is no longer finding its foundation in the state.

HEGEL AND TRUST INVESTED IN THE STATE

For Hegel, trust is a disposition (*Gesinnung*), an essential element of the ethical relationship that citizens have with the state. Hegel writes that trust (*Zutrauen*) "is the consciousness that my substantial and particular interest is preserved and contained in the interest and end of an other."[34] As Houlgate writes in his analysis of this passage, this means that trust is "the feeling that my well-being and freedom are secured by that other, and that in relating to the other I am in fact relating to myself and my own essence. Such trust can remain naive and immediate, or it can 'pass over into more or less educated insight' (PR: §§268, 147 Remark)."[35] As Adriaan Peperzak writes in his helpful commentary on this passage:

> The word *Gesinnung* is difficult to translate; "disposition" is too generic to capture the combination of attitude, mentality, and conviction expressed in it. The appropriate political disposition within a rational state is primarily trust (*Zutrauen*): well-disposed citizens will what the state wills because they are confident that their own true freedom and interests are contained in the state's substantial (i.e., universal, but particularized) interests. Citizens feel *at home* in their state when they are convinced that the state's endeavors are not alien to their own (§268). Education and reflection can transform this

basic trust into justified insight, but a *naïve consciousness of the free will's radical unity in its communitarian and individual realizations* is sufficient for a positive disposition with regard to the state's politics.³⁶

As Peperzak's commentary elucidates, trust for Hegel provides a sense of "home" in our world, and its content is based on a presumed and "naïve" congruence of the interest of the state with the individual. Such basic and naïve trust may transform into "justified insight," but such insight is only secondary. Reflecting upon how such a trusting disposition arises, Peperzak argues that it is for Hegel, in part, "a result of the historical situation in which we are born and educat[ed]."³⁷ Peperzak also references one of Hegel's courses, where Hegel speaks about the "invisibility" of trust, in that even if people critique the community of which they are part, their critique still operates within a more fundamental field of deep trust, a field that often remains invisible until its foundations would be disturbed.³⁸

Hegel defines trusting a person in the following way: "[To] believe that he has sufficient insight to treat my cause as if it were his own, and to deal with it in the light of his own best knowledge and conscience."³⁹ Underlying our ethical actions is trust, consisting of an "essentially theoretical relation to ethical life—a knowing of oneself in the other."⁴⁰ The consciousness that "right and freedom are indeed actualized in the world . . . principally takes the form of our trust in the institutions of ethical life. Action must, therefore, be rooted in trust, if it is to be truly ethical."⁴¹

Trust connects a citizen with its own freedom, its rights, and the institutions that embody that which is right and good. This also means that affect and understanding come to intersect in the phenomenon of trust. As Houlgate clarifies: "Trust and understanding are not at odds with one another, but true trust is itself a form of felt understanding and insight. Such trust is not merely peripheral to ethical life, for Hegel, but belongs to the very essence of the latter, because it is the appropriate subjective relation to objectively existing right."⁴²

We can discern a number of important aspects in Hegel's analysis that are worthwhile for my own analysis of elemental trust.

First, in trust, for Hegel, human beings not only relate to others and the state for their sense of security but also find, through connecting to the other, a way to relate to, and affirm, themselves. Thus, a double confirmation, of both the other and the self, takes place in establishing a relationship of trust. This is also important for my analysis of elemental trust because we find in our trusting relationship with the elemental *both* a sense of acknowledgment of the elemental constellation and an empowering sense of our own sense of being. In times of losing elemental trust, this means we not only lose a sense of trust in the elemental (i.e., "the elemental home") but also lose connection to our own sense of agency, power, and being (i.e., "the human home").

Second, trust for Hegel, as clarified by Bernstein, is fundamentally invisible when it operates well. Even those who critique a community do so on the basis of a fundamental trust that they would defend it if assailed. This also means that we need to think about what level we are talking about distrust regarding our relationship to the elemental: (a) does our sense of current distrust and critique toward elemental spaces still build upon a more profound and existing sense of trust, or (b) does our current critique and sense of losing trust actually mean that our most foundational—"elemental"—trust is disappearing or completely gone?

Third, trust for Hegel is inclusive of understanding. Houlgate in that sense translates trust as "a form of felt understanding and insight."[43] Over and against articulations of trust that make it *merely* affective and thereby at odds with insight, Hegel argues that it includes both affect and understanding.[44] Also, trust, for Hegel, can be both more basic (i.e., "naïve") or develop into what he calls "educated insight."[45] For my analysis of elemental change, this means that the analysis of trust needs to think in a sophisticated sense of trust—both as affect and as inclusive of insight—and negotiate various tiers—namely in speaking to both a very fundamental sense of embodied trust in our relationship to the elemental and more reasoned forms of trust that have been articulated through established, socialized practices.

Fourth, in Hegel's focus upon trust, he outlines that true trust is not antidotal to freedom but actually is, as Houlgate words it, "an essential element of modern freedom."[46] However, this also means, as Houlgate stipulates, that states need to merit trust: "[Modern states] must protect individual rights, maintain the division of powers, and protect themselves from public corruption."[47] While my analysis of the elemental moves beyond the notion of the state as the key institution, Hegel's idea that trust and freedom are mutually implied is important for thinking through the idea of elemental trust: the idea that elemental trust is dependent upon the ability to render intelligible the contingency of the elemental and thus be able to bring our being to act upon or react to the elements in their unfolding.

Additionally, Hegel's idea that institutions need to merit trust is helpful in terms of my analysis, as speaking to the need that trust entails, in an institutional context, clarifies the *normative stance* that institutions need to embody if we want to bestow them trust in mediating the elemental.

Fifth, it is important to provide trust to institutions that merit it. There is a danger, as Houlgate situates it in his reading of Hegel, that "we might refuse to ever place our trust in the institutions of ethical life, even when they do in fact merit it, and instead cultivate an attitude of perpetual vigilance and suspicion."[48] Criticism is key, but what is detrimental to society is ungrounded suspicion and degeneration into what Houlgate calls "a self-sustaining 'culture of suspicion.'"[49] For my analysis of elemental trust, this means that I would want to engage a *dialectics between trust and vigilance*, which allows a dialogical critique without giving up on the fundamental notion of trust.

In sum, Hegel offers a rich account of trust that shows how trust ideally serves as the actual foundation for our ethical life: reaffirming institutions, others, and ourselves. Trust can be lived on various levels—naïvely or educated—and it operates at the intersection of affect and understanding. Trust does not exclude critique or vigilance, but it may productively entail it as long as its foundation stands. Our institutions should ideally merit trust, but they need to live up to normative standards to do so.

My Definition of Trust

Overall, having moved now through Bernstein's, Godfrey's, and Hegel's analyses, we are better positioned to define trust. Trust, when operative, functions as the invisible glue that connects persons to others, to social institutions, and to themselves. Trust is foundational for our sense of belonging in the world, and it is precariously built around a sense of vulnerability that shows our co-dependence upon others for our perceived sense of self. Trust operates at the intersection of affect and understanding and can be either implicit or more explicitly formulated.

For my own analysis, particularly the ideas of (1) the invisibility of trust, (2) the foundational nature of trust for a sense of "home," and (3) the ontological vulnerability relayed by trust are crucial. They highlight, in the context of current-day senses of elemental loss, how much stands at risk if trust is lost. Overall, *these accounts allow me to define elemental trust as a social-affective interface that, invisibly, underpins our relationship with the elemental, resulting in a sense of elemental home.*

In the next section, I turn to Marx and Stiegler to explain the broader contours of losing trust and how, in their view, the collapse of authorities such as God and the state initiates an age of distrust and disenchantment sanctioned by capitalism. Their diagnostic simultaneously provides clues to how trust may reemerge.

Diagnosing the Loss of Trust in Modern Society

Marx and Stiegler on Economic Systems and the Fraying of Trust

Marx's analysis of trust is closely related to that of Hegel, in that it sees trust ideally as a fundamental affective and ethical glue that (a) binds citizens to the state and each other, and that (b) affirms the worth of each citizen. However, Marx points out that monetary relationships that rule our modern capitalist society—for instance, credit—are actually based on distrust, thereby showing that economic systems, rather than adding to trust, actually dissolve trust and dismantle broader cohesion in society.

While providing credit to another seems to establish a direct sense of "trust" and respectful acknowledgment between two or more individuals or between individuals and institutions, even appearing "to run counter to the market and capital-labor relation," debtor-creditor relations in fact are based on distrust, according to Marx: "It is a self-estrangement, dehumanization, all the more infamous and extreme because its element is no longer a commodity, metal or paper, but the moral existence, the social existence, the very heart of man, and because under the appearance of mutual trust between men it is really the greatest distrust and a total estrangement."[50] While debtor-creditor relationships *seem* to depend on the recognition of one person by another, pulling on "the belief of new possibilities" and "some noble sentiment towards oneself, others, and the world,"[51] as Lazaretto writes, in fact credit relations constitute the full completion of alienation, as credit does not invest in truly taking chances on the unknown or the creativity of another's accomplishments into the future but is simply part of establishing "security" and the "circulation of selfish and individual interests."[52]

Trust and distrust, and, with them, "the 'moral' concepts of good and bad," are limited, translated, and transformed into new categories: solvency and insolvency.[53] In Marx's words:

> What constitutes the essence of credit? We disregard here the *content* of credit which is once again money. We disregard then the content of this trust according to which a man accords *recognition* to another man by advancing money to him and—at best, i.e., when he does not call in the securities, that is to say, if he is no usurer—expresses his confidence that his fellow human being is a "good" man and not a scoundrel. By a "good" man the creditor, like Shylock, means a "sufficient" man.[54]

When good and bad are translated into the categories of "solvent" versus "insolvent," then this indicates that society's yardstick for measuring human beings' worth revolves around what Lazaretto calls the "measure of (the) economic reason (of debt)."[55]

Marx continues by exploring the invasive, privacy-violating, and fear-driven practice of risk assessment that constantly places the potential borrower under suspicion. This indicates that, paradoxically, the foundation of so-called "trust" in modern societies, that is, credit, is, in fact, the very opposite: mistrust.

> The mistrustful reflection about whether to extend credit or not; the spying-out of the secrets in the private life of the borrower; the revelation of temporary difficulties so as to embarrass a competitor by undermining his credit, etc. The whole system of bankruptcy, fictitious enterprises, etc. . . . *In state credit systems* the state is in the same position as the individual as described above. . . . The games played with state loans show to what extent it has become a toy in the hands of businessmen, etc.[56]

Lazzarato is keen to point out that the modern welfare state is similarly operating along the lines of distrust: "When social rights (unemployment insurance, the minimum wage, healthcare, etc.) are transformed into social debt and private debt, and beneficiaries into debtors whose repayment means adopting prescribed behavior, subjective relations between 'creditor' institutions, which allocate rights, and 'debtors,' who benefit from assistance of services, begin to function in a radically different way, just as Marx foresaw."[57]

Thus, in Lazzarato's view at least, the initial tendencies that Marx diagnosed with the rise of capitalism have been further extended to operate in modern society. While perhaps less visible than before, such structures as "unemployment insurance" still operate within the general logic of solvency, constantly placing individuals under the detective-like lens of mistrust.

All of this is to say that trust, as Hegel had worded it, with its focus on the—ideal—acknowledgment of human freedom and acknowledgments of "the logic of individual and collective rights," has been transformed into what Lazzarato, following Marx, names "a logic of credit (investments of human capital)."[58] Moreover, this distrustful regime is not limited to cases of monetary borrowing alone but, according to Lazzarato, informs the very operation of the contemporary welfare state as we know it: "[It] suspects all users, and especially the poorest, of being cheats, of living at society's expense by taking advantage of public assistance instead of working. Under the conditions of ubiquitous distrust created by neoliberal policies, hypocrisy and cynicism now form the content of social relations."[59] Marx and Lazzarato's analyses underline the importance of foundational trust for a society to operate well; in fact, their analyses of the rise of distrust are themselves an ode to the need for true trust. However, their accounts also raise the question of what exactly trust means in a society devoid of divine or state authority and where the only ruling mechanism is an economic and political one: that of a politics of debt and credit. If a society is guided by issues of solvency/insolvency for its key moral compass, then this frays a society not just at the (economic) edges but ruptures its cohesive foundational whole.

French contemporary philosopher Bernard Stiegler continues this Marxist diagnostic of distrust in modern society. Following Weber, he argues that it is not only the rise of capitalism that is to blame for the rise of distrust, but capitalism's rise was made possible by the void left in the wake of society's lost faith in God. In the trace of Weber, Stiegler states that capitalism "transformed the type of fidelity that had structured Western society, changing it from a society grounded in the faith of monotheistic religious belief to a society based on trust understood as fiduciary calculability."[60] Stiegler defines this development of infidelity in the following way, arguing that "the systematic organization of consumption presupposes *abandonment*; it presupposes abandoning objects, institutions, relations, places and everything that . . . is possible for markets to control, all of which must therefore be abandoned by the symbolic dimension [*le symbolique*], that is, de-symbolized."[61]

Stiegler's theoretical access point to grasping loss of trust is by theorizing the loss of what he calls the "thingly support" of the world.

That is, where things, until the twentieth century, had originally served as transitional objects for our care of and desire in the world, they now, due to their almost immediate obsolescence and "self-destructive short-termism," have done away with "the shared milieu within which relations of fidelity are formed." In the past, it had been the case that "things tie, seal and support relations, as objects of inheritance, work, the formation of knowledge, shared activities, games, commerce of all kinds, and so on, but also and above all as *transitional objects*."[62] With the rise of capitalism, however, things as part of the making-world and thus of making-trust have become disposable.

The new societal organization according to Stiegler is that of "dependence grounded in infidelity."[63] The "addictive" nature of the items we crave has nothing to do anymore with our trust and joy in things we care for. What results is life bereft of the key ideals that give it value, such as love, trust, and knowledge: "Disenchantment as the calculation of trust, and as fiduciary calculation, leads to the liquidation of fidelity, friendship, love, *philia*, knowledge, arts and letters, in a word, of what makes life worth living."[64] To counter this disenchantment, Stiegler proposes to transform pharmacology's current drive toward nihilism into a new form that "re-invests *pharmakon* as a remedy, cure, transitional mediation understood as transindividuation—to re-enchant this world confronted with a new pharmacology constituted by the digital milieu, its relational technologies and its completely *revolutionary* social practices."[65] Our world can again become reenchanted, according to Stiegler, if we return to the world via the reconstitution of a new—digital, technological, and social—interface that may turn our formerly problematic pathologies "into a new metastabilized milieu"—"into a new space of fidelity."[66] This turn toward finding new pharmacologies and techniques is all part of the Promethean project and promise that, according to Stiegler, underlies human existence. As also discussed in the chapter on fire, humanity is grounded in a non-origin and is essentially driven toward using prosthetics that can either lead to flourishing or our demise: "The prosthesis is a danger, that of artifacts, and artifacts can destroy what gathers within an effective and active being-together."[67]

In the following section, I will seek to address the issue of rebuilding trust. I will approach this notion of rebuilding trust by invoking a turn not to naïve trust but toward concrete practices that, in collaboration, seek to rebuild trust, sharing the elemental constellations of which we are part in a more equitable way, carving out futures for all living beings. In this, I will think through Elinor Ostrom's model of collective action, which moves us beyond the state-market dichotomy, so as to examine sharing the commons in a more equitable way using horizontal lines of power. Moreover, I will analyze, with Michel Serres, philosophical pathways that propose relational ontologies and epistemologies that more holistically track and propose changes to how we relate to the elemental. What I hope unfolds is a nuanced way of taking issues with distrust seriously and introducing possible conceptual frameworks that can rebuild elemental trust.

From Loss of Trust to Gaining Trust: Building Trust through Collective Action and Embodied Affect-Knowledges

In this third section, I will analyze two models of rebuilding trust that propose what I have argued for: returning trust to its place as a foundational affective interface capable of interpreting and interacting with the elemental ensuring a sense of orientation and agency; combatting a sheer economic short-term understanding of "fidelity" and "credit," which is built out of actual distrust; and rethinking trust in postmodern society as emerging from coalitions and collectives that are built from the ground up, rather than imposed from the top down from the perspective of the nation-state. However, the account of rebuilding trust must carefully navigate local communities in search of rebuilding trust in an age of climate change and straddle the register of larger global forces, given that these permeate localities through the shared elements of water, fire, air, and earth.

In the following subsection, I build upon two conceptual-practical models to cast possible future paths of rebuilding trust: (1) Ostrom's model of collective action, and (2) Michel Serres's proposal for developing ontological responsivities in our interaction with the elemental, which is complemented by Indigenous practices that can rebuild trust.

Rebuilding Trust through Elinor Ostrom's Model of Collective Action

Collective Action, the Commons, and Design Principles

Ostrom's model of collective action offers an alternative program for building trust. While she does not unpack the term "trust," the model of collective action she proposes aims at showing "how trust and cooperation could be nurtured to overcome the commons dilemmas and similar problems,"[68] where commons is defined as "[a] resource (including land) that is not privately owned and is available for use by a community or the wider public."[69] Her optimism that the commons may be shared contradicts Garrett Hardin, who argued for the "tragedy of the commons," which is based on the premise that each human being is "locked into a system that compels him to increase his herd without limit—in a world that is limited."[70] According to Hardin, this leads to ruin and tragedy, with "each pursuing his own best interest in a society that believes in the freedom of the commons. Freedom in a commons brings ruin to all."[71] Hardin's view here follows a long tradition starting with Aristotle, who argued already in the *Politics*—versus Plato—that what is deemed common rather than private stands to suffer in terms of care and attention.[72] Along these lines, Wall, voicing Hardin's position, argued that human beings, on their own, "could not cooperate to tackle ecological problems,"[73] thereby requiring public interference and central governmental control.

Opposite Hardin,[74] however, Ostrom showed that the tragedy of the commons is not unavoidable, as evidenced by successful historical examples of communities managing the commons over time.[75] What Hardin overlooked, in Ostrom's mind, "was the capacity of the individuals involved in such tragedies to have sufficient insight into the problems that they faced to restructure their own rules and change the incentives they faced."[76] To prove this point, Ostrom pulled evidence from many institutions that dealt with Common Pool Resources (CPR)—that is, "natural or man-made resource[s] that [are] not privately owned and [are] available for use by a community or (typically a limited subset of) the wider public."[77] As evidenced through Ostrom's research, the institutions studied proved resilient in that they "survived droughts, floods, wars, pestilence, and major economic and political changes."[78] Summarizing what these institutions did, as they successfully managed the commons collectively, Ostrom writes that "the participants designed basic operational rules, created organizations to undertake the operational management of their CPR, and modified the rules-in-use over time in light of past experience according to their own collective choice and constitutional rules."[79] Ostrom points out the stability of the population in these settings (versus the changing milieu) and the fact that "individuals shared a past and expected to share a future."[80] Reliability in these settings was key, as well as the evolution of what she calls "extensive norms."[81] Ostrom writes:

It was important to individuals to maintain their reputation as a reliable member of a community. Extensive norms have evolved in all of these settings that narrowly defined "proper" behavior. Many of these norms made it feasible for individuals to live in close interdependence on many fronts without excessive conflict. Further, gaining a reputation for keeping promises, honest dealings, and reliability in one arena was a valuable asset. Prudent, long-term self-interest reinforced the acceptance of the norms of proper behavior. The most notable similarity of all, of course, is the sheer perseverance of these resource systems and institutions.[82]

Across those institutions, the variety of settings makes it impossible to derive a general set of rules. However, as she argues, "there are similar design principles that characterize all of the robust CPR institutions."[83] Accordingly, Ostrom outlined eight specific design principles,[84] which I will briefly mention here:

1. Clear circumscribed boundaries: "Individuals or households who have rights to withdraw resource units from the CPR must be clearly defined, as must the boundaries of the CPR itself."[85]

2. Locally tailored rules: "Appropriation rules restricting time, place, technology, and/or quantity of resource-units are related to *local conditions* and to provision rules requiring labor, materials, and/or money."[86]

3. Participation open to those affected: "Most individuals affected by operational rules can participate in modifying operational rules." This means that "CPR institutions that use this principle are able to better tailor rules to local circumstances, since the individuals who directly interact with one another and with the physical world can modify the rules over time so as to better fit them to the specific characteristic of their setting."[87]

4. Monitoring: "Monitors, who actively audit CPR conditions and participant behavior, are accountable to the participants or are the participants."[88]

5. Graduated penalties: "Participants who violate operational rules are likely to be assessed graduated sanctions

(depending on the seriousness and context of the offense) from other participants, by officials accountable to these participants, or by both."[89]

6. Conflict management: "Participants and their officials have rapid access to low-cost, local arenas to resolve conflict among participants or between participants and officials."[90]

7. Right to self-organize: "The rights of participants to devise their own institutions are not challenged by external governmental authorities."[91]

8. Nested layers: "Appropriation, provision, monitoring, enforcement, conflict resolution, and governance activities are organized in multiple layers of nested enterprises."[92] This final principle stipulates that commons need to work within larger systems of networks. For instance, a locally and collectively managed irrigation system needs to function well within a larger water network to succeed.[93]

As Ostrom showed in examining historical case studies of collectively managed long-lasting commons, there is no overarching "blueprint"[94] to guide them all. Instead, she discerned eight important ways that have historically guided collective and successful sharing of the commons. Ranging from self-organization and accountability to open participation, these design principles work at organizing the emergent collective, in a way that is equitable and sustainable over time, and building collective resilient futures of managing the commons.

Since much of her earlier work was aimed at the specifics of the locality, Ostrom in her later work shifted context, arguing that many elements of sharing the commons at the local level can be scaled up. Specifically, she has argued that the eighth design principle, which is centered on acknowledging nested layers, can be further unpacked to imagine managing the commons more globally.[95]

Ways of Scaling Up Trust from the Local to the Global: Ostrom's Guidance

During the last decades of her life, Ostrom increasingly emphasized the importance of theorizing the commons not only in terms of discrete entities but also as placed within larger social-ecological systems (SESs),[96] thereby highlighting the relevance of the eighth design principle of "nesting." Especially in a time of climate change, losses of natural resources, and ranges of biodiversity, she argues that a holistic approach to grasping the larger world of which discrete commons are a part is essential. Thus, she suggests approaching the issue of scale in a way that connects the micro-parts to the macro-parts: "SESs are composed of multiple subsystems and internal variables within these subsystems at multiple levels analogous to organisms composed of organs, organs of tissues, tissues of cells, cells of proteins, etc."[97] Like living organisms composed of multiple sub-tiers, social-ecological systems are similarly constituted, with each part on a continuum with the subsystem within which it is nested as well as the lower-tier subsystem that it nests. Such approach requires complexity, thereby demanding research methods from both social and natural sciences "to dissect and harness complexity."[98] Additionally, Ostrom saw vital importance in learning from the communities that lived within such complex social-ecological systems.[99]

In theorizing global climate change, Ostrom argued for caution in scaling up, "since a change in scale frequently changes the structure of situations dramatically."[100] Still, this does not mean that we should dismiss the lessons learned from the local as not applying to the global "simply on the basis of a distinction between supposedly homogeneous local groups and the heterogeneous actors involved in the global system."[101] She argues that local CPR regimes often include actors that come from diverse cultural groups, which shows that homogeneity of actors is neither a prerequisite for successfully managing local commons nor an obstacle for scaling up from the local to the global.

Thus, while supporting complexity in analyzing SESs, Ostrom also argued that we may do well in discerning a continuum between certain locally applied CPR principles and principles that could work on the more global level. This is based on the following three reasons: "First, the substantive natures of many local and global problems are similar. Second, despite the vast differences in scale involved in local and global commons, the configurations of the situations at these levels are fundamentally similar. Thus, the theoretical principles underlying successful cooperation are also similar. Third, any global regime that undermines the requisites for successful cooperation at the local level is unlikely to be sustainable in the long run."[102] Accordingly, when Ostrom focused on the case of global warming in her work, she argued that some specific theoretic principles could be scaled up and applied to the global level for the following three reasons:

a. The analytical structure of some of the problems related to global warming shares similar features with the analytical structure of many local CPRs.

b. Starting with theories and models devised for the analysis of local CPRs may speed the work in developing theories and models at a global level.[103]

c. Many of the problems related to global warming (e.g., deforestation) are themselves the result of inadequate solutions at a microlevel of a complementary and interactive commons problem.[104]

For example, in terms of similar analytic structure, the CPR rules guiding local communities sharing fishing resources apply to the international community managing carbon emissions, since "if one thinks of carbon emissions as 'using up' a natural capacity to absorb carbon in the atmosphere, then the units of natural capacity used up by carbon emissions in one country are not available to be used up by any other country."[105] While the counted units thus are different—fish or units or plant units absorbing carbon emissions—the analytic structure is similar. Moreover, in terms of institutional organization there are similarities as well. In the case of local CPR sharing, communities find ways to cooperate absent an institutional authority. Similarly, on the international level, Ostrom argues, there is an opportunity for alternative means of organizing: "Research on international regimes has emphasized the ability of governments to cooperate in an environment of 'anarchy,' defined as the absence of any central authority at the global level."[106] Thus, the alternative co-emergent local setting of the micro-sharing of resources, independent of an institutional regime and enforcement, and the very fact that many of the micro institutions "are neither a market [n]or a state," show important parallels in proving the opportunities for "alternative international institutions."[107]

Finally, it needs mention that Ostrom's focus on the complexity of SESs also implies that she thinks that institutional meetings and treaties, for instance on carbon emissions, are flawed and likely ineffective: "Such meetings may indeed be crucially important if they provide an opportunity for open discussion of truly difficult and complex problems that need multiple solutions at multiple scales. But the change in human understanding of the nature of the problems involved may be far more important in the first instance for a change in behavior than a new international convention whose pronouncements are nothing much more than words on paper."[108] Since the problem of climate change involves recognition of the fact that individual choices are made within contexts that are differently structured and embedded in each case, "in a wide diversity of institutional and cultural settings," Ostrom argues that "no uniform set of rules" will solve the problems associated with climate change.[109]

Summarizing: Redefining Trust with Ostrom

While Ostrom does not philosophically analyze trust or define it, her analysis of the possibilities of sharing the commons involving collective action proves the very possibility of a collaborative sociality that works toward building and retaining trust. Ostrom shows that beyond visions of a human nature based on pure egotism or on pure solidarity there is another option, namely one in which—through communication and in building particular institutional settings in which the agents can collaborate according to community-generated and maintained rules—humans can move toward compassion once trust is able to flourish and be reciprocated: "When humans learn to value trust and reciprocity and use them as fundamental norms for organizing their lives, it is possible for them to agree on a set of rules that they agree to follow."[110] However, Ostrom is also enough of a realist, as reciprocity in this process is key: "If others do not reciprocate, one immediately returns to noncooperation and tries to exit and find other situations that are more productive."[111]

Trust, for Ostrom, is not a matter of ideality. Trust is fragile and can easily fall apart. It can, *materially*, be generated from the bottom-up, and certain principles of design in sharing the commons can help with generating the social fabric of trust. There are certain dos and don'ts for this practice. For instance, as she shows, direct communication and graduated penalties will generate trust; indirect communication and severe penalties will dismantle trust. Trust moves here beyond naïveté and enigma to emerge as a social affect informed by behavior *and* directing behavior, which has been proven in various historical contexts. Trust demonstrates itself in the context of reciprocity and proves to be multilayered. Trust is materially scaffolded, responding to communal needs, and preserved in time and place by rules and practices guiding behavior: "Rules and practices act to encourage some forms of behavior and to discourage others; they work as a support or scaffold."[112] If rules and practices can inform behavior and trust, then trust remains, for Ostrom, fundamentally a bottom-up principle. Trust can emerge beyond market and governmental interventions, finding traction in the collective actions of humans trying to negotiate the space of the commons to which they belong.

Shortcomings of Ostrom's Model

While Ostrom's model of collective action allows for a building of trust that reinserts agency along the lines of collective bodies—without being imposed through a state or through a system of capital—it also has shortcomings. Although the model shows the important emergence of building trust and emergent collective rulemaking adaptive to the localities it pertains to—and it may possibly, as Ostrom argues, be scaled up—this model of trust-building also fundamentally stays with the status quo of our relationship to the elemental. Thinking through notions of scarcity in our commons (water, crab fisheries, etc.), it is perceptive of the problematic issues there, but it (a) remains too focused on mitigating the issues arising rather than preventing the issues arising, (b) remains too focused on human agency, and (c) does not seek to think beyond the current economic and political system as we currently have it. In other words, Ostrom's model of trust offers a thoughtful bottom-up approach to deal with scarcity issues in the commons, but it is not imaginative enough to ponder, anticipate, and alter the very mindset and issues that got us to scarcity in the first place—namely, the Cartesian mindset that has sought to claim the earth, "to rule and master" nature, thereby preparing a world in which the elemental has been converted from a home to a stage whereby so-called "natural things" have become objects, standing in reserve for human needs, ready to be exploited. Overcoming the Cartesian mindset also implies overcoming the idea that the commons just consists of resources. What is needed is a radical new thought, namely the idea that humans are *part of the commons*.[113]

It is at this point that Michel Serres's philosophy can be brought in, as his thinking reclaims a different access point to the elemental—that is, he accesses life (*bios*) and the earth (*gea*) through his philosophical account of expressive content. This account is based on the idea of a nonhierarchical, always emerging, interrelated reality that emits and expresses itself along various intersecting tiers. Serres proposes to formulate an epistemology and a language that seeks to truly listen to the world's expressions. In stimulating earth-and-life sciences that, in interdisciplinarity, listen to and connect to this expressive content, we may begin to formulate a new ethics to accompany such interdisciplinary knowledge, one that is forceful enough to combat the prevailing Western objectifying and mastering attitude of the world that has led us to feel elemental loss.

Rebuilding Trust with Michel Serres: Engaging the Expressive Content of the Elemental

In his book *Biogea*, Michel Serres diagnoses our current climate predicament and seeks to find a new "birth," a new language, a new mindset and affective disposition that moves beyond our objectifying stance toward life (*bios*) and earth (*gea*)—a problematic stance that is rooted in Western classical thinking that seeks competition, is driven by war and human anthropocentrism, and has spoiled and soiled the earth. In his writing, Serres points to the mathematician Archimedes, whose scholarship was groundbreaking, but whose discovery of levies, pullies, and mirrors was used on warships defending Syracuse, unleashing an inferno of burning enemy ships.[114] Such uses of Archimedes's discoveries had the consequence of casting Western thought patterns that followed under the spell of the need to conquer, possess, and dominate.

However, in *Biogea*, Serres also discerns in the early Greek world another fruitful model for scientific thinking that is community driven, collaborative, and peaceful. This is the model of thinking that he attributes to the Greek Presocratic thinker Empedocles, whose scholarship was truly interdisciplinary in that it thought through the elemental and the forces of love and strife on both the larger, cosmic scale and on the level of the human body and mind. Thanks to this knowledge, Empedocles's philosophical thinking extended beyond narrow disciplinary boundaries to discern many forms of knowledge, including, as is reported, Empedocles's ability to discern the causes of a local plague, which he traced to a local marsh, thus leading to a solution (drainage) and consequent diminished suffering.[115]

Serres's turn to Empedocles provides another possible beginning to Western thinking than the model provided by Archimedes. Where Archimedes promotes a narrow model of knowledge that is trapped in conceptions of war and competition, the Empedoclean model is broad and interdisciplinary and cognizant of the need to track unity and bring peace and balance to living communities. Following Empedocles, Serres aims to think through interconnected earth and life sciences that no longer put life at risk through traditional, rationalizing, objectifying sciences (e.g., atomic science) but instead to think holistically about their role and commitment to our earth, thereby avoiding major human-imposed disasters (e.g., war, atomic bombs) that risk all life. The aim is to think unity and commonality rather than division and fragmentation.[116] As he states, "The contemporary time requires that we try to return to that unity in which the principles of love and hate are at the same time human, living, inert and global."[117] To this end, Serres provocatively asks: "How to speak in several voices, that of things, that of knowledge, of emotions, of each and every one, that of humanity? Will we, one day, by dint of listening to the voices of the Biogea, say this language?"[118] In his writings, Serres offers what I call an alternative model of affective understanding, indexing trust in both the elemental and the possibility of human responsiveness to the ontological layers of the elemental.[119]

A case in point is Serres's analysis of engaging the river Garonne and the community of bargemen skillfully collaborating with one another to navigate the violent currents and treacherous conditions of this river. In the scenario, as he sketches it from his childhood, the elemental emerges as a choric space of potentialities that can both be calm but, during floods, could all too easily cause havoc and death. As the son of one of the bargemen, Serres describes the river's dynamism as well as the community that sought to collectively survive. He describes harrowing times when the river flooded and where he, with four or five others, tried to keep the pontoon boat afloat and balanced:

> Occasionally, plunged in that intense rumbling and sometimes blinded by the fog, we no longer knew our position very well; lost, it was nonetheless necessary to stay in the low-water channel, for a sudden retreat on the part of the flood would have deposited our flat-bottomed and high-belfried old pontoon boat forever among the apple trees. Without detaching any cable, we had to keep them under tension. Give them slack and take it in again. . . . They mustn't break either. . . . Standing up to the force of the water, fighting against the debris it was bringing, saving what could be saved, boats, tools and persons: for how long?[120]

Serres does anything but romanticize the river. In his 24/7 struggles to stay safe and alive on the pontoon boat, the river shows itself in its dynamic forces—in its forcefulness, in its powerful collection of large and dangerous pieces of debris, in its sudden and abrupt swells and retreats. In this description, the full force of Serres's engagement with the diachronic nature of the elemental can be witnessed: Serres does not just speak to the current moment, but his embodied knowledge speaks to a history of the river's swells and (possibly sudden) retreats, acknowledging a sense of a landscape radically changing from times of retreat to times of the river's swelling. Amid those forces, not only is the boat surrounded by turbulent waters, but also all sense of orientation is lost due to the thick fog. The boat and its crew are in constant dialogical exchange with the river's forces as the crew constantly measures the boat's movement and ropes are slackened or fastened in symbiosis with the river's swells or dips. Thus, both a direct engagement with the river as well as the mediated boat encounter with the elemental are part of Serres's analysis, which proves to go beyond the current synchronic moment to cover the deeper diachronic trail of the water.

Furthermore, on the boat, balancing and navigating those forces, a tight community forms itself, gaining punctuation in the relationship between the so-called boss and the dredger: "In solidarity, they appreciated one another; they wouldn't have been able to live without each other; faced with risk, they formed a silent couple where each knew what the other was doing; they loved each other through Garonne, their common mistress."[121] Notwithstanding the problematic feminization of the river Garonne—called "their common mistress"—this excerpt shows how the elemental is a place for possibilities within which the norms of interaction between people emerge. The excerpt proves the power of the elemental generating a community built in full dependence upon each other, building reciprocal trust. The skipper and dredger's commonly desired object of love—the river—is what enables and generates their connection. This connection to the river is not simply generated out of naïve love or naïve trust in the river, but instead it is born out of a complex affective understanding of the river's episodic calmness and forcefulness, including violent upheavals. Moreover, if the skipper and the dredger were not able to trust each other and the mutual knowledge they embodied in navigating the boat on the river, then each could easily perish. This indicates the complexity of their connection—of their trustful diachronic relationship to the river and their reciprocal trust in each other. While each of their relationships with loved ones on land suffered, Serres notes the remarkable nature of this friendship born out of a dialogical relationship with the river—a relationship that is anything but easy.

Trust, for Serres, is thus the responsive-affective interface that entails the dialogical exchange with the (material) elemental and, through the norms of interaction with the elemental, this includes the (social) communal interrelationship as well. In this model, Serres can move beyond Ostrom's model of collective action to tap into the diachronic features of the elemental while simultaneously including the reciprocal trust of a community born out of engagement with the elemental. Overall, both models (1) return trust to its place as a foundational affect capable of building a home for ourselves and others, (2) combat a sheer economic short-term understanding of trust, and (3) rethink trust in a postmodern society as emerging from coalitions that are built from the ground up.

Still, both Serres's and Ostrom's ways of grasping trust need to be tested against the very climate reality we currently live in: namely that reality in which the elemental background conditions have shifted (and thereby the elemental possibilities), and our realization that the terms by which we relate to the elemental are faltering and need epistemic and affective adjustment. In my view, Wildcat's notions of familial trust can aid in addressing this and may help adjusting our epistemic and affective habitus.

Extending Out from Serres: Wildcat on Indigenous Forms of Familial Trust

On the basis of Serres's model of seeking to "speak in several voices," addressing the interconnected expressive content of the world, it is no far stretch to see how Indigenous forms of knowledge can add further concretion to Serres's focus on unity and being part of a shared world. As Daniel R. Wildcat, in *Red Alert*, indicates, we need to learn in this time of climate change from a form of knowledge that he calls "indigenous realism," which centers on "respect for the relationships and relatives that constitute the complex web of life."[122] What is needed is place-shaped knowledge, which allows us to "reconnect, in a deep spatial and spiritual sense, to the places where we live and the lifesystems that support us."[123] The key here is to allow a vision that perceives our lives as lived *in common* and that is "full of relatives":

> Indigenous realism places the most important life challenges Native peoples face—and, for that matter, those that all of

humankind face—on common ground, literally and figuratively. It affirms patterns and processes beyond our own human making—patterns residing in ancient environs, such as wetlands, mountain ranges, prairies, and coastal estuaries and seascapes, and processes emerging in these environs, some of relatively short duration and some extending far beyond directly observable human time frames, such as the processes embodied in the hydrologic cycle, nutrient cycling, and the rock cycle, to name a few.[124]

Renewed attention for discerning the—short-term and long-term—"patterns and processes" that Wildcat references with respect to various ecosystems (e.g., mountain ranges and prairies) aligns with Serres's invocation to more fully listen and understand the world's expressive content. However, Wildcat also highlights the importance of seeing our lives as lived in a commonality that is beyond the human world, where each of the various factors in an ecosystem has origins and dynamisms far beyond human timelines and places, thereby casting human lives in a—temporally—far deeper and—spatially—extensive framework than that of the human world. Deeper knowledge of such patterns is needed, and Wildcat argues that it is precisely through turning to Indigenous realism that we can understand that we need "to extend our notion of community to our natural relatives that make possible and constitute the ecosystems in which we reside."[125]

I would argue that the "common ground" and the "community [of] natural relatives" that Wildcat references directly correlates with my focus on rebuilding our relationship with the elemental, and specifically in wanting to think about a new language to address the common elemental home that we share. As Wildcat indicates, it is easier to respect and trust family members; if this is the case, then the practice of building trust that I have pleaded for may become more accessible through practices that describe and analyze the nonhuman participants in our world no longer in terms of strangers but rather as "family members" that solicit our respect and trust. Thus, building trust, from this perspective, entails practicing new forms of familial trust, where kinship is generated not along so-called bloodlines but rather along tentacular, weblike lines in shared dependence upon a common home.[126]

One example of a practice that drives home Wildcat's point—about kinship and trust—is that of the recent river reengineering and river restorations in the Pacific Northwest, which have led not only to an increased migratory fish population and the consequent ecosystem boost but also to renewal of Indigenous culture. While the global population of migratory fish such as salmon has plummeted in the last fifty years (by some estimates by three-quarters of their population[127]), Christopher Preston in his book *Tenacious Beasts* cites the example of the removal of the Elwha Dam (built in 1912) in the Elwha River to offer a sign of resilience. The dam's removal in 2011–2012 enabled the remarkable return of Chinook salmon,[128] and, with that, a boost for the 137 animal species that benefit from the salmon (e.g., killer whales, bears, mink, crows, ravens, songbirds).[129] The river's new flow and sedimentation also enabled a new estuary, and fish nutrients have altered the forest's entire ecosystem. Importantly, reengineering the water has also allowed the Lower Elwha Klallam tribe to imagine its future in direct connection to its past and current culture and heritage, oriented around the salmon. As tribal chairperson Dennis Sullivan said, "We are protectors of the salmon. Salmon and us are like family to each other. We need each other."[130] By concretely giving space to and trusting the power of the Elwha-salmon relationship, the river was able to be reborn, and, with that, its natural and cultural ecosystem.[131]

Concluding Thoughts

To regain trust, and transform our relationships with the elemental, we need to make use of this moment of crisis and felt loss to create new futures. If Michel Serres is correct, then moments of crisis such as these, stipulated by our sense of elemental loss, are also moments of *de-cision*, offering opportunities for making new cuts[132] in our perception and in our habits, thereby enabling a shift in our affective habitus. It is not easy to take on building trust, nor is it without risk. As the Covid-19 pandemic and its aftermath have shown, it is risky to share and trust the air and each other.[133]

Such risk-taking, as Michel Foucault has shown, can be part of a parrhesiastic practice, entailing frankness toward oneself and others in situations where much is at stake: "*Parrhesia* is a verbal activity in which a speaker expresses his personal relationship to truth, and risks his life because he recognizes truth-telling as a duty to improve or help other people (as well as himself)."[134] Truth and trust, which are, according to etymology, rooted in the same Indo-European root *deru* that also links them to the elemental—"be firm, solid, steadfast with specialized senses 'wood,' 'tree' and derivatives referring to objects made of wood"[135]—reconnect in this practice of truth-telling, which aims at improving lives by taking on risk through a commitment to that which is truthful and trustworthy. In times of climate change, the risk that is taken on here is not something that is only contemporaneously or individually assessed, but one that, following Hans Jonas, ideally takes into account the risk to *future* generations of life as a "fact" to be dealt with.[136]

This parrhesiastic practice, I argue, could become part of building up trust. Precisely not by starting in naïve trust, but instead through engagement in a *dialectics of trust*, where trust is the goal but vigilance provides constant correction. Truth-telling can offer helpful guidance toward balancing the oscillating movement between trust and vigilance, as frankness can keep the process of seeking and finding trust on task and open, facing uncomfortable "less visible and less flattering truths," while circumventing dogma and self-evident meanings.[137] In this way, certain practices that, on the surface, aim to inspire trust (e.g., greenwashing or superficial nods to sustainable practices such as recycling) can be dismantled as "confidence tricks,"[138] aimed at building so-called confidence while ultimately depriving us of truly sustainable and trustworthy futures. Thus, the dialectical process that I envision pleads for carefully judging trustworthiness and untrustworthiness along the lines of practical reason,[139] establishing in the context of institutional life a combination of what O'Neill calls "forward-looking and retrospective elements."[140]

Overall, I see the benefits of thinking through a dialectical movement that keeps the process of seeking trust open yet guarded, exposed yet protected, cooperative yet confrontational. Trust, which, ideally, functions as an invisible "background" or home to our lives, needs, in fact, to be materially and concretely fashioned through sophisticated practices of coalition forming, including dialectical and transparent processes including commitment to truth, and evidence-checking through commitment to vigilance. Additionally, it needs to entail a continuous assessment of the trustworthiness and untrustworthiness of certain practices and institutions. Cultivating "habits of perception" that can guide us in this practice is crucial, along with bottom-up procedures for building trust sharing the commons, as Ostrom's design principles show. If trust leads to "the building of trustworthy and trusted institutions and relationships,"[141] it can offer pathways to a new, more sustainable future. Thus, our current loss of trust is not an end—it can be a beginning. With an eye toward truly sustainable, futural possibilities, we can carve out a path from the current moment, and be transformed—beyond elemental loss.

Notes

Introduction

1. This fire came to be known as the Kincade fire, the source of which was traced back to a failed electric transmission line.
2. "Kincade Fire," *Cal Fire*, last modified October 23, 2019, accessed June 25, 2024, https://www.fire.ca.gov/incidents/2019/10/23/kincade-fire.
3. Nicholas Iovino, "PG&E Slapped with $125M Penalty for Sparking 2019 Kincade Fire," *Courthouse News Service*, November 2, 2021, accessed June 25, 2024, https://www.courthousenews.com/pge-slapped-with-125m-penalty-for-sparking-2019-kincade-fire/#:~:text=In%20an%20emailed%20statement%2C%20PG%26E,sparked%20by%20the%20utility's%20equipmentAccessed%20June%2025,%202024.
4. Our term "element" as we use it derives from "the Old French *element*, < Latin *elementum*, a word of which the etymology and primary meaning are uncertain, but which was employed as translation of Greek στοιχεῖον in the various senses < a component unit of a series; a constituent part of a complex whole (hence the 'four elements'); a member of the planetary system; a letter of the alphabet; a fundamental principle of a science." "Element, n.," *OED Online*, Oxford University Press, June 2020, accessed July 13, 2020, https://www.oed.com/view/Entry/60353?rskey=cvpVuF&result=1&isAdvanced=false.
5. John Sallis, *The Return of Nature: On the Beyond of Sense* (Bloomington: Indiana University Press, 2016).
6. Martin Heidegger, *Being and Time*, trans. John Macquarrie and Edward Robinson (Oxford: Blackwell, 1962), §53, E. 304, H. 260.
7. Hannah Arendt, *The Human Condition* (Chicago: University of Chicago Press, 1958), 52–53; my own italics.
8. Emmanuel Levinas, *God, Death, and Time*, trans. Bettina Bergo (Palto Alto, CA: Stanford University Press, 2000), 12–13.
9. Martin Buber, *I and Thou*, trans. Ronald Gregor Smith (New York: Charles Scribner's Sons, 1958), 6.

10. Judith Butler, "Violence, Mourning, Politics," *Studies in Gender and Sexuality* 4, no. 1 (2003): 13.

11. Butler, "Violence, Mourning, Politics," 11.

12. Annegret Haase, "Covid-19 as a Social Crisis and Justice Challenge for Cities," *Frontiers in Sociology* 5 (2020): 1–7, https://doi.org/10.3389/fsoc.2020.583638.

13. Judith Butler, *What World Is This? A Pandemic Phenomenology* (New York: Columbia University Press, 2022), 21–23.

14. Butler, *What World Is This?*, 25.

15. Pauline Boss, *The Myth of Closure: Ambiguous Loss in a Time of Pandemic and Change* (New York: W. W. Norton, 2021), 12.

16. Boss, *The Myth of Closure*, 6.

17. As Gupta et al. argue, "The rise in industrialization-related human activities has created a marked imbalance in the homeostasis of environmental factors such as temperature and other weather and these might even have imposed conditions for the emergence of future coronavirus cycles. . . . We surmise that pandemics will be more frequent in the future and more severely impactful unless climate changes are mitigated." S. Gupta, B. T. Rouse, and P. P. Sarangi, "Did Climate Change Influence the Emergence, Transmission, and Expression of the COVID-19 Pandemic?," *Frontiers in Medicine* (Lausanne) 8 (December 8, 2021): 769208. doi: 10.3389/fmed.2021.769208. PMID: 34957147; PMCID: PMC8694059.

18. Hans Henri P. Kluge, "Statement—Climate Change Is Already Killing Us, but Strong Action Now Can Prevent More Deaths," World Health Organization, November 7, 2022, accessed June 5, 2023, https://www.who.int/europe/news/item/07-11-2022-statement---climate-change-is-already-killing-us--but-strong-action-now-can-prevent-more-deaths.

19. Donna J. Haraway, *Staying with the Trouble: Making Kin in the Chthulucene* (Durham, NC: Duke University Press, 2016), 30.

20. Lauren Berlant, "Slow Death (Sovereignty, Obesity, Lateral Agency)," *Critical Inquiry* 33, no. 4 (Summer 2007): 761.

21. Glenn Albrecht, "Solastalgia and the New Mourning," in *Mourning Nature: Hope at the Heart of Ecological Loss and Grief*, ed. Ashlee Cunsolo and Karen Landman (Montreal: McGill-Queen's University Press, 2017), 300.

22. Albrecht, "Solastalgia and the New Mourning," 299.

23. Albrecht, "Solastalgia and the New Mourning," 299.

24. Albrecht, "Solastalgia and the New Mourning," 300.

25. Interestingly, Aristotle's account of the elements does not postulate such an underlying substance, since he argues in *On Generation and Corruption* that the "primary bodies" (*ta prota somata*) that others have called "elements" (*stoicheia*) are, in fact, *composites*. Although each is simple qua body, each is qua composite characterized by two different "elemental qualities": fire is hot (*thermon*) and dry (*kseron*), air is hot (*thermon*) and wet (*hygron*), water is cold (*psychron*) and wet (*hygron*), and earth is cold (*psychron*) and dry (*kseron*) (*GC*

II.3, 330b4–6). Aristotle subsequently argues that the generation and corruption of the simple bodies are derived from one another (*GC* II.4, 331a7–8), as they are by nature able to change into each other (*GC* II.4, 331a12–13). Aristotle, *On Generation and Corruption*, trans. E. S. Forster and D. J. Furley (Cambridge, MA: Harvard University Press, 1965).

26. As I have argued elsewhere, for nature to "fold back upon itself," we need to do more than to simply return to the idea of "natural potencies" actualizing themselves. Citing a problematic breeding-and-rearing program of whooping cranes held in captivity, I propose to view "nature as collaboratively designed and framed within a non-hierarchical politics of nature," where nature folds back upon itself and is constantly regenerated, in solidarity with others. Marjolein Oele, "Folding Nature Back upon Itself: Aristotle and the Rebirth of *Physis*," in *Ontologies of Nature: Continental Perspectives and Environmental Reorientations*, ed. Gerard Kuperus and Marjolein Oele (Dordrecht: Springer, 2017), 64.

27. Marjolein Oele, *E-Co-Affectivity: Exploring* Pathos *at Life's Material Interfaces* (Albany: State University of New York Press, 2020), 5. In my definition of affectivity, I appeal to the Greek term *pathos* as used by Aristotle, where the meaning of *pathos* includes a broad range of phenomena, including illness, suffering, qualitative change, and emotion.

28. Oele, *E-Co-Affectivity*, 10.

29. Ricoeur argues that memory and care are essentially connected: "If memory is in fact a capacity, the power of remembering (*faire-mémoire*), it is more fundamentally a figure of care, that basic anthropological structure of our historical condition. In memory-as-care we hold ourselves open to the past, we remain concerned about it." Paul Ricoeur, *Memory, History, Forgetting*, trans. Kathleen Blamey and David Pellauer (Chicago: University of Chicago Press, 2006), 505.

30. Anaximenes, DK 13 B2, as cited in Richard D. McKirahan, *Philosophy before Socrates: An Introduction with Texts and Commentary* (Indianapolis, IN: Hackett, 2011), 54.

31. J. Baird Callicott speaks to the natural environment of early Greek philosophy and how it may have contributed to the rise of philosophy, especially given what Jared Diamond has called the favorable environment and the postglacial endowment of the Eurasian continent. J. Baird Callicott, John van Buren, Keith Wayne Brown, *Greek Natural Philosophy: The Presocratics and Their Importance for Environmental Philosophy* (San Diego, CA: Cognella, 2018), 31.

32. Alison Stone, "Irigaray's Ecological Phenomenology: Towards an Elemental Materialism," *Journal of the British Society for Phenomenology* 46, no. 2 (2015): 125.

33. Stone, "Irigaray's Ecological Phenomenology," 126. I find Stone's interpretation of the elemental in Irigaray helpful not only in terms of Irigaray's specific account, but in clarifying my own methodological path as I seek to integrate notions of both the Presocratics and early Greek thought with insightful theoretical currents in twentieth-century and contemporary continental thought.

34. Stacy Alaimo, "Elemental Love in the Anthropocene," in *Elemental Ecocriticism: Thinking with Earth, Air, Water, and Fire*, ed. Jeffrey Jerome Cohen and Lowell Duckert (London: University of Minnesota Press, 2015), 298.

35. Jeffrey Jerome Cohen and Lowell Duckert, "Eleven Principles of the Elements," in *Elemental Ecocriticism: Thinking with Earth, Air, Water, and Fire*, ed. Jeffrey Jerome Cohen and Lowell Duckert (London: University of Minnesota Press, 2015), 7.

36. David Abram, *The Spell of the Sensuous: Perception and Language in a More-than-Human World* (New York: Vintage Books / Penguin Random House, 2017).

37. Michael Marshall, "The Event That Transformed Earth," BBC, July 2, 2015. Originally accessible at http://www.bbc.com/earth/story/20150701-the-origin-of-the-air-we-breathe. Reproduced under license from BBC / BBC Earth / bbc.co.uk—© [2015] BBC at: https://www.woodz.co/journal/the-origin-of-the-air-we-breathe/.

38. Stephanie D. Clare, *Earthly Encounters: Sensation, Feminist Theory, and the Anthropocene* (Albany: State University of New York Press, 2019), xiix.

39. Clare analyzes Ta-Nehisi Coates's book *Between the World and Me* and observes that the book ends with "rain coming down in sheets." She argues that this elemental water, in the form of rain, is more-than-human, not produced by us. Simultaneously, the rain cannot be seen other than through the lens of Coates's observance of the structures of socialization, which have enabled anthropogenic climate change, thereby altering the rain (with higher global temperatures affecting rain patterns) and producing patterns of racialization, so that the windshield through which the rain is visible reveals also the rain-drenched ghettos that are part of the cityscape that is Philadelphia. Clare, *Earthly Encounters*, xv–xiix.

40. In my view, new materialism's turn to the intricacies of bodies can both yield a turn to the intricacies of the minute details of elemental bodies as well as offering insight into the larger forces, such as economic-political forces, that striate elemental matter and its significance. In understanding materiality as tiered, I take my cues from Quentin Meillassoux's *After Finitude: An Essay on the Necessity of Contingency*, trans. Ray Brassier (London: Continuum, 2008).

41. John Sallis, *The Return of Nature: on the Beyond of Sense* (Bloomington: Indiana University Press, 2016), 58. Sallis addresses the fact that the elements resist appropriation by metaphysics while simultaneously being "displayed before our senses—in the blue of the sky, the brilliance of the light, the coolness of the wind, the sound of the falling rain. It is also by inclusion of the elements that nature exceeds the mere sum of sensible things."

42. John Sallis, *The Figure of Nature: On Greek Origins* (Bloomington: Indiana University Press, 2016), 49.

43. Sallis, *The Figure of Nature*, 25.

44. While Sallis's ideas on the elemental have limitations for our understanding given their abstract focus on what I have called its "expansive" features,

and thereby overlook the social, dynamic, and everyday engagement with the elements, a possible exception to this is his book *Stone*. For instance, in Sallis's description of the Jewish cemetery in Prague, he combines phenomenologically rich descriptions of the gravestones with the history of the Jewish ghetto, addressing the cruel history and politics of the ghetto. John Sallis, *Stone* (Bloomington: Indiana University Press, 1994), 27–28. I owe this helpful addition to the comments of the anonymous peer reviewer of the manuscript for this book.

45. Michel Serres and Bruno Latour, *Conversations on Science, Culture, and Time*, trans. Roxanne Lapidus (Ann Arbor: University of Michigan Press, 1995), 118. Furthermore, Paul Virilio's *Open Sky* argues that, in addition to discovering a hole in the ozone, "*our sky is vanishing*" because, due to plane and space travel, "*today, there is a way out up above.*" Virilio accordingly speaks of a "*fall upwards*" enabled by the speed of liberation from gravity. Paul Virilio, *Open Sky*, trans. Julie Rose (London: Verso, 1997), 2; his italics.

46. While the term "engineering" has a problematic *hue* due to its association with eugenics in the history of thought, my usage of it seeks to bracket and overcome this baggage by addressing how engineering speaks to the *strategic intervention* into the elemental, postulating that environmental factors are not outside of human purview, but actively co-fashioned alongside human existence. I argue that such interventions need to be reassessed ethically and politically in light of the climate crisis and elemental loss, and I point out ways for doing so in the various chapters, especially in chapter 5.

47. For Sloterdijk, Heidegger's ultimate turn away from the "where" to the "who" signals a move away from solidarity, intimacy, and place toward a lonely Dasein, who is on the way to death. Peter Sloterdijk, *Bubbles: Spheres Volume I: Microspherology*, trans. Wieland Hoban (Los Angeles, CA: Semiotext(e), 2011), 341.

48. Sloterdijk, *Bubbles*, 28.

49. Sloterdijk, *Bubbles*, 46.

50. Peter Sloterdijk, *Foams: Spheres Volume III: Plural Spherology*, trans. Wieland Hoban (Los Angeles, CA: Semiotext(e), 2016), 137.

51. Irigaray as quoted in David Macauley, *Elemental Philosophy: Earth, Air, Fire, and Water as Environmental Ideas* (Albany: State University of New York Press, 2010), 316. The quote is from Luce Irigaray, *Sexes and Genealogies*, trans. Gilliam C. Gill (New York: Columbia University Press, 1985), 57.

52. Luce Irigaray, *Marine Lover*, trans. Gillian C. Gill (New York: Columbia University Press, 1991), 20.

53. As Stone notes, Irigaray's unpublished notes also indicate that Irigaray wanted "to remind Marx" of the material depth of fire. However, this project never came to fruition. Stone, "Irigaray's Ecological Phenomenology," 124.

54. Luce Irigaray, "From *The Forgetting of Air* to *To Be Two*," in *Feminist Interpretations of Martin Heidegger*, ed. Nancy Holland and Patricia Huntington (University Park: Pennsylvania State University Press, 2001), 312.

55. Luce Irigaray, *The Forgetting of Air in Martin Heidegger*, trans. Mary Beth Mader (Austin: University of Texas Press, 1999), 15. She also argues that when Heidegger forgets air, "he forgets the cultivation of life itself and of its relation with the surrounding world, with others, mastery then without violence, without a technique that takes living matter in a fabricated exteriority where it is exiled from its own becoming." Irigaray, "From *The Forgetting of Air* to *To Be Two*," 311.

56. "The being is given first, and irrevocably, in the form of fluids." Irigaray, *The Forgetting of Air in Martin Heidegger*, 82.

57. Stone, "Irigaray's Ecological Phenomenology," 129.

58. See, for instance, Luce Irigaray, *Elemental Passions*, trans. Joanne Collie and Judith Still (New York: Routledge, 1992).

59. Macauley provides a splendid overview on Bachelard's thematizing the elemental. He writes: "Bachelard, who was trained in physics, chemistry, and the philosophy of science, dedicates a series of books to surveying each of the four elements in studies involving alchemical symbols, literary criticism, psychoanalysis, scientific history, dream images, and various other forms of reverie. In works ranging in name from *Water and Dreams* and *The Psychoanalysis of Fire* to *Earth and Reveries of Will* and *Air and Dreams*, Bachelard turns to images of matter and the "things themselves"—as Husserl puts it—in order to illustrate the importance of the material imagination and to study 'direct ontology' as well as the role of myth and metaphor in philosophy." Macauley, *Elemental Philosophy*, 295.

60. Gaston Bachelard, *Air and Dreams: An Essay on the Imagination of Movement*, trans. Edith R. Farrell and C. Frederick Farrell (Dallas, TX: Dallas Institute of Humanities and Culture, 1988), 11. In *The Psychoanalysis of Fire*, Bachelard writes about his method as one of exploring the "*unconscious of the scientific mind*" and of investigating how "unconscious values affect the very basis of empirical and scientific knowledge." Gaston Bachelard, *The Psychoanalysis of Fire*, trans. Alan C. M. Ross (Boston, MA: Beacon Press, 1964), 10, italics original. However, it is worth noting that even as Bachelard undertakes a rich psychoanalytic and poetic exploration of the elements, he keeps insisting on their material origination, writing, "If a reverie is to be pursued with the constancy a written work requires, to be more than simply a way of filling in time, it must discover its *matter*. A material element must provide its own substance, its particular rules and poetics." Gaston Bachelard, *Water and Dreams: An Essay on the Imagination of Matter*, trans. Edith R. Farrell (Dallas, TX: Dallas Institute of Humanities and Culture, 1983), 3. Admittedly, Bachelard's account of the imagination is thus very complex, also since it does not simply include "a mental image to be possessed, but a dynamic flow in which minds participate, often in unpredictable ways." Julian Evans, email message to the author, May 11, 2023.

61. Bachelard, *Air and Dreams*, 11.

62. I owe this nuance to the thoughtful comments of one of the peer reviewers of the manuscript for this book.

63. Macauley, *Elemental Philosophy*, 74. As one of the peer reviewers noted, particular elemental "outcroppings" such as sky, ice, stone, and wood could have become part of my discussion, although they lie outside the scope of the present work.

64. Elements other than water, fire, air, and earth surface in cross-cultural sources. For instance, in the Chinese text *The Three Characters*, there is mention of five elements from which all things are derived: "water, fire, wood, metal, and earth." Intriguingly, the elements mentioned in this text are not only conceptualized as exterior, environmental elements but also take on a role in our interior organs: "[Water, fire, wood, metal, and earth] correspond to inner organs—kidneys, heart, liver, lungs, and spleen." Macauley, *Elemental Philosophy*, 74.

65. Hesiod, *Works and Days and Theogony*, trans. Stanley Lombardo (Indianapolis, IN: Hackett, 1993), ll.126–133.

66. Empedocles, as preserved in Simplicius *Physics* 158.1–159.4 (B17), as quoted in: Daniel W. Graham, *The Texts of Early Greek Philosophy: The Complete Fragments and Selected Testimonies of the Major Presocratics*, part 1 (Cambridge: Cambridge University Press, 2010), 350–355.

67. John Sallis, "The Elemental Earth," in *Rethinking Nature: Essays in Environmental Philosophy*, ed. Bruce V. Foltz and Robert Frodeman (Bloomington: Indiana University Press, 2004), 145.

68. J. M. Bernstein. "Trust: On the Real but Almost Unnoticed, Ever-Changing Foundation of Ethical Life," *Metaphilosophy* 42, no. 4 (July 2011): 395.

69. Joseph Godfrey, *Trust of People, Words, and God: A Route for Philosophy of Religion* (Notre Dame, IN: University of Notre Dame Press, 2012), 45.

70. Thus, my argument partly converges and diverges from Macauley's centrally hopeful claim, that "with some patience, fortune, and persistence, we might be able to rediscover and recover a deeper and more lasting connection with the elemental world and in the process find our place—reside in our own element or elements, with the bewildered and bewildering beauty everywhere around us." My argument precisely starts with elemental loss and shows both opportunities for generation (in the spirit of Macauley; albeit less in terms of recovery and more in terms of creating anew) but also the broader social-political economic problems that may hamper such regeneration. In the end, my project on elemental loss thus has more of a political edge than Macauley's poetic tone. Macauley, *Elemental Philosophy*, 355.

Chapter 1. Water—Living and Speaking Oceanic Loss: On Extinction, Migration, and Language(s)

1. The 1953 North Sea flood was a major flood caused by a heavy storm that occurred on the night of Saturday, January 31, 1953, and morning of Sunday,

February 1, 1953. A combination of a high spring tide and a severe European windstorm over the North Sea caused a storm tide; the combination of wind, high tide, and low pressure led to a water level of more than 5.6 meters (18.4 ft.) above mean sea level in some locations. The storm caused great damage to the coastline in both England and Scotland, breaching seawalls and inundating large areas. The History Press, "The Devastating Storm of 1953," accessed October 31, 2022, https://www.thehistorypress.co.uk/articles/the-devastating-storm-of-1953.

2. While beginning with personal reflections on my mother's swimming excursions, my own chapter seeks to avoid romanticism and channels personal anecdotes toward broader ecological-cultural issues occurring at sea or in relationship to the sea. Thus, my approach is radically different from that of David Krell's *The Sea*, which incorporates various philosophical registers of analyzing the sea (the personal-poetic, Presocratic, phenomenological, and psychoanalytic), but which, despite these varieties in register, shies away from directly analyzing the "problems" that occur in our seas. Thus, his personal reflections on cradling and floating on the sea and his musings on Chopin's barcarolles (18) tend toward romanticism, far removed from the current oceanic crisis. Krell thereby offers no answer to these ecological issues, even as he briefly mentions them and is aware that he offers no answer to such issues as plastic oceanic waste. David Farrell Krell, *The Sea: A Philosophical Encounter* (London: Bloomsbury Academic, 2019), xxxi, 29.

3. See the Editors of *Encyclopedia Britannica*, "Zeeland," *Encyclopedia Britannica*, last modified June 20, 2011, https://www.britannica.com/place/Zeeland-province-Netherlands. The name of Zeeland can be found in various places around the world connected with its colonial history, such as in the names of four fortresses, all called "Fort Zeelandia" in current-day Taiwan, Suriname, and Guyana. See Round Taiwan Round, "Fort Zeelandia," accessed October 31, 2022, https://www.rtaiwanr.com/tainan/fort-zeelandia; Amazonian-Museum-Network. Org, "De Stichting Surinaams Museum," accessed October 31, 2022, http://amazonian-museum-network.org/nl/amazone-museum/stichting-surinaams-museum-nl; National Trust of Guyana, "Fort Zeelandia," last modified December 17, 2021, https://ntg.gov.gy/monument/fort-zeelandia. Cf. also Gert Oostindie, "Index of Geographical Names," in *Dutch Colonialism, Migration and Cultural Heritage*, ed. Gert Oostindie (Leiden: Brill, 2008), 343–350; 346–347.

4. As discussed in Ryan Heryford's chapter in *Contesting Extinctions*, a point in case is the slave ship *Zong*, originally called *Zorg*, which means, paradoxically and cruelly in Dutch, "care." While the case Heryford discusses pertains to the genocide that took place under British ownership of the slave ship, the ship itself originally was a Dutch boat, owned by the Middelburgsche Commercie Compagnie, based in Middelburg, in what is now the province of Zeeland in the Netherlands. In 1777, it delivered enslaved people to Suriname and the ship was later captured by the British. Jane Webster, "The *Zong* in the Context of the Eighteenth-Century Slave Trade," *Journal of Legal History* 28, no. 3 (November

2007): 288, doi:10.1080/01440360701698403. Reference is to Ryan Heryford, "'The Word for Bringing Bodies Back from Water': Black Oceanic Ecopoetics and the Re-imagining of Extinction," in *Contesting Extinctions: Decolonial and Regenerative Futures*, ed. Suzanne M. McCullagh et al. (Lanham, MD: Lexington Books, 2021), 70.

5. Michel Serres, *Biogea*, trans. Randolph Burks (Minneapolis, MN: Univocal, 2012), 88.

6. Karin Amimoto Ingersoll, *Waves of Knowing: A Seascape Epistemology* (Durham, NC: Duke University Press, 2016). Ingersoll's proposal for a seascape epistemology fills in the need for a reclamation of language and reality. In his writings on language, Wesley Leonard clarifies the importance of restoring language anchored in Indigenous needs and ways of knowing. He differentiates this from language "revitalization" projects, which follow dominant notions that language is to be "fixed." Wesley Y. Leonard, "Contesting Extinction through a Praxis of Language Reclamation," in *Contesting Extinctions: Decolonial and Regenerative Futures*, ed. Suzanne M. McCullagh et al. (Lanham, MD: Lexington Books, 2021), 145–146. As should become clear in this chapter, my own use of the term "revitalization" is more closely aligned with Leonard's term "restoration" than with what he denotes as the problematic practice of language "revitalization" (145–146).

7. Alanna Mitchell, *Seasick: Ocean Change and the Extinction of Life on Earth* (Chicago: University of Chicago Press, 2009), 9–10.

8. "Atmosphere and ocean are ineluctably joined. . . . The ocean has absorbed about a third of the extra carbon dioxide that we have pumped into the atmosphere since we started using fossil fuels, digging up grasslands, and cutting down forests." Mitchell, *Seasick*, 8–9.

9. Elizabeth Kolbert, *The Sixth Extinction: An Unnatural History* (New York: Picador, 2014), 120.

10. Kolbert, *The Sixth Extinction*, 120.

11. Heidegger's account of being-toward-death has been critiqued from multiple angles, for instance by Edith Stein. Stein shows, versus Heidegger, the importance of socialization for our sense of death, and how experiencing the death of others is crucial in relationship to our own understanding of death. Edith Stein, "Martin Heidegger's Existential Philosophy," trans. Mette Lebech, *Maynooth Philosophical Papers* 4 (2007): 76–77.

12. Peter Sloterdijk, *Foams: Spheres Volume III: Plural Spherology*, trans. Wieland Hoban (Los Angeles, CA: Semiotext(e), 2016), 48.

13. According to Sloterdijk, there is however not only dissolution but also the possibility of sublation: "Human death thus always has two faces: one that leaves behind a rigid body and one that shows sphere residues—those that are sublated into higher spaces and re-animated and those that, as the waste products of things, fallen out of former spaces of animation, are left lying there. Sloterdijk, *Foams: Spheres Volume III: Plural Spherology*, 48.

14. Vinciane Despret, "Afterword: It Is an Entire World That Has Disappeared," in *Extinction Studies: Stories of Time, Death, and Generations*, ed. Deborah Bird Rose, Thom Van Dooren, and Matthew Chrulew (New York: Columbia University Press, 2017), 219–220.

15. Despret, "Afterword: It Is an Entire World That Has Disappeared," 219–220.

16. Despret, "Afterword: It Is an Entire World That Has Disappeared," 219–220.

17. "It is likely that, with a further rise in temperature, the North Sea will become more livable for southern species and that the number of northern species will decrease. Climate change can also have indirect effects on species by acting on the food web. Because of warming up, seawater can contain less oxygen, which is unfavorable for certain species" (my translation). Ralf van Hal, Oscar Georg Bos, and Robert Gerbrand Jak, "Noordzee: Systeemdynamiek, Klimaatverandering, Natuurtypen en Benthos; Achtergronddocument bij Natuurverkenning 2011," *Wageningen, Wettelijke Onderzoekstaken Natuur en Milieu* 255 (2011): 1–93; 9.

18. "Crustaceans include commonly-known marine life such as crabs, lobsters, barnacles, and shrimps. . . . There are over 52,000 species of crustaceans." Jennifer Kennedy, "Crustaceans: Species, Characteristics, and Diet," last modified December 13, 2019, https://www.thoughtco.com/crustaceans-profile-and-facts-2291816.

19. "Kalkhoudende soorten, zoals schelpdieren, zullen hier in de toekomst mogelijk hinder van ondervinden, omdat hun schelp kan oplossen" (my translation: "crustaceans, such as shellfish, may be affected by this in the future because their shell can dissolve"). Hal, Bos, and Jak, "Noordzee: Systeemdynamiek, Klimaatverandering, Natuurtypen en Benthos; Achtergronddocument bij Natuurverkenning 2011," 9.

20. Emily, Grade 11, 2004 Young Naturalist Winner, "Morphologic Variation in the Common Periwinkle," American Museum of Natural History, accessed October 31, 2022, https://www.amnh.org/learn-teach/curriculum-collections/young-naturalist-awards/winning-essays/2004/morphologic-variation-in-the-common-periwinkle. Cf. also: Samuel Kinuthia, "What Is the Intertidal Zone?," *World Atlas*, last modified January 10, 2018, https://www.worldatlas.com/articles/what-is-the-intertidal-zone.html.

21. Kolbert, *The Sixth Great Extinction*, 121.

22. Robert Nordsieck, "Amazing Facts about Snails," *The Living World of Molluscs*, accessed August 31, 2019, https://molluscs.at/gastropoda/index.html.

23. Nordsieck, "Amazing Facts about Snails."

24. Serres, *Biogea*, 17.

25. Serres, *Biogea*, 22.

26. Serres, *Biogea*, 32. Additionally, speaking to so-called "natural disasters," Serres points out that it is problematic "political, economic, social conditions—

poverty for example—[that] prevail" (29) in exacerbating death counts, thus clarifying that the suffering experienced is unequally and dramatically experienced most by those who are marginalized.

27. Serres, *Biogea*, 67. Serres's way of framing the collective in this passage, namely in terms of Western history and science, indicates that he is not blaming the entirety of humanity for pollution and extinction, but the destructive and polluting Western systems of thought that humans participate in. For more examples of the destructive power of such systems, see Leonardo E. Figueroa Helland, Abigail Perez Aguilera, and Felix Mantz, "Decolonize, ReIndigenize: Planetary Crisis, Bioculture Diversity, Indigenous Resurgence, and Land Rematriation," in *Contesting Extinctions: Decolonial and Regenerative Futures*, ed. Suzanne M. McCullagh et al. (Lanham, MD: Lexington Books, 2021), 23–62. They argue that, in contrast to Indigenous practices, "colonial, Eurocentric, patriarchal and capitalist industrial civilization has pushed the planet to mass extinction, biocultural obliteration and climate catastrophe in a few hundred years" (28).

28. In the case of Archimedes, Serres discusses his brilliance in math and physics, as well as his involvement in warfare, setting up gigantic mirrors in the landscape that, when attracting sunlight, would set the ships of the Roman enemy fleet ablaze. Serres, *Biogea*, 67.

29. Serres, *Biogea*, 38.
30. Serres, *Biogea*, 38–39.
31. Serres, *Biogea*, 38–39.
32. Serres, *Biogea*, 129.
33. Serres, *Biogea*, 128.
34. Serres, *Biogea*, 129.
35. Serres, *Biogea*, 154.

36. Rather than simple interactions, much more is at stake. Serres points at orchestral music to capture the emergence of rhythms and patterns in the world. However, pattern here is not all there is: sound is accompanied by background noise, order is bound by disorder. Serres, *Biogea*, 111.

37. Serres, *Biogea*, 196.

38. A similar focus on reciprocity is discussed by Figueroa, Aguilera, and Mantz, for instance, in this passage: "For Indigenous peoples, interpersonal relational intimacy weaves humans and the land into integrated communities where the holistic regeneration of life depends on reciprocal human-nonhuman nurturance" (29).

39. Brandon Guerrero, "Hell Is a Place on Earth: USF Existentialism Paper," University of San Francisco, San Francisco, California, May 15, 2020, 1.

40. Aldo Leopold, *A Sand County Almanac: And Sketches Here and There* (Oxford: Oxford University Press, 1989), 113.

41. Serres, *Biogea*, 23.

42. Daniel O'Connell, email correspondence with the author, May 21, 2020.

43. In "Loanwords to Live With," the introduction to their *Ecotopian Lexicon*, coeditors Matthew Schneider-Mayerson and Brent Ryan Bellamy provide us with "an assortment of conceptual tools and a prismatic window into the ecological multiverse," offering "thirty terms and concepts to jump-start the critical process of imagining and eventually realizing better futures." Matthew Schneider-Mayerson and Brent Ryan Bellamy, "Introduction: Loanwords to Live With," in *An Ecotopian Lexicon*, ed. Matthew Schneider-Mayerson and Brent Ryan Bellamy (Minneapolis: University of Minnesota Press, 2019), 1–14; 5.

Schneider-Mayerson and Bellamy thereby seek to offer "conceptual tools for reckoning with the environmental, political, social and philosophical challenges of the Anthropocene, today and in the decades to come" (7). Their critical lexicon thereby "does not merely describe unfolding disasters but offers buoyant linguistic and conceptual tools for the collective construction of a future that is more just, equitable, pleasurable, and truly sustainable for *Homo sapiens* and the millions of species with whom we gratefully share this planet" (7–8).

44. Brian Treanor, "Mind the Gap: The Challenge of Matter," in *Carnal Hermeneutics*, ed. Richard Kearney and Brian Treanor (New York: Fordham University Press, 2015), 67.

45. Serres, *Biogea*, 51.

46. Serres, *Biogea*, 117.

47. Serres, *Biogea*, 198.

48. Serres, *Biogea*, 40.

49. Serres, *Biogea*, 131.

50. Similar to how Serres highlights prepositions, Wesley Leonard emphasizes how, for the Miami community, language is defined in terms of *interactions* with special emphasis on strong relationships as expressed by what are called "'the R-words' such as respect, reciprocity, and responsibility" (152) that are key to the notion of strong relationship that stands at the core of Miami culture (153).

51. Cf. also Serres's "philosophy of prepositions." Serres and Latour, *Conversations on Science, Culture, and Time*, 103. Serres wants to turn away from a thinking and language that is centered around substantives and verbs, to a language of prepositions that emphasizes relations. Serres writes: "To talk only by means of substantives or verbs, and thus to write in a telegraphic code, as ordinary philosophy does, defines a different form of abstraction from the one I propose, which relies on prepositions" (103).

52. Posthumus argues that, for Serres, "language does not remove us from the material world; it is part of this world, as the water in which thinking swims." Stephanie Posthumus, *French Écocritique: Reading Contemporary French Theory and Fiction Ecologically* (Toronto: University of Toronto Press, 2017), 67. She continues: "Ecological dwelling thus necessarily includes the practices of language" (67).

53. Ingersoll, *Waves of Knowing*, 5.

54. Ingersoll, *Waves of Knowing*, 3.

55. Ingersoll, *Waves of Knowing*, 3.
56. Ingersoll, *Waves of Knowing*, 6.
57. Ingersoll, *Waves of Knowing*, 6.
58. Ingersoll, *Waves of Knowing*, 136.
59. Ingersoll, *Waves of Knowing*, 5.
60. Leonard, "Contesting Extinction through a Praxis of Language Reclamation," 145–146.
61. Leonard, "Contesting Extinction through a Praxis of Language Reclamation," 150.
62. Sally Anderson Boström, "*Waves of Knowing: A Seascape Epistemology.* By Karin Amimoto Ingersoll," *Interdisciplinary Studies in Literature and Environment* 24, no. 4 (2017): 829–831; 831.
63. Boström, "*Waves of Knowing: A Seascape Epistemology.* By Karin Amimoto Ingersoll," 831.
64. See Harmannus Hoetink, "Netherlands Antilles," *Encyclopedia Britannica*, last modified September 27, 2022, https://www.britannica.com/place/Netherlands-Antilles. The Dutch Caribbean includes the islands of Bonaire, Sint Eustatius, and Saba (also known as the "Caribbean Netherlands") and the islands of Curaçao, Bonaire, and Sint Maarten (which are part of the Kingdom of the Netherlands). Government of the Netherlands, "What Are the Different Parts of the Kingdom of the Netherlands?," accessed May 20, 2021, https://www.government.nl/topics/caribbean-parts-of-the-kingdom/question-and-answer/what-are-the-different-parts-of-the-kingdom-of-the-netherlands.
65. Cf. the analysis of the transatlantic slave trade as discussed in Heryford, "'The Word for Bringing Bodies Back from Water,'" 70.
66. Édouard Glissant, *Poetics of Relation*, trans. Betsy Wing (Ann Arbor: University of Michigan Press, 1997). He writes: "Without necessarily inferring any advantage whatsoever to their situation, the reality of archipelagos in the Caribbean or the Pacific provides a natural illustration of the thought of Relation" (33).
67. Glissant, *Poetics of Relation*, 8.
68. Miguel Gualdrón Ramírez, "To 'Stay Where You Are' as a Decolonial Gesture: Glissant's Philosophy of Antillean Space in the Context of Césaire and Fanon Chapter," in *Memory, Migration and (De)Colonisation in the Caribbean and Beyond*, ed. Jack Webb et al. (London: University of London Press, 2020), 133–152; 134.
69. For instance, as Ramírez explains, the beach and waves crashing on the shore signifies the draining of a life force being sucked away, the arrival of death, and decomposition. Ramírez, "To 'Stay Where You Are' as a Decolonial Gesture: Glissant's Philosophy of Antillean Space in the Context of Césaire and Fanon Chapter," 138.
70. Cf. Jacques Van Keymeulen, "Zeeuws Overzee," *Nehalennia* 198 (2017): 18–19, who reports on a Creole language based on Zeelandic known as "Negerhollands" (negro Dutch) that used to be spoken on the Danish Antilles (St.

Thomas, St. Croix, and St. John). "[The Danish Antilles] were sold by Denmark to the United States in 1917 and are currently called the American Virgin Island (Virgin Islands of the United States). When in 1666 the British attacked the Dutch island St. Eustatius, numerous Zeelandic and West-Flemish 'planters' fled to the Danish island and their slaves brought the creole Dutch with them as 'plantation language.' White people were also able to speak the language. The last speaker of the mother tongue of Negerhollands, Alice Stevens, died in 1987." Van Keymeulen, "Zeeuws Overzee," 2–3, my translation.

71. Glissant, *Poetics of Relation*, 34.

72. Celia Britton, *Edouard Glissant and Postcolonial Theory: Strategies of Language and Resistance* (Charlottesville: University of Virginia Press, 1999), 15.

73. Drabinski contrasts diffraction helpfully with transmission, which "*promises* (even if it cannot realize) the preservation of what is prior in what is later" (his italics). Drabinski, *Glissant and the Middle Passage: Philosophy, Beginning, Abyss*, 82.

74. Curaçao Maritime Museum, "Curaçao, an Island of Harbors," accessed May 11, 2020, https://www.curacaomaritime.com/history.

75. de Jong, "The Tambú of Curaçao: Historical Projections and the Ritual Map of Experience," 199–202. See also de Jong, "Curaçao and the Folding Diaspora," 69. Only since 1969 has the tambú become legal. de Jong, "Curaçao and the Folding Diaspora," 70. In 2015, tambú was placed on the National Inventory of Intangible Cultural Heritage in the Netherlands on the initiative of the SPLIKA Foundation. SPLIKA, "Ontdek Tambú!"

76. SPLIKA, "Ontdek Tambú!"

77. de Jong, "Curaçao and the Folding Diaspora," 76.

78. de Jong, "Curaçao and the Folding Diaspora," 74.

79. de Jong, "Curaçao and the Folding Diaspora," 77.

80. de Jong, "Curaçao and the Folding Diaspora," 77.

81. "Like Aldo Leopold, Empedocles wanted to think like the mountain; to live like the earth on fire, the fire that warms with love and consumes with hate: to think like the elements of a science that was being born in its totality. Like I would like to think." Serres, *Biogea*, 79.

82. Serres, *Genesis*, 24.

83. Ton Emmen, *De kwetsbaarheid van de Zeeuwen: Factoren die de kwetsbaarheid en veerkracht van de bevolking ten aanzien van dreiging van overstromingen vanuit zee beïnvloeden*, online publication (2002), accessed May 16, 2020, https://www.ifv.nl/kennisplein/Documents/emmen-4-de-kwetsbaarheid-van-de-zeeuwen.pdf.

84. Marieke van Katwijk writes that "many things have changed since the construction and completion of the Oosterschelde: the climate (higher temperature),

there are more seals and porpoises (which eat fish), there is less seagrass." Marieke van Katwijk, email message to author, April 18, 2024.

85. I. M. Mulder, I. Tulp, and T. Ysebaert, "Ontwikkelingen van bodemgebonden vis en epibenthos in de Oosterschelde in de periode 1970–2018," *Wageningen Marine Research rapport*, no. C024/20 (2020): https://doi.org/10.18174/518404.

86. BN DeStem, "Onder water zit het niet goed in de Oosterschelde," *Total Fishing*, accessed May 16, 2020, http://www.totalfishing.nl/laatste-nieuws/articles/onder-water-zit-het-niet-goed-in-de-oosterschelde. However, given dynamic changes associated with interfering with waterways, "static management goals should be carefully considered in environmental planning, as ecosystems develop, causing new and unexpected features to emerge." Francesco Cozzoli et al., "A Modeling Approach to Assess Coastal Management Effects on Benthic Habitat Quality: A Case Study on Coastal Defense and Navigability," *Estuarine, Coastal and Shelf Science* 184 (2017): 72. For instance, the Oosterschelde's subtidal benthic habitat has experienced a notable improvement in quality as an unexpected consequence of the construction of the storm surge barrier.

87. Wittgenstein, *Philosophical Investigations*, §19/11e.

88. Schneider-Mayerson and Bellamy, "Introduction: Loanwords to Live With," 7–8.

89. Michel Serres, *The Natural Contract*, trans. Elizabeth MacArthur and William Paulson (Ann Arbor: University of Michigan Press, 1995), 40.

90. Astrid Neimanis, *Bodies of Water: Posthuman Feminist Phenomenology* (London: Bloomsbury, 2017), 160.

91. Neimanis, *Bodies of Water*, 160.

92. Neimanis, *Bodies of Water*, 157.

Chapter 2. Fire—Pyrogenic Creation and Destruction: Contemplating the Meaning of Fire, Affect, and Loss in the Pyrocene

1. Bachelard, *The Psychoanalysis of Fire*, 16.

2. Bachelard, *The Psychoanalysis of Fire*, 7.

3. As for its future impact, Stengers writes: "It seems clear that the regions of the earth that will be affected first will be the poorest on the planet, to say nothing of all those living beings that have nothing to do with the affair." Isabelle Stengers, *In Catastrophic Times: Resisting the Coming Barbarism*, trans. Andrew Goffey (London: Open Humanities Press, 2015), 46; cf. Haraway, *Staying with the Trouble*, 47.

4. Also known as *Homo industrialis*: Janine M. Benyus, *Biomimicry: Innovation Inspired by Nature* (New York: Quill, 1998), 1.

5. As I am using the term "sustainability," I seek to use it in a critical way, not simply in its current form that promotes so-called sustainability while

preserving the status quo of the neocapitalist regime, which is in my view fundamentally unsustainable. Read further in this chapter on my analysis of California's giant sequoias for a critical account of sustainability.

6. Bernard Stiegler, *Technics and Time, 1: The Fault of Epimetheus*, trans. Richard Beardsworth and George Collins (Stanford, CA: Stanford University Press, 1998), 193.

7. In using the term "posthuman," I am playfully following Roden's definition of posthumanism, which builds upon the idea that various technologies have arisen that may have "the potential to engender posthuman successors," for instance, through "cybernetic hookups between organisms or between organisms and machines" or biologically modifying current humans with certain features yet unimaginable. David Roden, *Posthuman Life: Philosophy at the Edge of the Human* (London: Routledge, 2015), 5.

8. "Pyrocene" is a term found in Edward Struzik, *Firestorm: How Wildfire Will Shape Our Future* (Washington, DC: Island Press, 2017), 103.

9. Bachelard, *The Psychoanalysis of Fire*, 10.

10. Hesiod, *Works and Days and Theogony*, ll. 563–573. The *Theogony* presents fire as something naturally belonging to humans. Zeus's act of taking fire away from humans out of revenge for their disrespect, as well as his punishment for having Prometheus steal fire back (sending humans the "irresistible" yet troublesome first woman, Pandora) indicates the *crucial and irresistible* value of fire, both from a human and divine perspective. And maybe we could argue that the supposed "irresistible" trouble that Pandora brings to humanity is the other side—the punishment—of the *seductive ease* that (domesticated) fire brings. Certainly, this reading of the ease that fire brings finds additional proof in Hesiod's *Works and Days*, where Zeus, out of anger, keeps both fire and "the means of life" (l. 66) away from humans. Cf. Stiegler, *Technics and Time, 1*, 192.

11. Stiegler, *Technics and Time, 1*, 192.

12. Plato, *Laches, Protagoras, Meno, Euthydemus*, trans. W. R. M. Lamb (Cambridge, MA: Harvard University Press, 2006), 320d.

13. This seems a *compensatory* attribution system, a protection against the seasons and ability to obtain food.

14. Stiegler, *Technics and Time, 1*, 188.

15. Stiegler, *Technics and Time, 1*, 193.

16. Stiegler, *Technics and Time, 1*, 198.

17. Stiegler, *Technics and Time, 1*, 193; his italics.

18. Stiegler, *Technics and Time, 1*, 188.

19. Stiegler, *Technics and Time, 1*, 193.

20. Stiegler, *Technics and Time, 1*, 198.

21. Stiegler, *Technics and Time, 1*, 199.

22. Stephen J. Pyne, *Fire: A Brief History* (London: British Museum Press, 2001), 25.

23. James C. Scott, *Against the Grain: A Deep History of the Earliest States* (New Haven, CT: Yale University Press, 2017), 39–40.
24. Scott, *Against the Grain*, 42. See also Richard W. Wrangham, *Catching Fire: How Cooking Made Us Human* (London: Basic Books, 2009), 2. Wrangham's "cooking hypothesis" argues that cooking informed and modified human evolution. It provided for more digestible and efficiently energy-dense food, allowing more energy for the brain to grow. He dates this transition to the time of the emergence of *Homo erectus*, around 1.8 million years ago: "The extra energy gave the first cooks biological advantages. They survived and reproduced better than before. Their genes spread. Their bodies responded by biologically adapting to cooked food, shaped by natural selection to take maximum advantage of the new diet. There were changes in anatomy, physiology, ecology, life history, psychology, and society" (14).
25. Scott, *Against the Grain*, 42.
26. A helpful account of commensality can be found in H. Jönsson, M. Michaud, and N. Neuman, "What Is Commensality? A Critical Discussion of an Expanding Research Field," *International Journal of Environmental Research and Public Health* 18, no. 12 (June 2021): 6235, doi: 10.3390/ijerph18126235; PMID: 34207626; PMCID: PMC8295993.
27. Wrangham, *Catching Fire*, 184–186.
28. Scott, *Against the Grain*, 42.
29. Scott, *Against the Grain*, 42.
30. Scott, *Against the Grain*, 38.
31. Stiegler, *Technics and Time, 1*, 194; his italics.
32. Brian Seitz, "Grids of Power: Toward a Phenomenology of Fuel," *Environmental Philosophy* 15, no. 2 (Fall 2018): 319.
33. Stephen J. Pyne, "Consumed by Either Fire or Fire: A Prolegomenon to Anthropogenic Fire," in *Earth, Air, Fire, Water: Humanistic Studies of the Environment*, ed. Jill Ker Conway, Kenneth Keniston, and Leo Marx (Amherst: University of Massachusetts Press, 1999), 91.
34. Pyne, *Fire*, 156.
35. Pyne, *Fire*, 183.
36. Pyne, *Fire*, 156.
37. Pyne, *Fire*, 155.
38. Pyne, *Fire*, 155.
39. Pyne, *Fire*, 184.
40. Struzik, *Firestorm*, 2. We can discern as major factors, contributing to the cause and consequences of these megafires, a warmer, drier (forest) environment, more lightning and longer fire seasons, more burnable fuel on the ground (due to drought, invasive species, and disease), and more people living in the forest-wildland interface. Cf. Struzik, *Firestorm*, 8–9, 13.
41. Cronon, foreword to *Fire*, xiv.

42. Struzik, *Firestorm*, 6, 26, 47, 60, 89, 111, 122.
43. Albrecht, "Solastalgia and the New Mourning," 297.
44. Albrecht, "Solastalgia and the New Mourning," 296.
45. Artists Amiko Matsuo and Brad Monsma provide in their art a look into both the constructive and destructive features of art. For instance in their exhibit, *Pyrometric: Earth and Ash in the Anthropocene*, which was on display in the Kwan Fong Gallery of Art and Culture on the Thousand Oaks campus in 2018. "There are hand-built and -thrown ceramic traffic cones that Ventura County firefighters placed in controlled burns and cones that were fired with a dusting of ash from previous fires. Like pyrometric cones, which are used to gauge heat in kilns, the cones suggest the nature of the fires they experienced. The artists used contemporary and ancient techniques, including a Japanese coil-building method called nejitate." See California Lutheran University, "Fire-Inspired Art Exhibit at Cal Lutheran," October 4, 2018, https://www.callutheran.edu/news/story.html?id=13655#story.
46. Pyne, *Fire*, 181.
47. In Adriaan Peperzak's words: "Trust creates a kind of participation between you and me, and this changes my life, including my feeling, working, and thinking, at least in some aspect and to a certain extent." Adriaan T. Peperzak, *Trust: Who or What Might Support Us?* (New York: Fordham University Press, 2013), 10.
48. Cf. Marjolein Oele, "Priam's Despair and Courage: An Aristotelian Reading of Fear, Hope and Suffering in Homer's *Iliad*," in *Logoi and Muthoi: Further Essays in Greek Philosophy and Literature*, ed. William Wians (Albany: State University of New York Press, 2019), 298–304.
49. Kent Lightfoot et al., *California Indians and Their Environment: An Introduction* (Berkeley: University of California Press, 2009), 143.
50. Lightfoot et al., *California Indians*, 114.
51. Lightfoot et al., *California Indians*, 117.
52. Lightfoot et al., *California Indians*, 143.
53. Such trees can become 3,200 years old. Neil Purslow, *Redwood National Park* (New York: Weigl, 2006), 4–8.
54. Bruce M. Kilgore, "Fire's Role in a Sequoia Forest," Sequoia and Kings Canyon, National Park Service, updated May 20, 2017, https://www.nps.gov/seki/learn/nature/fic_firerole.htm.
55. Kilgore, "Fire's Role in a Sequoia Forest."
56. As Albrecht critically writes in "Solastalgia and the New Mourning" about problematic uses of resilience: "Instead of helping us rebound into configurations of successful models of living after disturbance, we are now seeing resilience being used to justify the ongoing existence of processes and activities that are driving humans to extinction" (304).

57. David Wood's book *Deep Time, Dark Times: On Being Geologically Human* investigates the question of how deep time, and thinking about multiple durations that have taken on geological shapes, put to the test the question of who "we" are and what "life" is. David Wood, *Deep Time, Dark Times: On Being Geologically Human* (New York: Fordham University Press, 2019), 17. Rather than focusing upon geological time, David Roden in *Posthuman Life* emphasizes deep technological time, articulating that certain properties cannot be understood on the basis of their initial conditions, but rather through grasping the "temporally extended process" (118).

58. He continues: "One report describes a colony of forty-five redwood trunks that formed a third-generation fair ring 17 m by 15 m across, whereas another illustrates a lignotuber exposed by erosion that was 12.5 m across and weighted 475,000 kg." Reed F. Noss, *The Redwood Forest: History, Ecology, and Conservation of the Coast Redwoods* (Washington, DC: Island Press, 1999), 114.

59. The following article lucidly maps out this practice as it unfolds in fire belts: Reveal News, "Burning Hotter and Faster," November 24, 2018, https://revealnews.org/podcast/burning-hotter-and-faster/.

60. David R. Baker, "The California Rule That Doomed PG&E: Inverse Condemnation," *Bloomberg*, January 15, 2019, https://www.bloomberg.com/news/articles/2019-01-15/the-california-rule-that-doomed-pg-e-inverse-condemnation.

61. Louis S. Warren tells us that the California Dream is often seen as "a popular ideal of California life that is said to have originated in the gold rush and to have energized California's ascent." However, Warren also critiques the idea that the California Dream originates from the gold rush. Louis S. Warren, "The California Dream: History of a Myth," *Pacific Historical Review* 92, no. 2 (May 2023): 260–298, doi: https://doi.org/10.1525/phr.2023.92.2.260.

62. Donald A. Krueckeberg, "The Difficult Character of Property: To Whom Do Things Belong?," *Journal of the American Planning Association* 61, no. 3 (Fall 1995): 306–307.

63. Krueckeberg, "The Difficult Character," 306–307.

64. Krueckeberg, "The Difficult Character," 307.

65. Gregory S. Alexander et al., "A Statement of Progressive Property," *Cornell Law Faculty Publications* 11 (2009): https://scholarship.law.cornell.edu/facpub/11.

66. Thomas C. Blackburn and Kat Anderson, "Introduction: Managing the Domesticated Environment," in *Before the Wilderness: Environmental Management by Native Californians*, ed. Thomas C. Blackburn and Kat Anderson (Menlo Park, CA: Ballena Press, 1993), 19.

67. Tirso A. Gonzales and Melissa K. Nelson, "Contemporary Native American Responses to Environmental Threats in Indian Country," in *Indigenous Traditions and Ecology: The Interbeing of Cosmology and Community*, ed. John Grim (Cambridge, MA: Harvard University Press, 2001), 499.

68. As Bobroff specifies: "Among tribes in what is now northern California, along the Klamath River and the nearby Pacific coast, property was held in individual private ownership and included ownership rights in other tribes' territories. . . . Ownership could be divided over time, with several individuals each having rights to the same fishing spot at different times of the year. . . . In much drier areas further south, the native peoples recognized property rights of various kinds at the time of Spanish contact." Kenneth H. Bobroff, "Retelling Allotment: Indian Property Rights and the Myth of Common Ownership," *Vanderbilt Law Review* 54, no. 4 (2001): 1589–1590. As Bobroff continues, it included both individual and family ownership, special ownership connected to shamanism and medicinal plants, and intellectual property privately owned, such as songs and dances (1589–1590).

69. Bobroff, "Retelling Allotment," 1563.

70. Bobroff, "Retelling Allotment," 1622. While Bobroff specifies this in the context of addressing Native American issues of allotment, the issue itself is applicable to our entire situation, in my view.

71. Brandon Collins, US Forest Service—PSW; UC Berkeley—Center for Fire Research and Outreach, email message to author, June 30, 2019.

72. Scott L. Stephens et al., "U.S. Federal Fire and Forest Policy: Emphasizing Resilience in Dry Forests," *Ecosphere* 7, no. 11 (2016): https://doi.org/10.1002/ecs2.1584.

73. On the centrality of trust for collective action in relationship to the commons, see also chapter 5 of this monograph. A helpful resource on this topic is Amy R. Poteete, Marco A. Janssen, and Elinor Ostrom, *Working Together: Collective Action, the Commons, and Multiple Methods in Practice* (Princeton, NJ: Princeton University Press, 2010), 226–227.

74. Stephen Pyne as quoted in: Tara Lohan, "How Do We Solve Our Wildfire Challenges?," *The Revelator: Wild, Incisive, Fearless* (October 2018): https://therevelator.org/solve-wildfire-problems, accessed April 11, 2024.

75. Pyne, *Fire*, 185.

76. Pyne, *Fire*, 185.

77. Pyne, *Fire*, 185.

78. Roy Scranton, *Learning to Die in the Anthropocene: Reflections on the End of a Civilization* (San Francisco, CA: City Lights Books, 2015), 23.

79. Scranton, *Learning to Die*, 24.

80. Stiegler, *Technics and Time, 1*, 200–202.

81. Stiegler addresses that another *technē* is needed that will ground community and politics: "Politics is the feeling of the default." It is this technics that we need—through *aidōs*—to battle *ēris* and to come together: "Politics is an art, a technics, imprinted in every mortal as the originary feeling of the divine coup of technicity itself." Stiegler, *Technics and Time, 1*, 201.

82. Mary Shelley, *Frankenstein: or, The Modern Prometheus* (New York: Modern Library, 1984). This idea concerning Dr. Frankenstein's loss of trust is based upon Bruno Latour's interpretation: Bruno Latour, "Love Your Monsters: Why We Must Care for Our Technologies as We Do Our Children," *Breakthrough Journal*, no. 2 (2011): 22.

83. As Derrida quotes Francisco de Quevedo's sonnet "To Vesuvius / Al Vesubio": "I am cinder that darkens in the flame/ nothing that remains to consume the fire/ that in amorous conflagration" is dispersed, and "will be cinder, but will remain sentient/ will be dust, but amorous dust." Jacques Derrida, *Cinders* (Minneapolis: University of Minnesota Press, 2014), 55–57.

Chapter 3. Air—The Breath of Decaying Constellations: A Phenomenology of Loss, Illness, Allergies, and Bad Air

1. Katerina Stamati, Vivek Mudera, and Umber Cheema, "Evolution of Oxygen Utilization in Multicellular Organisms and Implications for Cell Signaling in Tissue Engineering," *Journal of Tissue Engineering* 2, no. 1 (2011): 1.

2. Marshall, "The Event That Transformed Earth."

3. Sallis emphasizes Hegel's reading of Anaximenes: "Air is virtually unique among the elements in that it is invisible." Sallis, *The Figure of Nature*, 18.

4. McKirahan, *Philosophy before Socrates*, 50.

5. Daniel W. Graham, "Anaximenes," *Internet Encyclopedia of Philosophy*, last accessed February 8, 2023, https://www.iep.utm.edu/anaximen/.

6. Graham argues, based upon Plato's rendition of Anaximenes in the *Timaeus*, that Anaximenes's ideas on air need not be understood through the lens of Aristotle's interpretation, namely that Anaximenes is a material monist focusing upon air. Rather, his ideas need to be understood more in terms of process philosophy. Daniel W. Graham, "Plato and Anaximenes," *Études Platoniciennes* 12 (2015): 6, https://doi.org/10.4000/etudesplatoniciennes.706.

7. Graham, "Plato and Anaximenes," 5.

8. Sallis argues that air somehow "remains largely out of sight, withholding itself in order that things can appear. And yet, it is nothing apart from the elements and indeed can show itself only in its dyadic, differentiated connection with them. It is an *archē* withdrawn from the elements, which nonetheless belongs with them." Sallis, *The Figure of Nature*, 25. Sallis's remarks are perceptive in that air, in and of itself, remains difficult to visualize. While during Covid these remarks could be contested given that scientific accounts of various sorts sought to visualize air, air currents, and air particles, I tend to agree with Sallis's remarks but want to refocus them on the invisibility of the *genealogy* of air. While we often seem to encounter air directly—through the immediacy of our breath or

through the touch of our fingers on the air quality apps on our technological devices—the question I raise in this chapter is the following: If air is a material space that has a deep genealogy, and it is subject to social and natural factors that underpin our existence, then what exactly are the invisible factors that make certain subjects increasingly more vulnerable to bad air and how can it be that these factors usually escape our perception?

9. In *What World Is This?* Butler argues that, despite the fact that the Covid-19 pandemic affected all ("pan"), it has been anything but a "leveler" for all. Notions of differential precarity played an enormous role as certain lives were marked dispensable whereas other lives were to be protected at all costs. Butler, *What World Is This?*, 52–55.

10. "Atopy involves the capacity to produce IgE in response to common environmental proteins such as house dust mites, grass pollen, and food allergens." "Medical Definition of Atopy," MedicineNet, last reviewed March 29, 2021, https://www.medicinenet.com/script/main/art.asp?articlekey=31081.

11. While medicine has made great strides in perfecting itself—due to increased knowledge of biochemistry, genetics, statistics, and so on—phenomenology of illness has allowed us to show the enduring *other* side of modern medicine. Cf. Fredrik Svenaeus, "A Defense of the Phenomenological Account of Health and Illness," *Journal of Medicine and Philosophy* 44 (2019): 459–478. Even if medicine in its modern incarnation has greatly progressed in terms of scientific understanding and evidence-based treatments, illness is still lived and suffered, and this dimension of illness cannot be wiped away with treatments and statistics. Illness, treatment, bodies, disability, and life are inextricably bound together and need to be studied from multiple levels. Thus, even despite the increasingly positive success of new cures, the living reality of patients presents itself with changes, obstacles, and modified ways of negotiating the world.

12. Fredrik Svenaeus, "Medicine," in *A Companion to Phenomenology and Existentialism*, ed. Hubert L. Dreyfus and Mark A. Wrathall, 412–424 (Hoboken, NJ: Wiley-Blackwell, 2009), 416; my emphasis.

13. Svenaeus, "Medicine," 422.

14. My account seeks to rectify Svenaeus's account of the uncanny in Heidegger, thereby offering a different kind of critique than Ahlzén offers of Svenaeus. Ahlzén critiques the fact that the phenomenological language of home may not serve well in the context of practical lives living with illness. Rolf Ahlzén, "Illness as Unhomelike Being-in-the-World? Phenomenology and Medical Practice," *Medical Health Care and Philosophy* 14 (2011): 325–326. He finds that the word "home" has already a "strong everyday understanding" and that "hoping for a broad metaphorical interpretation of it seems hazardous. Patients will not easily come to terms with physicians telling them that they will get this analgesic in order to make their being more homelike" (328). While he critiques Svenaeus, and the problems caused by the transition from ontology to psychology, he does not

critique Svenaeus's reading of Heidegger as such. Ahlzén, "Illness as Unhomelike Being-in-the-World?," 328.

15. Martin Heidegger, *Introduction to Metaphysics*, trans. Ralph Manheim (New Haven, CT: Yale University Press, 1973), 158.

16. Heidegger, *Being and Time*, §57, H. 277, E. 322.

17. Robert Mugerauer, *Heidegger and Homecoming: The Leitmotif in the Later Writings* (Toronto: University of Toronto Press, 2008), 41–42; Mugerauer's emphasis.

18. Heidegger, *Being and Time*, §57, E. 322, H. 277.

19. Heidegger contests that "the They" is negatively valued since it is an existential, primordial structure; however, as its connection to negatively laden terms such as "fallenness" indicates, it would be hard to take "the They" purely neutral and not in a negative fashion. Heidegger, *Being and Time*, §27, E. 167, H. 129.

20. Sloterdijk, *Foams*, 56.

21. Sloterdijk, *Foams*, 135.

22. Sloterdijk, *Foams*, 165.

23. Sloterdijk, *Foams*, 165.

24. Sloterdijk, *Foams*, 122.

25. The First World War was the first war in which chemical weapons (gases) were used on a large scale: "Historians now refer to the Great War as the chemist's war because of the scientific and engineering mobilization efforts by the major belligerents. The development, production, and deployment of war gases such as chlorine, phosgene, and mustard created a new and complex public health threat that endangered not only soldiers and civilians on the battlefield but also chemical workers on the home front involved in the large-scale manufacturing processes." Quoted from an abstract of Gerard J. Fitzgerald, "Chemical Warfare and Medical Response During World War I," *American Journal of Public Health* 98, no. 4 (April 2008): 611–625, 10.2105/AJPH.2007.11930. In *Foams*, Peter Sloterdijk offers a philosophical analysis of the manipulation of air in the form of airfare and toxic gases at the beginning of the twentieth century, which he rightfully calls a "caesura" in time, after which those living in zones synchronized with modernity had to deal with climactic concern or atmospheric design in one way or another. Sloterdijk, *Foams*, 122.

26. Irigaray argues that when Heidegger forgets air, "he forgets the cultivation of life itself and of its relation with the surrounding world, with others, mastery then without violence, without a technique that takes living matter in a fabricated exteriority where it is exiled from its own becoming." Irigaray, "From *The Forgetting of Air* to *To Be Two*," 311.

27. Anaximenes, fragment 141, Hippolytus *Refutation* 1.7.1–3 = DK 13 A7. As cited in McKirahan, *Philosophy before Socrates*, 48–49; translation slightly modified by author.

28. In *Greek Natural Philosophy*, Callicott et al. argue that Anaximenes had two reasons for naming air as the *archē*: "(1) Air is the most *apeiron* (indefinite)

state of the *archē*. It is colorless, odorless and tasteless (even more so than water) and is only noticeably experienced as wind, significantly, the first step on the rarefaction-condensation spectrum towards stone. (2) Air is what we breathe. And phenomenologically speaking, the most obvious differences between a living person and a dead one is that the former moves and breathes and the latter does neither, while metaphysically speaking, the difference between a living person and a dead one is that the soul has departed from the latter." Callicott et al., *Greek Natural Philosophy*, 99.

29. M. Laura Gemelli Marciano, *Die Vorsokratiker: Band I: Thales, Anaximander, Anaximenes, Pythagoras und die Pythagoreer, Xenophanes, Heraklit* (Düsseldorf: Artemis & Winkler, 2007), 88.

30. Daniel W. Graham, "A New Look at Anaximenes," *History of Philosophy Quarterly* 20, no. 1 (2003): 13.

31. Graham, "A New Look at Anaximenes," 13.

32. Graham, "A New Look at Anaximenes," 13.

33. Stamati et al, "Evolution of Oxygen Utilization in Multicellular Organisms and Implications for Cell Signaling in Tissue Engineering," 1–2.

34. Marshall, "The Event That Transformed Earth."

35. This is the case since it allows for "producing 16–18 times more adenosine triphosphate (ATP) per hexose sugar than anaerobic metabolism, thus generating more energy." Stamati et al., "Evolution of Oxygen Utilization in Multicellular Organisms and Implications for Cell Signaling in Tissue Engineering," 2.

36. Marshall, "The Event That Transformed Earth."

37. Anaximenes, as cited by Plutarch, *The Principle of Cold* 7 947F = DK 13 B1, in McKirahan, *Philosophy before Socrates*, 50.

38. Anaximenes, DK 13 B2; as cited in McKirahan, *Philosophy before Socrates*, 54.

39. McKirahan, *Philosophy before Socrates*, 54.

40. McKirahan, *Philosophy before Socrates*, 54.

41. Densely populated areas, such as cities, are particularly grim examples of how geographical locations and their built infrastructures affect people's relationships with air. This is apparent in Engels's writing, commenting on the living conditions in Manchester during the time of industrialization: "Such is the Old Town of Manchester, and on re-reading my description, I am forced to admit that instead of being exaggerated, it is far from black enough to convey a true impression of the filth, ruin, and uninhabitableness, *the defiance of all considerations of cleanliness, ventilation, and health* which characterise the construction of this single district, containing at least twenty to thirty thousand inhabitants. And such a district exists in the heart of the second city of England, the first manufacturing city of the world. If any one wishes to see in how little space a human being can move, *how little air—and such air!—he can breathe*, how little of civilisation he may share and yet live, it is only necessary to travel hither."

Friedrich Engels, *The Condition of the Working Class in England* (London: Panther, 1969), 60; emphasis added. Engels continues: "These courts were built in this way from the beginning, and communicate with the streets by means of covered passages. *If the totally planless construction is injurious to the health of the workers by preventing ventilation, this method of shutting them up in courts surrounded on all sides by buildings is far more so. The air simply cannot escape*; the chimneys of the houses are the sole drains for the imprisoned atmosphere of the courts, and they serve the purpose only so long as fire is kept burning. Moreover, the houses surrounding such courts are usually built back to back, having the rear wall in common; and this alone suffices to prevent any sufficient through ventilation. And, as the police charged with care of the streets does not trouble itself about the condition of these courts, as everything quietly lies where it is thrown, there is no cause for wonder at the filth and heaps of ashes and offal to be found here" (61; emphasis added).

42. Gregg Mitman, *Breathing Space: How Allergies Shape Our Lives and Landscapes* (New Haven, CT: Yale University Press, 2007), 2.

43. Mitman, *Breathing Space*, 8.

44. As made clear by Engels, those of the lower class are typically the most impacted by illness because they lack access to a healthy environment, and they lack the means to live a healthy life: "The manner in which the great multitude of the poor is treated by society today is revolting. They are drawn into the large cities where they breathe a poorer atmosphere than in the country; they are relegated to districts which, by reason of the method of construction, are worse ventilated than any others; they are deprived of all means of cleanliness, of water itself, since pipes are laid only when paid for, and the rivers so polluted that they are useless for such purposes; they are obliged to throw all offal and garbage, all dirty water, often all disgusting drainage and excrement into the streets, being without other means of disposing of them; they are thus compelled to infect the region of their own dwellings" (84). Furthermore, Engels notes, "that the dwellings of the workers in the worst portions of the cities, together with the other conditions of life of this class, engender numerous diseases, is attested on all sides. The article already quoted from the *Artisan* asserts with perfect truth, that *lung diseases must be the inevitable consequence of such conditions, and that, indeed, cases of this kind are disproportionately frequent in this class.* That the bad air of London, and especially of the working-people's districts, is in the highest degree favourable to the development of consumption, the hectic appearance of great numbers of persons sufficiently indicates. If one roams the streets a little in the early morning, when the multitudes are on their way to their work, one is amazed at the number of persons who look wholly or half-consumptive. Even in Manchester the people have not the same appearance; these pale, lank, narrow-chested, hollow-eyed ghosts, whom one passes at every step, these languid, flabby faces, incapable of the slightest energetic expression, I have seen in such startling numbers only in

London, though consumption carries off a horde of victims annually in the factory towns of the North. In competition with consumption stands typhus, to say nothing of scarlet fever, a disease which brings most frightful devastation into the ranks of the working-class. *Typhus, that universally diffused affliction, is attributed by the official report on the sanitary condition of the working-class, directly to the bad state of the dwellings in the matters of ventilation, drainage, and cleanliness"* (ibid., 84; emphasis added).

45. Mitman, *Breathing Space*, 8. As mentioned earlier, Butler in *What World Is This?* argues that Covid-19 affected people differently based on their social, economic, racial, and gender positionalities (52–55). Annegret Haase offers further exploration of Butler's point, in that she argues that people from a lower social-economic class also tend to live in poorer housing conditions. These living conditions often have limited or no ventilation or air-conditioning options and thus make those of the lower social-economic class both more vulnerable to air pollution as well as to pathogens such as the coronavirus. Annegret Haase, "Covid-19 as a Social Crisis and Justice Challenge for Cities," *Frontiers in Sociology* 5 (2020): 1–7.

46. Mitman, *Breathing Space*, 39.

47. Mitman, *Breathing Space*, 21–36.

48. It has been debated that the rise of hay fever also partly has to do with "botanical sexism": because "female" trees bear fruit, they were less popular to plant in cities and densely populated areas since they would create a "mess" (i.e., fruit being spilled on the streets, etc.). Thus, mostly "male" trees were planted in cities, which produced more pollen. It is still debated if "botanical sexism" has any real measurable impact on the pollen production in cities, but it is interesting to keep this debate in mind as we ponder the (unintentional) implications of cultural (and possibly sexist) presuppositions on the environment, and the way the recreated environment, in turn, informs humanity's lifeworld and its air. See chapter 4.4, "Sex Bias ('Botanical Sexism') in Tree Planting," in Daniel S. W. Katz et al., "The Effects of Tree Planting on Allergenic Pollen Production in New York City," *Urban Forestry and Urban Greening* 92, no. 128208 (2024): 1–10.

49. Mitman, *Breathing Space*, 80.

50. Mitman, *Breathing Space*, 80, 94, 128.

51. Mitman, *Breathing Space*, 123.

52. Mitman, *Breathing Space*, 120–121. In line with Mitman's thoughts, Engels observed that "in all the coal-mines which [were] properly ventilated [the disease known as 'black spittle'] [was] unknown, while it frequently [happened] that miners who [went] from well- to ill-ventilated mines [were] seized by it. The profit-greed of mine owners which prevent[ed] the use of ventilators is therefore responsible for the fact . . . that this working-men's disease exists at all." Engels, *Condition of the Working Class in England*, 167.

53. Mitman, *Breathing Space*, 204.

54. For instance, many people lack the privilege to decide the environments that they would like to work in. Jaclynn Knecht, "5 Reasons to Take the Job You Don't Want," Career Contesta, last accessed February 15, 2023, https://www.careercontessa.com/advice/the-job-you-dont-want/. Accordingly, people may expose themselves to toxins, carcinogens, and overall "bad air" on a daily basis for the sake of financially supporting themselves and their families. This was made especially evident during the industrial revolution: "It is impossible to wonder at the almost unanimous testimony of the physicians in the Factories' Report, that they find a great lack of ability to resist disease, a general depression in vital activity, a constant relaxation of the mental and physical powers." Engels, *Condition of the Working Class in England*, 116. Engels continues, "But besides all this, there are some branches of factory-work which have an especially injurious effect. In many rooms of the cotton and flax-spinning mills, the air is filled with fibrous dust, which produces chest affections, especially among workers in the carding and combing-rooms. Some constitutions can bear it, some cannot; but *the operative has no choice. He must take the room in which he finds work, whether his chest is sound or not.* The most common effects of this breathing of dust are blood-spitting, hard, noisy breathing, pains in the chest, coughs, sleeplessness—in short, all the symptoms of asthma ending in the worst cases in consumption" (120).

55. Vicky Walters and J. C. Gaillard, "Disaster Risk at the Margins: Homelessness, Vulnerability and Hazards," *Habitat International* 44 (2014): 212. For the term "silent disasters" they refer to a campaign by the Internal Federation of Red Cross and Red Cross Crescent Societies 2013. Walters and Gaillard, "Disaster Risk at the Margins," 212, 218.

56. Anand 1998 as cited in Walters and Gaillard, "Disaster Risk at the Margins," 212.

57. Bull-Kamanga et al. 2013, as cited in Walters and Gaillard, "Disaster Risk at the Margins," 212.

58. Berlant, "Slow Death (Sovereignty, Obesity, Lateral Agency)," 761.

59. Friedrich Nietzsche, *On the Genealogy of Morality*, ed. Keith Ansell-Pearson, trans. Carol Diethe (Cambridge: Cambridge University Press, 2007), III.14, 89.

60. Nietzsche, *On the Genealogy of Morality*, III.8, 78.

61. Nietzsche, *On the Genealogy of Morality*, III.26, 117–118.

62. Stephen Graham, "Life Support: The Political Ecology of Urban Air," *City* 19, nos. 2–3 (2015): 203.

63. Stephen Buraniyi, "The Air Conditioning Trap: How Cold Air Is Heating the World," *The Guardian*, August 29, 2019, https://www.theguardian.com/environment/2019/aug/29/the-air-conditioning-trap-how-cold-air-is-heating-the-world.

64. Buraniyi, "The Air Conditioning Trap." He writes: "There are just over 1bn single-room air conditioning units in the world right now—about one for every seven people on earth. Numerous reports have projected that by 2050 there are likely

to be more than 4.5bn, making them as ubiquitous as the mobile phone is today. The US already uses as much electricity for air conditioning each year as the UK uses in total. The IEA projects that as the rest of the world reaches similar levels, air conditioning will use about 13% of all electricity worldwide, and produce 2bn tonnes of $CO2$ a year—about the same amount as India, the world's third-largest emitter, produces today." Buraniyi, "The Air Conditioning Trap." See also Cécile de Munck et al., "How Much Can Air Conditioning Increase Air Temperature for a City Like Paris, France?," *International Journal of Climatology* 33, no. 1 (2013): 210–227.

65. Buraniyi, "The Air Conditioning Trap." In the United States, they became indispensable as large post-WWII building projects came underway, and "architects and construction companies no longer had to worry much about differences in climate—they could sell the same style of home just as easily in New Mexico as in Delaware. The prevailing mentality was that just about any problems caused by hot climates, cheap building materials, shoddy design or poor city planning could be overcome, as the American Institute of Architects wrote in 1973, 'by the brute application of more air conditioning' [sic]. As Cooper writes, 'Architects, builders and bankers accepted air conditioning first, and consumers were faced with a fait accompli that they merely had to ratify.'"

66. Buraniyi, "The Air Conditioning Trap."

67. Buraniyi, "The Air Conditioning Trap."

68. Stamati et al., "Evolution of Oxygen Utilization in Multicellular Organisms and Implications for Cell Signaling in Tissue Engineering," 1–2.

69. Sergio Gallegos, Zoom conversation with author, May 2, 2021.

70. Peter Steeves, email conversation with author, May 2, 2021.

71. Pope, as cited in Graham, "Life Support," 200. Graham references Alexander Pope, "An Airquake in China," Zoneresearch.org, November 29, 2013.

Chapter 4. Earth—Silent Tremors: Earthquakes and the Question of Balance and (Dis)Orientation

1. In *E-Co-Affectivity*, which examines life's e-co-affective interfaces, I devoted the last chapter to soil, the "skin of the earth." In that chapter, I focused on the tiny pores and interstitial spaces of soil, and on the messy, creative, and co-affective nature of dirt as it connects different forms of being—both organic and nonorganic. By contrast, in this chapter, I focus on the larger, deeper destabilizing movements of earth and how they connect to our own human (dis)orientation. Oele, *E-Co-Affectivity*, 139–164.

2. Macauley, *Elemental Philosophy*, 15.

3. Carol Svec, *Balance: A Dizzying Journey through the Science of Our Most Delicate Sense* (Chicago: Chicago Review Press, 2017), 29. The quote is attributed to Dr. Isaac Jones.

4. Svec, *Balance*, ix.
5. Svec, *Balance*, ix.
6. Bill McGuire, *Waking the Giant: How a Changing Climate Triggers Earthquakes, Tsunamis, and Volcanoes* (New York: Oxford University Press, 2012), x.
7. Craig Stanford, *Upright: The Evolutionary Key to Becoming Human* (Boston, MA: Houghton Mifflin, 2003), 5.
8. Serres, *Biogea*, 28.
9. Hesiod, *Works and Days and Theogony*, ll. 116–119.
10. Hesiod, *Works and Days and Theogony*, ll. 126–131.
11. Hesiod, *Works and Days and Theogony*, l. 15.
12. Hesiod, *Works and Days and Theogony*, l. 460. Poseidon is characterized as "deep-booming Poseidon" (l. 824).
13. Paolo Vivante, "On the Representation of Nature and Reality in Homer," *Arion: A Journal of Humanities and the Classics* 5, no. 2 (1966): 188.
14. Vivante, "On the Representation of Nature and Reality in Homer," 160.
15. Homer, *The Iliad*, trans. R. Lattimore (Chicago: University of Chicago Press, 1951), book 15, ll. 187–193; translation slightly modified by the author.
16. Eric A. Havelock, "The Cosmic Myths of Homer and Hesiod," *Oral Tradition* 2, no. 1 (1987): 37.
17. Walter Burkert, *Greek Religion: Archaic and Classical*, trans. John Raffan (Malden, MA: Blackwell, 1991), 139; emphasis added.
18. Burkert, *Greek Religion*, 139.
19. Homer, *The Iliad*, trans. R. Lattimore, book 20, ll. 54–67.
20. Burkert, *Greek Religion*, 139. Cf. Elizabeth J. W. Barber and Paul Barber, *When They Severed Earth from Sky: How the Human Mind Shapes Myth* (Princeton, NJ: Princeton University Press, 2004), 50.
21. "Two powerful sons of Kronos, hearts divided against each other, were wreaking bitter agonies of the fighting warriors, since Zeus willed the victory for the Trojans and Hektor, glorifying swift-footed Achilleus, yet not utterly did he wish the Agaian people to be destroyed before Ilion, but only was giving glory to Thetis and her strong-spirited son, while Poseidon emerging unseen from the grey salt water went among the Argives and stirred them, since he was angered that they were beaten by the Trojans and blamed Zeus for it bitterly. Indeed, the two were of one generation and a single father, but Zeus was the elder born and knew more. Therefore Poseidon shrank from openly defending them, but secretly in a man's likeness was forever stirring them up through the army. So these two had looped over both sides a crossing cable of strong discord and the closing of battle, not to be slipped, not to be broken, which unstrung the knees of many." Homer, *The Iliad*, trans. Robert Fagles (New York: Penguin Books, 1991), ll. 345–359.
22. Burkert, *Greek Religion*, 139.
23. In early Greek philosophy, we find several theories about the origin of earthquakes. Thales postulated that, since the earth is floating on water, it is the

movement of water that causes the earth to shake. Alternatively, Anaximenes proposes a theory of collapse, Democritus a theory regarding rainfall mixing with underground water, and Anaxagoras argued that the entry of ether into the earth causes quakes. Erhard Oeser, "Historical Earthquake Theories from Aristotle to Kant," in *Historical Earthquakes in Central Europe: Monographs* (Vienna: Geologische Bundesanstalt, 1992), 13.

24. Oeser, "Historical Earthquake Theories from Aristotle to Kant," 14.

25. Oeser, "Historical Earthquake Theories from Aristotle to Kant," 15.

26. In Shakespeare's *Henry IV*, we find a similar image of "diseased nature" that breaks forth in "strange eruptions" addressing colic and "imprisoning of unruly wind." Aristotle, *Meteorologica*, trans. H. D. P. Lee (Cambridge, MA: Harvard University Press, 1952), 204–205.

27. Aristotle, *De Caelo*, trans. C. D. C. Reeve (Indianapolis, IN: Hackett, 2020), 14; Helen S. Lang, *The Order of Nature in Aristotle's Physics: Place and the Elements* (Cambridge: Cambridge University Press, 1998), 187.

28. Oele, *E-Co-Affectivity*, 120–121.

29. "Lisbon Earthquake of 1755," *Britannica*, last updated October 25, 2022, https://www.britannica.com/event/Lisbon-earthquake-of-1755.

30. "Magnitude of Great Lisbon Earthquake May Have Been Lower than Previous Estimates," *ScienceDaily*, January 7, 2020, https://www.sciencedaily.com/releases/2020/01/200107104942.htm.

31. "Lisbon Earthquake of 1755."

32. Theodore Besterman, *Voltaire Essays, and Another* (Oxford: Oxford University Press, 1962), 26.

33. Besterman, *Voltaire Essays*, 26.

34. Voltaire, "Poem on the Lisbon Disaster; or an Examination of the Axiom, 'All Is Well' (1755)," in *Toleration and Other Essays by Voltaire*, trans. Joseph McCabe (New York: G. P. Putnam's Sons, 1912), 256.

35. Voltaire, "Poem on the Lisbon Disaster," 255.

36. Besterman, *Voltaire Essays*, 39.

37. The ultimate version of the poem was based on various drafts, as Voltaire was carefully deliberating between sounding either too pessimistic or too optimistic. He ultimately contemplated yet another revision to downplay the too optimistically sounding "hope" at the very end. He annotated the lines quoted here with "what a frail [sic] hope." G. R. Havens, "Voltaire's Pessimistic Revision of the Conclusion of His *Poème sur le désastre de Lisbonne*," *Modern Language Notes* 44, no. 8 (December 1929): 491. The ultimate line of the poem, which also appeals to hope in the published version, runs like this: "He might have added one thing further—hope" ("Mais il pouvait encore ajouter l'espérance"). However, Voltaire later, in his own private library copy, added a question mark: "But might he have added one thing further—hope?" ("Mais pouvait-il encor ajouter l'espérance?").

38. Immanuel Kant, "History and Natural Description of the Most Noteworthy Occurrences of the Earthquake That Struck a Large Part of the Earth at

the End of the Year 1755 (1756)," in Immanuel Kant, *Natural Science*, ed. Eric Watkins (Cambridge: Cambridge University Press, 2012), 337–364.

39. Kant, "History and Natural Description of the Most Noteworthy Occurrences of the Earthquake That Struck a Large Part of the Earth at the End of the Year 1755 (1756)," E2, 431; trans. 340.

40. E1, 426; trans. 335.

41. E2, 431; trans. 340.

42. E3, 465; trans. 368.

43. Eric Watkins, "Editor's Introduction," in Kant, *Natural Science*, 327.

44. E1, 421; trans. 331.

45. E1, 420; trans. 331.

46. E2, 456; trans. 360.

47. E2, 434, trans. 342. In addition to pointing out the horror of the earthquake, Kant also points to the "usefulness" of earthquakes, for instance, in providing hot mineral springs (E2, 456). As Jones points out, we should feel uneasy about Kant's idea that the usefulness of mineral baths for humans can somehow compensate for the tragic loss associated with the earthquake. Rachel Jones, "Kant, Irigaray, and Earthquakes: Adventures in the Abyss," *Symposium* 17, no. 1 (2013): 281.

48. Watkins, "Editor's Introduction," 337.

49. Jones, "Kant, Irigaray, and Earthquakes," 282. Jones references E2, 456 and 460.

50. E2, 455, trans. 359.

51. Jones, "Kant, Irigaray, and Earthquakes," 282.

52. E2, 460; trans. 363.

53. E2, 461; trans. 363.

54. E2, 461; trans. 364.

55. Jones, "Kant, Irigaray, and Earthquakes," 284.

56. Immanuel Kant, *Critique of Judgment*, translated by Werner S. Pluhar. Indianapolis, IN: Hackett, 1987), §28, 261–262.

57. Kant, *Critique of Judgment*, §23, 245.

58. "To re-establish the balance that has been so dangerously disturbed, the philosopher decides that from now on nature overall will be put under the control of the human spirit and her origins will be based on her necessary obedience to the law. So the ground will now rest upon a transcendental ceiling that is propped up by the forms and rules of representation and is thus unshakeable." Luce Irigaray, *Speculum of the Other Woman*, translated by Gillian C. Gill (Ithaca, NY: Cornell University Press, 1985), 203–204.

59. This idea surfaced early in the twentieth century but was only considered correct once proven on the basis of forty years of scholarship. Naomi Oreskes, ed., *Plate Tectonics: An Insider's History of the Modern Theory of the Earth* (New York: CRC Press, 2003), 1.

60. The plates in question are about a dozen, and the plates comprise about "45–60 miles (80 to 100 kilometers) of the earth's surface (now called

the lithosphere), and move at a rate of 1 to 4 inches (3 to 10 centimeters) per year. . . . Moreover, the global configuration of continents and oceans is constantly changing." Naomi Oreskes, "From Continental Drift to Plate Tectonics," in *Plate Tectonics: An Insider's History of the Modern Theory of the Earth*, ed. Naomi Oreskes (New York: CRC Press, 2003), 3–4.

61. National Geographic Society, "Plate Tectonics," *National Geographic*, last updated August 17, 2022, https://education.nationalgeographic.org/resource/plate-tectonics-video/.

62. "Plate Tectonics," *National Geographic*, last accessed April 5, 2023.

63. "Plate Tectonics," *National Geographic*, last accessed April 5, 2023.

64. Oreskes, "From Continental Drift to Plate Tectonics," 7.

65. David T. Sandwell, "Plate Tectonics: A Martian View," in *Plate Tectonics: An Insider's History of the Modern Theory of the Earth*, ed. Naomi Oreskes (New York: CRC Press, 2003), 331.

66. National Geographic Society, "Plate Tectonics," *National Geographic*, last updated August 17, 2022, https://education.nationalgeographic.org/resource/plate-tectonics/.

67. "Plate Tectonics," *National Geographic*, last updated August 17, 2022.

68. Less than 10 percent of earthquakes take place in the middle of a plate. National Geographic Society, "Earthquakes," *National Geographic*, last updated May 19, 2022, https://education.nationalgeographic.org/resource/earthquakes/.

69. "Earthquakes," *National Geographic*, last updated May 19, 2022.

70. Sandwell, "Plate Tectonics," 332.

71. Sandwell, "Plate Tectonics," 332.

72. Sandwell, "Plate Tectonics," 331.

73. Sandwell, "Plate Tectonics," 334.

74. For instance, the San Andreas Fault, close to my home in Marin, is part of a large boundary intersection between the North American and the Pacific Plate. It runs from the Pacific to Colorado. See John Dvorak, *Earthquake Storms: The Fascinating History and Volatile Future of the San Andreas Fault* (New York: Pegasus Books, 2014), xvi.

75. Dvorak, *Earthquake Storms*, xvi.

76. "California is not going to fall catastrophically into the ocean. . . . But it is being sliced and slid apart incrementally, most of the sliding occurring during the occasional large earthquake." Dvorak, *Earthquake Storms*, 207.

77. Serres, *Biogea*, 29.

78. Interestingly, in *Seismic City*, Joanna Dyl analyzes the 1906 earthquake in San Francisco, coming to very similar conclusions as Serres in his analysis of the 1989 earthquake. Dyl writes: "Understanding the disaster requires consideration of the dynamic interplay of seismic forces, urban fire regimes, social circumstances, and the built environment of San Francisco." Joanna Leslie Dyl and Paul Sutter,

Seismic City: An Environmental History of San Francisco's 1906 Earthquake (Seattle: University of Washington Press, 2017), 53.

79. Paul Cohen (@paul_e_cohen@mastodon.social), "On the one hand, the @nytimes in-depth piece on Haitian 'reparations' to France brings much-needed attention onto a decisive moment in world history." Twitter, May 21, 2022, https://twitter.com/Paul_E_Cohen/status/1528053592946528256.

80. "In 1825, France conditioned its grant of recognition to the new nation of Haiti on the payment of 150 million francs plus trade benefits." Kim Oosterlinck et al., "A Debt of Dishonor," *Boston University Law Review* 102 (2022): 1247.

81. These are the words of President René Préval, speaking to Jonathan Katz on the nature of unsafe buildings in Haiti. The problem, he argues, is not that there are no building codes, but no agencies or "political stability" to enforce building codes. Jonathan M. Katz, *The Big Truck That Went By: How the World Came to Save Haiti and Left Behind a Disaster* (New York: Palgrave Macmillan, 2013), 11.

82. Berlant's analysis of slow death is done in the context of examining obesity in the United States. In my view, Berlant's argument can be expanded to include the global economic and political regimes gradually diminishing the strength or effectiveness of certain groups of people. Berlant, "Slow Death," 761.

83. Katz, *The Big Truck That Went By*, 2.
84. McGuire, *Waking the Giant*, x.
85. McGuire, *Waking the Giant*, x.
86. McGuire, *Waking the Giant*, x.
87. McGuire, *Waking the Giant*, x; Javier Yanes, "Will Climate Change Also Trigger Earthquakes, Tsunamis and Volcanic Eruptions?," last accessed April 5, 2023, https://www.bbvaopenmind.com/en/science/environment/climate-change-trigger-earthquakes-tsunamis-volcanic-eruptions/.
88. McGuire, *Waking the Giant*, 125.
89. Adven Masih, "An Enhanced Seismic Activity Observed Due to Climate Change: Preliminary Results from Alaska," *IOP Conference Series: Earth and Environmental Science* 167 (2018): 2.
90. In a recent analysis of Alaska, Masih argues that "even though the postglacial stress due to rapid shrinkage of sea ice cover and melting glaciers has not yet started influencing the major earthquakes of magnitude 6 or more on Richter scale much, however the noticeable rise in the frequency of moderate earthquakes of magnitudes ranging from 4 to 5.9 points to a seismically turbulent future, if the present trend of glaciers and sea ice melting due to rise in temperature due to anthropogenic activity remains the same, soon many of the countless subsurface faults will start responding in the form of major earthquakes." Masih, "An Enhanced Seismic Activity Observed Due to Climate Change," 7.
91. "Does the Production of Oil and Gas from Shales Cause Earthquakes? If So, How Are the Earthquakes Related to These Operations?," United States Geolog-

ical Survey, last accessed April 5, 2023, https://www.usgs.gov/faqs/does-production-oil-and-gas-shales-cause-earthquakes-if-so-how-are-earthquakes-related-these.

92. "How Oil and Gas Disposal Wells Can Cause Earthquakes," *StateImpact*, last accessed April 5, 2023, https://stateimpact.npr.org/texas/tag/earthquake/.

93. "How Oil and Gas Disposal Wells Can Cause Earthquakes," *StateImpact*, last accessed April 5, 2023, https://stateimpact.npr.org/texas/tag/earthquake/.

94. "Does the Production of Oil and Gas from Shales Cause Earthquakes? If So, How Are the Earthquakes Related to These Operations?"

95. In *Gas: Het verhaal van een Nederlandse bodemschat*, Emiel Hakkenes provides a provocative biographic genealogy of the various characters involved in the discovery, and ultimate drilling and distribution of gas. Emiel Hakkenes, *Gas: Het Verhaal van een Nederlandse Bodemschat* (Amsterdam: Thomas Rap, 2020).

96. Stanley Reed, "Earthquakes Are Jolting the Netherlands. Gas Drilling Is to Blame," *New York Times*, October 24, 2019, https://www.nytimes.com/2019/10/24/business/energy-environment/netherlands-gas-earthquakes.html.

97. Mark Middel, "Het openen van de subsidiepot leidde in Groningen tot een 'vernederende' tombola," *NRC*, January 13, 2022, https://www.nrc.nl/nieuws/2022/01/13/een-subsidietombola-die-de-groningers-vernederde-a4079235.

98. Serres, *The Natural Contract*, 1–3.

99. Serres, *Biogea*, 171–172. In order to establish a more peaceful symbiosis or "pact" with the world, he writes about the need for conjuring up a new language. He writes, "Through deciphering, better and better, these codes attached to things, I can imagine what language this pact could be drawn up in." Serres, *Biogea*, 172.

100. Jane Bennett in *Influx and Efflux: Writing Up with Walt Whitman* is providing an intriguing analysis of Whitman's interest in the relationship between personality and posture, also known as pathognomy. Jane Bennett, *Influx and Efflux: Writing Up with Walt Whitman* (Durham, NC: Duke University Press, 2020), 8. I find Bennett's reading of Whitman fascinating in that she rethinks, like I do, the causal relationships between position and disposition (9). However, while Bennett—with Whitman—pursues this topic in an individuated (or in her words: dividuated) setting, my argument in this chapter, and book, is aimed at the broader, communal outlines for rethinking our dispositions given the experience of elemental loss.

101. Svec, *Balance*, 76.

102. Stanford, *Upright*, 50.

103. Richard P. Allan et al., *Climate Change 2021: The Physical Science Basis—Summary for Policy Makers* (Geneva: IPCC, 2021), https://www.ipcc.ch/report/ar6/wg1/downloads/report/IPCC_AR6_WGI_SPM_final.pdf.

104. Paul Auster, introduction to Philippe Petit, *On the High Wire* (New York: New Directions Books, 2019), xiv.

105. Philippe Petit, *On the High Wire*, trans. Paul Auster (New York: New Directions Books, 2019), 20.

106. Auster, Introduction to *On the High Wire*, xxv.
107. Friedrich Nietzsche, "Zarathustra's Prologue," in *Thus Spoke Zarathustra: A Book for All and None* (New York: Modern Library, 1995), §6.
108. Caitlin Sims, "About Rhoden's *The Promised Land*," San Francisco Ballet, last accessed April 14, 2023, https://www.sfballet.org/about-rhodens-the-promised-land/.
109. San Francisco Ballet, "Pointes of View Lecture Series, *The Promised Land* with Dwight Rhoden and Ariel Osterweis, Ph.D.," YouTube, https://www.youtube.com/watch?v=KA9aslpL1hg.
110. At the very end of the piece, the dancers on stage all link hands, and principal dancer Esteban "rushes towards the chain and breaks through—but he cannot break back again. If you allow a struggle to change you, 'The Promised Land' suggests, there is no going back to who you used to be." Rachel Howard, "Review: S.F. Ballet Brings Audiences to 'The Promised Land' and Beyond with Electric New Works," *San Francisco Chronicle*, last updated April 11, 2022, https://datebook.sfchronicle.com/dance/review-s-f-ballet-brings-audiences-to-the-promised-land-and-beyond-with-electric-new-works.

Chapter 5. Elemental Trust—Transforming Elemental Loss into Elemental Change

1. Bernstein, "Trust," 395.
2. Godfrey, *Trust of People, Words, and God*, 45.
3. Albrecht speaks of "changes that one is powerless to prevent" and that "manifest in a feeling of disorientation." Albrecht, "Solastalgia and the New Mourning," 300.
4. Boss, *The Myth of Closure*, 58.
5. The Covid-19 pandemic provided Boss a new access point for grasping the ambiguity of loss in terms of broader societal frameworks unraveling, a theme that she elaborated in *The Myth of Closure*: "Ambiguous losses are ubiquitous but rarely acknowledged because they are difficult to see, even by those of us experiencing them. While all loss is stressful, ambiguous loss adds additional stress because both the loss and grief are frozen" (6). She addresses the need for us to "increase our tolerance for ambiguity." Boss distinguishes two kinds of loss, physical and psychological (10–11). Boss also addresses the evolution of her own thinking, which developed from thinking about ambiguous loss on the level of the family to include (within the context of the Covid-19 pandemic) not only a person or family but "a local community, or the global community" (12).
6. Rather than trust, Glenn Albrecht, in his book *Earth Emotions: New Words for a New World*, petitions for love as a proper affective counter-emotion to earth-destructive emotions such as solastalgia. He proposes to "take love from the domain of individual humans and project it out into the realm of the earth,

as alive, as a 'person.'" Glenn A. Albrecht, *Earth Emotions: New Words for a New World* (Ithaca, NY: Cornell University Press, 2019), 133. Additionally, he writes: "I appeal to my fellow humans to see their connection to the Earth as a loving relationship" (194). Versus Albrecht, I think trust can carry larger projects (given that it can include impersonal things much more strongly than love, which remains very much individual-bound), thereby having the potential to more easily, and pragmatically, be "scaled up."

7. Grund and Brock state in their research that "hope and optimism are strongly connected to psychological and physical health. . . . Research has shown that hope is connected to pre-environmental behavior." Julius Grund, and Antje Brock, "Why We Should Empty Pandora's Box to Create a Sustainable Future: Hope, Sustainability and Its Implications for Education," *Sustainability* 11, no. 3 (2019): 1, https://doi.org/10.3390/su11030893.

8. The complete text is:

A man out of work, a man with empty hopes (κενεὴν ἐπί ἐλπίδα μίμνων)
And no livelihood, has a mind that runs to mischief (κακά).
It's [a] no good (οὐκ ἀγαθη) kind of hope [that] comes to a man who's broke
Sitting in the blacksmith's with no sure living. (Hesiod, *Works and Days*, ll. 498–501)

Cf. Oele, "Priam's Despair and Courage," 298–304.

9. Aristotle, *Nicomachean Ethics*, translated, glossary, and introduction by Joe Sachs (Newburyport, MA: Focus, 2002), III.8, 1117a10–14.

10. J. R. Marlon et al., "How Hope and Doubt Affect Climate Change Mobilization," *Frontiers in Communication* 4, no. 20 (2019): 1, doi: 10.3389/fcomm.2019.00020.

11. Christian Morgner, "Trust and Confidence: History, Theory and Socio-Political Implications," *Human Studies* 36 (2013): 516.

12. Esteban Marín-Ávila, "Hope and Trust as Conditions for Rational Actions in Society: A Phenomenological Approach," *Husserl Studies* 37, no. 3 (2021): 241.

13. "Trust, n.," *OED Online*, December 2021, last accessed May 10, 2023, https://www.oed.com/view/Entry/207004?rskey=787rIv&result=1&isAdvanced=false#eid.

14. *OED* lists the etymology accordingly: "Probably the reflex of an unattested Old English **trust* (perhaps cognate with Middle High German *getrüste* company, troop, and the Frankish etymon of post-classical Latin *trustis* retinue, bodyguard [*c*800 in the *Lex Salica*]) < the Germanic base of trust adj. Compare trust v., and also *traist* n., *trest* n.1, *trist* n.1 Related words in other Germanic languages. Compare (from an ablaut variant [*o* -grade] of the same Germanic base) Old Frisian *trāst* help, comfort, confidence (West Frisian *treast*), Old Dutch *trōst* consolation, encouragement

(Middle Dutch *troost* help, faith, courage, hope, support, encouragement, Dutch *troost* comfort), Old Saxon *trōst* support (Middle Low German *trōst* consolation, comfort, help, helper), Old High German *trōst* help, comfort, consolation (Middle High German *trōst* confidence, courage, comfort, help, security, protection, encouragement, German *Trost* emotional support, confidence, consolation), Old Icelandic *traust* faith, protection, shelter, safety, confidence, Old Swedish *tröst* confidence, assurance, security, help, consent, encouragement, Old Danish *trøst* (Danish *trøst*), and also (with different suffix) Gothic *trausti* bon." "Trust, n.," *OED Online*.

15. Victoria McGeer, "Trust, Hope and Empowerment," *Australasian Journal of Philosophy* 86, no. 2 (2008): 240.

16. Bernstein, "Trust," 395.

17. Bernstein, "Trust," 395.

18. Bernstein, "Trust," 402.

19. Bernstein, "Trust," 395.

20. Bernstein, "Trust," 399.

21. Butler, "Violence, Mourning, Politics," 13.

22. Annette C. Baier, *Moral Prejudices: Essays on Ethics* (Cambridge, MA: Harvard University Press, 1995), 149.

23. Godfrey, *Trust of People, Words, and God*, 59.

24. Godfrey, *Trust of People, Words and God*, 49.

25. Godfrey, *Trust of People, Words and God*, 39.

26. Godfrey, *Trust of People, Words, and God*, 45.

27. Godfrey, *Trust of People, Words, and God*, 49.

28. Godfrey, *Trust of People, Words, and God*, 87.

29. Godfrey, *Trust of People, Words, and God*, 87.

30. Godfrey, *Trust of People, Words, and God*, 88. He explains: "To trust is to have some good within the causal range or power of another, with beliefs, at least implied, that one is not thereby subject to ill will or impotence for effecting benefit; plus a non-veto of that affectability situation. In the case of affectability that one cannot avoid, to be receptive is to permit being affected, is to permit-to-affect" (88).

31. Bernstein, "Trust," 401.

32. Oele, *E-Co-Affectivity*, 134.

33. Katherine Hawley, "Trust, Distrust and Commitment," *Noûs* 48, no. 1 (2014): 2.

34. Georg Wilhelm Friedrich Hegel, *Elements of the Philosophy of Right*, ed. Allen W. Wood, trans. H. B. Nisbet (Cambridge: Cambridge University Press, 1991), §268.

35. Hegel, *Elements of the Philosophy of Right*; Stephen Houlgate, "Right and Trust in Hegel's *Philosophy of Right*," *Hegel Bulletin* 37, no. 1 (2016): 112.

36. Adriaan Peperzak, *Modern Freedom: Hegel's Legal, Moral, and Political Philosophy* (Dordrecht: Kluwer Academic, 2001), 500; emphasis added. In addition

to Peperzak's commentary, this section on Hegel is indebted to the helpful comments of Christian Lotz on the role of trust in Hegel.

37. Peperzak, *Modern Freedom*, 500.

38. Peperzak references Hegel's course Ilt 4 (642–643), citing the following passage: "Even when people reason very much about their time [and] their state, they stand completely in it; it is their soil. If it were taken away, they would fall into a void. *They have thus more trust than they themselves and others believe.* . . . If destruction began, they would do whatever they could to stop it; for they are children of their time [and] their state . . . Everybody is more patriotic than he thinks." Peperzak, *Modern Freedom*, 503; emphasis added.

39. Hegel, *Elements of the Philosophy of Right*, §309, 348.

40. Houlgate, "Right and Trust in Hegel's *Philosophy of Right*," 112.

41. Houlgate, "Right and Trust in Hegel's *Philosophy of Right*," 112.

42. Houlgate, "Right and Trust in Hegel's *Philosophy of Right*," 113.

43. Houlgate, "Right and Trust in Hegel's *Philosophy of Right*," 113.

44. Interestingly, Bernstein argues that "trust precedes practical reason as its condition of possibility." Bernstein, "Trust," 407.

45. Hegel, *Elements of the Philosophy of Right*, §309.

46. Houlgate, "Right and Trust in Hegel's *Philosophy of Right*," 114.

47. Houlgate, 'Right and Trust in Hegel's *Philosophy of Right*," 114.

48. Houlgate, 'Right and Trust in Hegel's *Philosophy of Right*," 115.

49. Houlgate, 'Right and Trust in Hegel's *Philosophy of Right*," 115.

50. Karl Marx, "Excerpts from James Mill's *Elements of Political Economy*" (1844), in Karl Marx, *Early Writings*, trans. Rodney Livingstone and Gregor Benton (New York: Penguin Classics, 1992), 263.

51. Maurizio Lazzarato, *The Making of the Indebted Man* (Los Angeles, CA: Semiotext(e), 2012), 58.

52. Lazzarato, *The Making of the Indebted Man*, 57.

53. Lazzarato, *The Making of the Indebted Man*, 58.

54. Marx, "Excerpts from James Mill's *Elements of Political Economy*," 263; Marx's italics.

55. Lazzarato, *The Making of the Indebted Man*, 58.

56. Marx, "Excerpts from James Mill's *Elements of Political Economy*," 265; Marx's italics.

57. Lazzarato, *The Making of the Indebted Man*, 130.

58. Lazzarato, *The Making of the Indebted Man*, 130.

59. Lazzarato, *The Making of the Indebted Man*, 136.

60. Bernard Stiegler, *What Makes Life Worth Living: On Pharmacology*, trans. Daniel Ross (Malden, MA: Polity Press, 2013), 59.

61. Stiegler, *What Makes Life Worth Living*, 64.

62. Stiegler, *What Makes Life Worth Living*, 62–63.

63. Stiegler, *What Makes Life Worth Living*, 64.

64. Stiegler, *What Makes Life Worth Living*, 65.
65. Stiegler, *What Makes Life Worth Living*, 76.
66. Stiegler, *What Makes Life Worth Living*, 65.
67. Stiegler, *Technics and Time, 1*, 198.
68. Derek Wall, *Elinor Ostrom's Rules for Radicals: Cooperative Alternatives beyond Markets and States* (London: Pluto Press, 2017), 79.
69. As example for the commons, *OED* references "natural global resources, such as the atmosphere, space, wilderness areas, fish in the oceans, etc. "Commons, n.," *OED Online*, last accessed May 10, 2023, https://www.oed.com/view/Entry/37254?isAdvanced=false&result=4&rskey=VSaUlW&.
70. Garrett Hardin, "The Tragedy of the Commons," *Science* 162, no. 3859 (1968): 1243–1244.
71. Hardin, "The Tragedy of the Commons," 1243–1244.
72. Aristotle, *Politics*, trans. C. D. C. Reeve (Indianapolis, IN: Hackett, 1998), 1261b.
73. Wall, *Elinor Ostrom's Rules for Radicals*, 21.
74. Another fierce critic of Hardin is Gary Snyder, who argues in *The Practice of the Wild* that what Hardin calls a problem of the commons is actually a modern economic dilemma, that of "the dilemma of common-pool resources," which has to do with the problem of "overexploitation of 'unowned' resources" (35) and is different from the commons. Snyder defines the commons as "a social institution which, historically, was never without rules and did not allow unlimited access" (35), or, said differently, included "a level of organization of human society that includes the non-human" (36). Gary Snyder, *The Practice of the Wild: Essays* (Berkeley, CA: North Point Press, 1990).
75. Paul Dragos Aligica, "Rethinking Institutional Analysis: Interviews with Vincent and Elinor Ostrom," Mercatus Center, October 12, 2009, https://www.mercatus.org/research/research-papers/rethinking-institutional-analysis-interviews-vincent-and-elinor-ostrom.
76. Michael McGinnis and Elinor Ostrom, "Institutional Analysis and Global Climate Change: Design Principles for Robust International Regimes," *Global Climate Change: Social and Economic Research Issues* (1992): 52.
77. "Common, adj. and adv.," *OED Online*, last accessed May 10, 2023, https://www.oed.com/view/Entry/37216?rskey=KgiP7C&result=3&isAdvanced=false#eid.
78. "The robust CPR institutions originally included grazing and forest CPR institutions in Switzerland and Japan and irrigation systems in Spain and the Philippine Islands. Since then, many more cases of robust CPR institutions have been studied, particularly related to irrigation systems." McGinnis and Ostrom, "Institutional Analysis and Global Climate Change," 54.
79. McGinnis and Ostrom, "Institutional Analysis and Global Climate Change," 54.

80. McGinnis and Ostrom, "Institutional Analysis and Global Climate Change," 54.
81. McGinnis and Ostrom, "Institutional Analysis and Global Climate Change," 54.
82. McGinnis and Ostrom, "Institutional Analysis and Global Climate Change," 54.
83. McGinnis and Ostrom, "Institutional Analysis and Global Climate Change," 54.
84. For a helpful overview, see also Erik Nordman, *The Uncommon Knowledge of Elinor Ostrom: Essential Lessons for Collective Action* (Washington, DC: Island Press, 2021), 76.
85. Thus, for any participants to have a minimal interest in coordinating patterns of appropriation and provision, some set of participants has to be able to exclude others from access and appropriation rights. McGinnis and Ostrom, "Institutional Analysis and Global Climate Change," 55.
86. Illustration in the case of Zanjeras in the Philippines: "These self-organized systems obtain use-rights to previously unirrigated land from a large landowner by building a canal that irrigates the landowner's land and that of a zanjera. At the time that the land is allocated, each farmer willing to abide by the rules of the system receives a bundle of rights and duties in the form of Atars. Each Atar defines three parcels of land located in the head, middle, and tail sections of the service area where the holder grows his or her crops. Responsibilities for construction and maintenance are allocated by Atars, as are voting rights. In the rainy seasons, water is allocated freely. In a dry year, water may be allocated only to the parcels located in the head and middle portions. Thus, everyone receives water in plentiful and scarce times in rough proportion to the amount of Atars they possess. Atars may be sold to others with the permission of the irrigation association and they are heritable." McGinnis and Ostrom, "Institutional Analysis and Global Climate Change," 55.
87. McGinnis and Ostrom, "Institutional Analysis and Global Climate Change," 56.
88. McGinnis and Ostrom, "Institutional Analysis and Global Climate Change," 56.
89. Example: "The costs of monitoring are kept relatively low in many of the long-enduring CPUs as a result of the rules-in-use. Water rotation systems, for example, usually place the two actors most concerned with cheating in direct contact with one another. The irrigator who nears the end of a rotation turn would like to extend the time of his turn (and thus the amount of water obtained). The next irrigator in the rotation system waits nearby for him to finish and would even like to start early. The presence of the first irrigator deters the second from an early start, and the presence of the second irrigator deters the first from a late ending. Neither has to invest additional resources in monitoring activities.

Monitoring is a by-product of their own strong motivations to use their water rotation turn to the fullest extent." McGinnis and Ostrom, "Institutional Analysis and Global Climate Change," 57.

90. McGinnis and Ostrom, "Institutional Analysis and Global Climate Change," 58.

91. McGinnis and Ostrom, "Institutional Analysis and Global Climate Change," 58.

92. McGinnis and Ostrom, "Institutional Analysis and Global Climate Change," 58.

93. Wall, *Elinor Ostrom's Rules for Radicals*, 32.

94. Wall, *Elinor Ostrom's Rules for Radicals*, 32.

95. "All of the more complex, enduring CPRs meet this last design principle. This is probably one of the most important design principles when one begins to think about global rather than local CPRs. If different environmental zones need to be regulated in diverse manners in order to achieve the same outcomes, it is quite essential that there be governance mechanisms at all levels and ways of effectively communicating and resolving conflict between units at one level and across levels." McGinnis and Ostrom, "Institutional Analysis and Global Climate Change," 58.

96. Wall, *Elinor Ostrom's Rules for Radicals*, 36.

97. Elinor Ostrom, "A General Framework for Analyzing Sustainability of Social-Ecological Systems," *Science* 325, no. 5939 (2009): 419.

98. Ostrom, "A General Framework for Analyzing Sustainability of Social-Ecological Systems," 420.

99. Wall, *Elinor Ostrom's Rules for Radicals*, 38.

100. McGinnis and Ostrom, "Institutional Analysis and Global Climate Change," 59.

101. McGinnis and Ostrom, "Institutional Analysis and Global Climate Change," 59.

102. McGinnis and Ostrom, "Institutional Analysis and Global Climate Change," 50.

103. They argue, "Even though it is impossible to completely decompose global problems into entirely discrete subproblems, working upward may enable solutions to be reached faster than starting from the global and working downward—at least for some subset of problems." McGinnis and Ostrom, "Institutional Analysis and Global Climate Change," 59.

104. McGinnis and Ostrom, "Institutional Analysis and Global Climate Change," 50.

105. McGinnis and Ostrom, "Institutional Analysis and Global Climate Change," 50.

106. McGinnis and Ostrom, "Institutional Analysis and Global Climate Change," 50.

107. McGinnis and Ostrom, "Institutional Analysis and Global Climate Change," 59.

108. McGinnis and Ostrom, "Institutional Analysis and Global Climate Change," 60.

109. McGinnis and Ostrom, "Institutional Analysis and Global Climate Change," 60.

110. Elinor Ostrom, "Building Trust to Solve Commons Dilemmas: Taking Small Steps to Test an Evolving Theory of Collective Action," in *Games, Groups, and the Global Good*, ed. Simon A. Levin (New York: Springer, 2008), 25, available at SSRN: https://ssrn.com/abstract=1304695, accessed June 28, 2024.

111. Ostrom, "Building Trust to Solve Commons Dilemmas," 12.

112. Wall, *Elinor Ostrom's Rules for Radicals*, 86. Reference is to Elinor Ostrom, "A Behavioral Approach to the Rational Choice Theory of Collective Action: Presidential Address, American Political Science Association, 1997," *American Political Science Review* 92, no. 1 (1998): 1–22.

113. I owe this phrasing to Jason Wirth, "Life beyond the Anthropocene: The Human and Ecological Attunement," London, Ontario, March 17–19, 2023. Wirth's phrasing resonates with Gary Snyder's view on the commons, and the "resolution" he has in mind for a new age beyond thinking in terms of common pool resources: "We need to make a world-scale 'Natural Contract' with the oceans, the air, the birds in the sky. The challenge is to bring the whole victimized world of 'common pool resources' into the Mind of the Commons. . . . Take back, like the night, that which is shared by all of us, that which is our larger being. There will be no 'tragedy of the commons' greater that this: if we do not recover the commons—regain personal, local, community, and peoples' direct involvement in sharing (in *being*) the web of the wild world—that world will keep slipping away." Snyder, *The Practice of the Wild*, 36.

114. Serres, *Biogea*, 77.

115. Serres, *Biogea*, 72.

116. Serres, *Biogea*, 71, 75.

117. Serres, *Biogea*, 71.

118. Serres, *Biogea*, 79.

119. In what follows here, I use some of the arguments I have made elsewhere, for instance, in this co-written chapter: "Michel Serres and Ecological Crisis: Listening to the World's Expressions," co-authored with Brian Treanor, in *Continental Philosophy and the History of Thought: Inaugural Volume*, ed. Antonio Calcagno and Christian Lotz (Lanham, MD: Lexington Books, 2023), 79–100.

120. Serres, *Biogea*, 13–14.

121. Serres, *Biogea*, 16.

122. Daniel R. Wildcat, *Red Alert: Saving the Planet with Indigenous Knowledge* (Wheat Ridge, CO: Fulcrum, 2009), 9.

123. Wildcat, *Red Alert*, 133.
124. Wildcat, *Red Alert*, 102–103.
125. Wildcat, *Red Alert*, 103.
126. Haraway, *Staying with the Trouble*, 2.
127. Christopher J. Preston, *Tenacious Beasts: Wildlife Recoveries That Change How We Think about Animals* (Cambridge, MA: MIT Press, 2023), 103.
128. Preston, *Tenacious Beasts*, 107.
129. Preston, *Tenacious Beasts*, 113–114.
130. Preston, *Tenacious Beasts*, 106.
131. As Preston also accedes, to rebuild ecosystems, not just removal of dams is needed. At times, it may include the need for certain human-made dams, or seeking to allow other nonhuman engineers, such as beavers, to do the work. Preston, *Tenacious Beasts*, 115.
132. He traces this idea back to the etymology of decision: "'de-cision' means to cut in two, as with scissors." Michel Serres, *Times of Crisis: What the Financial Crisis Revealed and How to Reinvent Our Lives and Future*, trans. Anne-Marie Feenberg-Dibon (New York: Bloomsbury, 2014), xi.
133. I owe this idea to Chiara Cappelletto, in our conversation on October 21, 2022.
134. Michel Foucault, *Fearless Speech*, ed. Joseph Pearson (Los Angeles, CA: Semiotext(e), 2001), 19.
135. "Deru-/Proto-Indo-European Roots," *Etymology Online*, https://www.etymonline.com/word/*deru-, accessed June 26, 2024. I owe this insight to Jeremy Bendik-Keymer. Interestingly, the etymology of *deru* also relates to trees (and wood) and is thus reminiscent of the earlier discussion of sequoia trees in chapter 2. I owe this latter thoughtful insight to one of the anonymous peer reviewers of the manuscript for this book.
136. Jonas's position is clarified here: "If there is a risk that our actions could do harm to future existence, we should treat this hypothetical knowledge as if it is a fact. The slightest possibility of future harm should guide our actions. Our fear for disaster must be a guiding principle: It is through our fear of disasters that we notice what is valuable, and this will in turn affect our moral character." Hein Berdinesen, "On Hans Jonas' 'The Imperative of Responsibility,'" *Philosophia* 17 (2017): https://philosophia-bg.com/archive/philosophia-17-2017/on-hans-jonas-the-imperative-of-responsibility.
137. Rita Felski, "Critique and the Hermeneutics of Suspicion," *M/C Journal* 15, no. 1 (2012): 2, https://doi.org/10.5204/mcj.431.
138. I owe this idea to Jason Wirth, in our conversation on March 18, 2023.
139. As Onora O'Neill writes: "Aligning trust with trustworthiness and mistrust with untrustworthiness is not simple. It requires intelligent judgment of others' trustworthiness or untrustworthiness, and the available evidence may

not reveal clearly which agents and which institutions are trustworthy in which matters." Onora O'Neill, "Questioning Truth," in *The Routledge Handbook of Trust and Philosophy*, ed. Judith Simon (New York: Routledge, 2020), 19.

140. In the context of institutional life, O'Neill defines this practice in the following way: "Forward-looking measures include establishing clearer and stricter requirements for trustworthy action, and for demonstrating trustworthiness, as well as strong measures to deter and penalize untrustworthy action." O'Neill, "Questioning Truth," 21.

141. In this observation, Scheman is referencing the historical case of building trust in the context of distrust in medication for HIV. Naomi Scheman, "Trust and Trustworthiness," in *The Routledge Handbook of Trust and Philosophy*, ed. Judith Simon (New York: Routledge, 2020), 37.

Bibliography

Abram, David. *The Spell of the Sensuous: Perception and Language in a More-than-Human World.* New York: Vintage Books / Penguin Random House, 2017.
Adey, Peter. *Air.* London: Reaktion Books, 2014.
Ahlzén, Rolf. "Illness as Unhomelike Being-in-the-World? Phenomenology and Medical Practice." *Medical Health Care and Philosophy* 14 (2011): 323–331.
Alaimo, Stacy. "Elemental Love in the Anthropocene." In *Elemental Ecocriticism: Thinking with Earth, Air, Water, and Fire,* edited by Jeffrey Jerome Cohen and Lowell Duckert, 298–309. London: University of Minnesota Press, 2015.
Albrecht, Glenn A. *Earth Emotions: New Words for a New World.* Ithaca, NY: Cornell University Press, 2019.
Albrecht, Glenn. "Solastalgia and the New Mourning." In *Mourning Nature: Hope at the Heart of Ecological Loss and Grief,* edited by Ashlee Cunsolo and Karen Landman, 292–315. Montreal: McGill-Queen's University Press, 2017.
Alexander, Gregory S., Eduardo M. Peñalver, Joseph W. Singer, and Laura S. Underkuffler. "A Statement of Progressive Property." *Cornell Law Faculty Publications* 11 (2009): https://scholarship.law.cornell.edu/facpub/11.
Aligica, Paul Dragos. "Rethinking Institutional Analysis: Interviews with Vincent and Elinor Ostrom." Mercatus Center, October 12, 2009. https://www.mercatus.org/research/research-papers/rethinking-institutional-analysis-interviews-vincent-and-elinor-ostrom.
Allan, Richard P., Paola A. Arias, Sophie Berger, Josep G. Canadell, Christophe Cassou, Deliang Chen, Annalisa Cherchi, et al. *Climate Change 2021: The Physical Science Basis—Summary for Policy Makers.* Geneva: IPCC, 2021. https://www.ipcc.ch/report/ar6/wg1/downloads/report/IPCC_AR6_WGI_SPM_final.pdf.
Amazonian-Museum-Network.Org. "De Stichting Surinaams Museum." Accessed October 31, 2022. http://amazonian-museum-network.org/nl/amazone-museum/stichting-surinaams-museum-nl.
Aristotle. *De Caelo.* Translated by C. D. C. Reeve. Indianapolis, IN: Hackett, 2020.

Bibliography

Aristotle. *Meteorologica*. Translated by H. D. P. Lee. Cambridge, MA: Harvard University Press, 1952.

Aristotle. *Nicomachean Ethics*. Translated, glossary, and introduction by Joe Sachs. Newburyport, MA: Focus, 2002.

Aristotle. *On Generation and Corruption*. Translated by E. S. Forster and D. J. Furley. Cambridge, MA: Harvard University Press, 1965.

Aristotle. *Politics*. Translated by C. D. C. Reeve. Indianapolis, IN: Hackett, 1998.

Auster, Paul. Introduction to *On the High Wire*, by Philippe Petit, ix–xxv. New York: New Directions Books, 2019.

Bachelard, Gaston. *Air and Dreams: An Essay on the Imagination of Movement*. Translated by Edith R. Farrell and C. Frederick Farrell. Dallas, TX: Dallas Institute of Humanities and Culture, 1988.

Bachelard, Gaston. *The Psychoanalysis of Fire*. Translated by Alan C. M. Ross. Boston, MA: Beacon Press, 1964.

Bachelard, Gaston. *Water and Dreams: An Essay on the Imagination of Matter*. Translated by Edith R. Farrell. Dallas, TX: Dallas Institute of Humanities and Culture, 1983.

Baier, Annette C. *Moral Prejudices: Essays on Ethics*. Cambridge, MA: Harvard University Press, 1995.

Baker, David R. "The California Rule That Doomed PG&E: Inverse Condemnation." *Bloomberg*, January 15, 2019. https://www.bloomberg.com/news/articles/2019-01-15/the-california-rule-that-doomed-pg-e-inverse-condemnation.

Barber, Elizabeth J. W., and Paul Barber. *When They Severed Earth from Sky: How the Human Mind Shapes Myth*. Princeton, NJ: Princeton University Press, 2004.

Bennett, Jane. *Influx and Efflux: Writing Up with Walt Whitman*. Durham, NC: Duke University Press, 2020.

Benyus, Janine M. *Biomimicry: Innovation Inspired by Nature*. New York: Quill, 1998.

Berdinesen, Hein. "On Hans Jonas' 'The Imperative of Responsibility.'" *Philosophia* 17 (2017): https://philosophia-bg.com/archive/philosophia-17-2017/on-hans-jonas-the-imperative-of-responsibility.

Berlant, Lauren. "Slow Death (Sovereignty, Obesity, Lateral Agency)." *Critical Inquiry* 33, no. 4 (2007): 754–780.

Bernstein, J. M. "Trust: On the Real but Almost Unnoticed, Ever-Changing Foundation of Ethical Life," *Metaphilosophy* 42, no. 4 (July 2011): 395–416.

Besterman, Theodore. *Voltaire Essays, and Another*. Oxford: Oxford University Press, 1962.

Blackburn, Thomas C., and Kat Anderson. "Introduction: Managing the Domesticated Environment." In *Before the Wilderness: Environmental Management by Native Californians*, ed. Thomas C. Blackburn and Kat Anderson, 1–12. Menlo Park, CA: Ballena Press, 1993.

BN DeStem. "Onder water zit het niet goed in de Oosterschelde." *Total Fishing.* Accessed May 16, 2020. http://www.totalfishing.nl/laatste-nieuws/articles/onder-water-zit-het-niet-goed-in-de-oosterschelde.

Bobroff, Kenneth H. "Retelling Allotment: Indian Property Rights and the Myth of Common Ownership." *Vanderbilt Law Review* 54, no. 4 (May 2001): 1559–1623.

Boss, Pauline. *The Myth of Closure: Ambiguous Loss in a Time of Pandemic and Change.* New York: W. W. Norton, 2021.

Boström, Sally Anderson. "*Waves of Knowing: A Seascape Epistemology.* By Karin Amimoto Ingersoll." *Interdisciplinary Studies in Literature and Environment* 24, no. 4 (2017): 829–831.

Britton, Celia. *Edouard Glissant and Postcolonial Theory: Strategies of Language and Resistance.* Charlottesville: University of Virginia Press, 1999.

Buber, Martin. *I and Thou.* Translated by Ronald Gregor Smith. New York: Charles Scribner's Sons, 1958.

Buraniyi, Stephen. "The Air Conditioning Trap: How Cold Air Is Heating the World." *The Guardian*, August 29, 2019. https://www.theguardian.com/environment/2019/aug/29/the-air-conditioning-trap-how-cold-air-is-heating-the-world.

Burkert, Walter. *Greek Religion: Archaic and Classical.* Translated by John Raffan. Malden, MA: Blackwell, 1991.

Butler, Judith. "Violence, Mourning, Politics." *Studies in Gender and Sexuality* 4, no. 1 (2003): 9–37.

Butler, Judith. *What World Is This? A Pandemic Phenomenology.* New York: Columbia University Press, 2022.

CAL Fire. "Kincade Fire." Last modified October 23, 2019, accessed on June 25, 2024. https://www.fire.ca.gov/incidents/2019/10/23/kincade-fire.

California Lutheran University. "Fire-Inspired Art Exhibit at Cal Lutheran." October 4, 2018. https://www.callutheran.edu/news/story.html?id=13655#story.

Callicott, J. Baird, John van Buren, and Keith Wayne Brown. *Greek Natural Philosophy: The Presocratics and Their Importance for Environmental Philosophy.* San Diego, CA: Cognella Academic, 2018.

Chawla, Saroj. "Linguistic and Philosophical Roots of Our Environmental Crisis." In *The Ecolinguistics Reader: Language, Ecology, and Environment*, edited by Alwin Fill and Peter Mühlhäusler, 115–112. London: Continuum, 2001.

Clare, Stephanie D. *Earthly Encounters: Sensation, Feminist Theory, and the Anthropocene.* Albany: State University of New York Press, 2019.

Coates, Ta-Nehisi. *Between the World and Me.* New York: One World / Random House, 2015.

Cohen, Jeffrey Jerome, and Lowell Duckert. "Introduction: Eleven Principles of the Elements." In *Elemental Ecocriticism: Thinking with Earth, Air, Water, and Fire*, edited by Jeffrey Jerome Cohen and Lowell Duckert, 1–26. London: University of Minnesota Press, 2015.

Cohen, Paul (@paul_e_cohen@mastodon.social). "On the one hand, the @nytimes in-depth piece on Haitian 'reparations' to France brings much-needed attention onto a decisive moment in world history . . ." Twitter, May 21, 2022. https://twitter.com/Paul_E_Cohen/status/1528053592946528256.
"Common, adj. and adv." *OED Online*, last accessed May 10, 2023. https://www.oed.com/view/Entry/37216?rskey=KgiP7C&result=3&isAdvanced=false#eid.
"Commons, n." *OED Online*, last accessed May 10, 2023. https://www.oed.com/view/Entry/37254?isAdvanced=false&result=4&rskey=VSaUlW&.
Cozzoli, Francesco, Sven Smolders, Menno Eelkema, Tom Ysebaert, Vincent Escaravage, Stijn Temmerman, Patrick Meire, Peter M. J. Herman, and Tjeerd J. Bouma. "A Modeling Approach to Assess Coastal Management Effects on Benthic Habitat Quality: A Case Study on Coastal Defense and Navigability." *Estuarine, Coastal and Shelf Science* 184 (2017): 67–82.
Cronon, William. Foreword to Stephen J. Pyne, *Fire: A Brief History*. London: British Museum Press, 2001, xi–xiv.
Curaçao Maritime Museum. "Curaçao, an Island of Harbors." Accessed May 11, 2020. https://www.curacaomaritime.com/history.
Darwin, Charles. *The Voyage of the Beagle*. New York: Penguin Books, 1989.
Day, Brian L., and Richard C. Fitzpatrick. "The Vestibular System." *Current Biology* 15, no. 15 (2005): https://doi.org/10.1016/j.cub.2005.07.053.
de Jong, Nanette. "Curaçao and the Folding Diaspora: Contesting the Party Tambú in the Netherlands." *Black Music Research Journal* 32, no. 2 (2012): 67–81.
de Jong, Nanette. "The Tambú of Curaçao: Historical Projections and the Ritual Map of Experience." *Black Music Research Journal* 30, no. 2 (2010): 197–214.
de Munck, Cécile, Grégoire Pigeon, Valéry Masson, Francis Meunier, Pierre Bousquet, Brice Tréméac, Michèle Merchat, Pierre Poeuf, and Colette Marchadier. "How Much Can Air Conditioning Increase Air Temperature for a City Like Paris, France?" *International Journal of Climatology* 33, no. 1 (2013): 210–227.
Derrida, Jacques. *Cinders*. Minneapolis: University of Minnesota Press, 2014.
"Deru- / Proto-Indo-European Root." *Etymology Online*, last accessed June 26, 2024. https://www.etymonline.com/word/*deru-.
Despret, Vinciane. "Afterword: It Is an Entire World That Has Disappeared." In *Extinction Studies: Stories of Time, Death, and Generations*, edited by Deborah Bird Rose, Thom van Dooren, and Matthew Chrulew, 217–222. New York: Columbia University Press, 2017.
"Does the Production of Oil and Gas from Shales Cause Earthquakes? If So, How Are the Earthquakes Related to These Operations?" United States Geological Survey. Last accessed April 5, 2023. https://www.usgs.gov/faqs/does-production-oil-and-gas-shales-cause-earthquakes-if-so-how-are-earthquakes-related-these.

Doyle, Timothy, and Melissa Risely. *Crucible for Survival: Environmental Security and Justice in the Indian Ocean Region*. New Brunswick, NJ: Rutgers University Press, 2008.

Drabinski, John E. *Glissant and the Middle Passage: Philosophy, Beginning, Abyss*. Minneapolis: University of Minnesota Press, 2019.

Dvorak, John. *Earthquake Storms: The Fascinating History and Volatile Future of the San Andreas Fault*. New York: Pegasus Books, 2014.

Dyl, Joanna Leslie, and Paul Sutter. *Seismic City: An Environmental History of San Francisco's 1906 Earthquake*. Seattle: University of Washington Press, 2017.

The Editors of Encyclopedia Britannica. "Zeeland." *Encyclopedia Britannica*, last modified June 20, 2011. https://www.britannica.com/place/Zeeland-province-Netherlands.

Emily, Grade 11, 2004 Young Naturalist Winner. "Morphologic Variation in the Common Periwinkle." American Museum of Natural History, accessed October 31, 2022. https://www.amnh.org/learn-teach/curriculum-collections/young-naturalist-awards/winning-essays/2004/morphologic-variation-in-the-common-periwinkle.

Emmen, Ton. *De kwetsbaarheid van de Zeeuwen: Factoren die de kwetsbaarheid en veerkracht van de bevolking ten aanzien van dreiging van overstromingen vanuit zee beïnvloeden*. Online publication, 2002, accessed May 16, 2020. https://www.ifv.nl/kennisplein/Documents/emmen-4-de-kwetsbaarheid-van-de-zeeuwen.pdf.

Empedocles. *The Fragments of Empedocles*. Edited and translated by William Ellery Leonard. LaSalle, IL: Open Court, 1973.

Engels, Friedrich. *The Condition of the Working Class in England*. London: Panther, 1969.

Felski, Rita. "Critique and the Hermeneutics of Suspicion." *M/C Journal* 15, no. 1 (2012): https://doi.org/10.5204/mcj.431.

Fitzgerald, Gerard J. "Chemical Warfare and Medical Response during World War I." *American Journal of Public Health* 98, no. 4 (April 2008): 611–625, 10.2105/AJPH.2007.11930.

Foucault, Michel. *Fearless Speech*. Edited by Joseph Pearson. Los Angeles, CA: Semiotext(e), 2001.

Glissant, Édouard. *Poetics of Relation*. Translated by Betsy Wing. Ann Arbor: University of Michigan Press, 1997.

Godfrey, Joseph. *Trust of People, Words, and God: A Route for Philosophy of Religion*. Notre Dame, IN: University of Notre Dame Press, 2012.

Gonzales, Tirso A., and Melissa K. Nelson. "Contemporary Native American Responses to Environmental Threats in Indian Country." In *Indigenous Traditions and Ecology: The Interbeing of Cosmology and Community*, edited by John Grim, 495–538. Cambridge, MA: Harvard University Press, 2001.

Government of the Netherlands. "What Are the Different Parts of the Kingdom of the Netherlands?" Accessed May 20, 2021. https://www.government.nl/topics/caribbean-parts-of-the-kingdom/question-and-answer/what-are-the-different-parts-of-the-kingdom-of-the-netherlands.

Graham, Daniel W. "Anaximenes." *Internet Encyclopedia of Philosophy*, last accessed February 8, 2023. https://iep.utm.edu/anaximenes/.

Graham, Daniel W. "A New Look at Anaximenes." *History of Philosophy Quarterly* 20, no. 1 (2003): 1–20.

Graham, Daniel W. "Plato and Anaximenes." *Études Platoniciennes* 12 (2015): 1–28, https://doi.org/10.4000/etudesplatoniciennes.706.

Graham, Daniel W. *The Texts of Early Greek Philosophy: The Complete Fragments and Selected Testimonies of the Major Presocratics*, part 1. Cambridge: Cambridge University Press, 2010.

Graham, Stephen. "Life Support: The Political Ecology of Urban Air." *City* 19, nos. 2–3 (2015): 192–215.

Grund, Julius, and Antje Brock. "Why We Should Empty Pandora's Box to Create a Sustainable Future: Hope, Sustainability and Its Implications for Education." *Sustainability* 11, no. 3 (2019): 1–20, https://doi.org/10.3390/su11030893.

Guenther, Lisa. *Solitary Confinement: Social Death and Its Afterlives*. Minneapolis: University of Minnesota Press, 2013.

Guerrero, Brandon. "Hell Is a Place on Earth: USF Existentialism Paper." University of San Francisco, San Francisco, California, May 15, 2020.

Gupta, Saloni, Barry T. Rouse, and Pranita P. Sarangi. "Did Climate Change Influence the Emergence, Transmission, and Expression of the COVID-19 Pandemic?" *Frontiers in Medicine* (Lausanne) 8, no. 8 (December 2021):769208, doi: 10.3389/fmed.2021.769208. PMID: 34957147; PMCID: PMC8694059.

Haase, Annegret. "Covid-19 as a Social Crisis and Justice Challenge for Cities." *Frontiers in Sociology* 5 (2020): 1–7, https://doi.org/10.3389/fsoc.2020.583638.

Hakkenes, Emiel. *Gas: Het Verhaal van een Nederlandse Bodemschat*. Amsterdam: Thomas Rap, 2020.

Hal, Ralf van, Oscar Georg Bos, and Robbert Gerbrand Jak. "Noordzee: Systeemdynamiek, Klimaatverandering, Natuurtypen en Benthos; Achtergronddocument bij Natuurverkenning 2011." *Wageningen, Wettelijke Onderzoekstaken Natuur en Milieu* 255 (2011): 1–93.

Haraway, Donna J. *Staying with the Trouble: Making Kin in the Chthulucene*. Durham, NC: Duke University Press, 2016.

Hardin, Garrett. "The Tragedy of the Commons." *Science* 162, no. 3859 (1968): 1243–1248.

Havelock, Eric A. "The Cosmic Myths of Homer and Hesiod." *Oral Tradition* 2, no. 1 (1987): 31–53.

Havens, G. R. "Voltaire's Pessimistic Revision of the Conclusion of His *Poème sur le désastre de Lisbonne*." *Modern Language Notes* 44, no. 8 (December 1929): 489–492.

Hawley, Katherine. "Trust, Distrust and Commitment." *Noûs* 48, no. 1 (2014): 1–20.
Helland, Leonardo E. Figueroa, Abigail Perez Aguilera, and Felix Mantz. "Decolonize, ReIndigenize: Planetary Crisis, Bioculture Diversity, Indigenous Resurgence, and Land Rematriation." In *Contesting Extinctions: Decolonial and Regenerative Futures*, edited by Suzanne M. McCullagh, Luis I. Prádanos, Ilaria Tabusso Marcyan, and Catherine Wagner, 23–62. Lanham, MD: Lexington Books, 2021.
Hegel, Georg Wilhelm Friedrich. *Elements of the Philosophy of Right*. Edited by Allen W. Wood. Translated by H. B. Nisbet. Cambridge: Cambridge University Press, 1991.
Heidegger, Martin. *Being and Time*. Translated by John Macquarrie and Edward Robinson. Oxford: Blackwell, 1962.
Heidegger, Martin. *An Introduction to Metaphysics*. Translated by Ralph Manheim. New Haven, CT: Yale University Press, 1973.
Heraclitus. "Fragments." In *Ancient Greek Philosophy: From Thales to Aristotle*, edited by S. Marc Cohen, Patricia Curd, and C. D. C. Reeve. Indianapolis, IN: Hackett, 2005.
Herder, Johann Gottfried. *Outlines of a Philosophy of the History of Man*. Translated by T. Churchill. New York: Bergman, 1966.
Heryford, Ryan. "'The Word for Bringing Bodies Back from Water': Black Oceanic Ecopoetics and the Re-imagining of Extinction." In *Contesting Extinctions: Decolonial and Regenerative Futures*, edited by Suzanne M. McCullagh, Luis I. Prádanos, Ilaria Tabusso Marcyan, and Catherine Wagner, 63–84. Lanham, MD: Lexington Books, 2021.
Hesiod. *Works and Days and Theogony*. Translated by Stanley Lombardo. Indianapolis, IN: Hackett, 1993.
The History Press. "The Devastating Storm of 1953." Accessed October 31, 2022. https://www.thehistorypress.co.uk/articles/the-devastating-storm-of-1953.
Hoetink, Harmannus. "Netherlands Antilles." *Encyclopedia Britannica*, last modified September 27, 2022. https://www.britannica.com/place/Netherlands-Antilles.
Homer. *The Iliad*. Translated by Richmond Lattimore. Chicago: University of Chicago Press, 1951.
Houlgate, Stephen. "Right and Trust in Hegel's *Philosophy of Right*." *Hegel Bulletin* 37, no. 1 (2016): 104–116.
"How Oil and Gas Disposal Wells Can Cause Earthquakes." *StateImpact*, last accessed April 5, 2023. https://stateimpact.npr.org/texas/tag/earthquake/.
Howard, Rachel. "Review: S.F. Ballet Brings Audiences to 'The Promised Land' and beyond with Electric New Works." *San Francisco Chronicle*, last updated April 11, 2022. https://datebook.sfchronicle.com/dance/review-s-f-ballet-brings-audiences-to-the-promised-land-and-beyond-with-electric-new-works.
Ingersoll, Karin Amimoto. *Waves of Knowing: A Seascape Epistemology*. Durham, NC: Duke University Press, 2016.

Iovino, Nicholas. "PG&E Slapped with $125M Penalty for Sparking 2019 Kincade Fire." *Courthouse News Service*, November 2, 2021, accessed on June 25, 2024. https://www.courthousenews.com/pge-slapped-with-125m-penalty-for-sparking-2019-kincade-fire.

Irigaray, Luce. *Elemental Passions*. Translated by Joanne Collie and Judith Still. New York: Routledge, 1992.

Irigaray, Luce. *The Forgetting of Air in Martin Heidegger*. Translated by Mary Beth Mader. Austin: University of Texas Press, 1999.

Irigaray, Luce. "From *The Forgetting of Air* to *To Be Two*." In *Feminist Interpretations of Martin Heidegger*, edited by Nancy J. Holland and Patricia Huntington, 309–315. University Park: Pennsylvania State University Press, 2001.

Irigaray, Luce. *Marine Lover*. Translated by Gillian C. Gill. New York: Columbia University Press, 1991.

Irigaray, Luce. *Speculum of the Other Woman*. Translated by Gillian C. Gill. Ithaca, NY: Cornell University Press, 1985.

Jones, Rachel. "Kant, Irigaray, and Earthquakes: Adventures in the Abyss." *Symposium* 17, no. 1 (2013): 273–299.

Jönsson, Håkan, Maxime Michaud, and Niklas Neuman. "What Is Commensality? A Critical Discussion of an Expanding Research Field." *International Journal of Environmental Research and Public Health* 18, no. 12 (June 2021): doi: 10.3390.

Kant, Immanuel. "Continued Observations on the Earthquakes That Have Been Experienced for Some Time (1756)." In *Natural Science*, edited by Eric Watkins, 365–373. Cambridge: Cambridge University Press, 2012.

Kant, Immanuel. *Critique of Judgment*. Translated by Werner S. Pluhar. Indianapolis, IN: Hackett, 1987.

Kant, Immanuel. "History and Natural Description of the Most Noteworthy Occurrences of the Earthquake That Struck a Large Part of the Earth at the End of the Year 1755 (1756)." In *Natural Science*, edited by Eric Watkins, 337–364. Cambridge: Cambridge University Press, 2012.

Kant, Immanuel. Introduction to *Natural Science*, edited by Eric Watkins, xiii–xviii. Cambridge: Cambridge University Press, 2012.

Kant, Immanuel. "On the Causes of Earthquakes on the Occasion of the Calamity That Befell the Western Countries of Europe toward the End of Last Year (1756)." In *Natural Science*, edited by Eric Watkins, 327–336. Cambridge: Cambridge University Press, 2012.

Katz, Daniel S. W., et al. "The Effects of Tree Planting on Allergenic Pollen Production in New York City." *Urban Forestry and Urban Greening* 92, no. 128208 (2024): 1–10.

Katz, Jonathan M. *The Big Truck That Went By: How the World Came to Save Haiti and Left Behind a Disaster*. New York: Palgrave Macmillan, 2013.

Kennedy, Jennifer. "Crustaceans: Species, Characteristics, and Diet." ThoughtCo, last modified December 13, 2019. https://www.thoughtco.com/crustaceans-profile-and-facts-2291816.

Kilgore, Bruce M. "Fire's Role in a Sequoia Forest." Sequoia and Kings Canyon, National Park Service, last modified May 20, 2017. https://www.nps.gov/seki/learn/nature/fic_firerole.htm.

Kinuthia, Samuel. "What Is the Intertidal Zone?" *World Atlas*, last modified January 10, 2018. https://www.worldatlas.com/articles/what-is-the-intertidal-zone.html.

Kirk, G. S., J. E. Raven, and M. Schofield. *The Presocratic Philosophers: A Critical History with a Selection of Texts*. Cambridge: Cambridge University Press, 2007.

Kirk, G. S, J. E. Raven, and M. Schofield. "Xenophanes of Colophon." In *The Prehistoric Philosophers: A Critical History with a Selection of Texts, Second Edition*, 163–180. Cambridge: Cambridge University Press, 1983.

Kluge, Hans Henri P. "Statement—Climate Change Is Already Killing Us, but Strong Action Now Can Prevent More Deaths." World Health Organization, November 2022. https://www.who.int/europe/news/item/07-11-2022-statement---climate-change-is-already-killing-us--but-strong-action-now-can-prevent-more-deaths.

Knecht, Jaclynn. "5 Reasons to Take the Job You Don't Want." Career Contessa, last accessed February 15, 2023. https://www.careercontessa.com/advice/the-job-you-dont-want/.

Kolbert, Elizabeth. *The Sixth Extinction: An Unnatural History*. New York: Picador, 2014.

Krell, David Farrell. *The Sea: A Philosophical Encounter*. London: Bloomsbury Academic, 2019.

Krueckeberg, Donald A. "The Difficult Character of Property: To Whom Do Things Belong?" *Journal of the American Planning Association* 61, no. 3 (1995): 301–309.

Lang, Helen S. *The Order of Nature in Aristotle's* Physics: *Place and the Elements*. Cambridge: Cambridge University Press, 1998.

Latour, Bruno. "Love Your Monsters: Why We Must Care for Our Technologies as We Do Our Children." *Breakthrough Journal*, no. 2 (2011): 21–28.

Lazzarato, Maurizio. *The Making of the Indebted Man*. Los Angeles, CA: Semiotext(e), 2012.

Leonard, Wesley Y. "Contesting Extinction through a Praxis of Language Reclamation." In *Contesting Extinctions: Decolonial and Regenerative Futures*, edited by Suzanne M. McCullagh, Luis I. Prádanos, Ilaria Tabusso Marcyan, and Catherine Wagner, 143–160. Lanham, MD: Lexington Books, 2021.

Leopold, Aldo. *A Sand County Almanac: And Sketches Here and There*. Oxford: Oxford University Press, 1989.

Levinas, Emmanuel. *God, Death, and Time*. Translated by Bettina Bergo. Palo Alto, CA: Stanford University Press, 2000.
Lightfoot, Kent G., Lee M. Panich, Otis Parrish, Tsim D. Schneider, and K. Elizabeth Soluri. *California Indians and Their Environment: An Introduction*. Berkeley: University of California Press, 2009.
"Life beyond the Anthropocene: The Human and Ecological Attunement." Conference at King's University College at Western University, London, Ontario, March 17–19, 2023.
"Lisbon Earthquake of 1755." *Britannica*, last updated October 25, 2022. https://www.britannica.com/event/Lisbon-earthquake-of-1755.
Lohan, Tara. "How Do We Solve Our Wildfire Challenges?" *The Revelator: Wild, Incisive, Fearless* (October 2018): https://therevelator.org/solve-wildfire-problems.
Macauley, David. *Elemental Philosophy: Earth, Air, Fire, and Water as Environmental Ideas*. Albany: State University of New York Press, 2010.
"Magnitude of Great Lisbon Earthquake May Have Been Lower than Previous Estimates." *ScienceDaily*, January 7, 2020. https://www.sciencedaily.com/releases/2020/01/200107104942.htm.
Marcel, Gabriel. "Testimony and Existentialism." In *The Philosophy of Existentialism*. Translated by Manya Harari, 91–103. New York: New Citadel Press, 1967.
Marciano, M. Laura Gemelli. *Die Vorsokratiker: Band I: Thales, Anaximander, Anaximenes, Pythagoras und die Pythagoreer, Xenophanes, Heraklit*. Düsseldorf: Artemis & Winkler, 2007.
Marshall, Michael. "The Event That Transformed Earth." BBC, July 2, 2015, originally accessible at http://www.bbc.com/earth/story/20150701-the-origin-of-the-air-we-breathe. Reproduced under license from BBC / BBC Earth / bbc.co.uk – © [2015] BBC at: https://www.woodz.co/journal/the-origin-of-the-air-we-breathe/.
Marx, Karl. "Excerpts from James Mill's *Elements of Political Economy*." 1844. In *Early Writings*. Translated by Rodney Livingstone and Gregor Benton, 259–278. New York: Penguin Classics, 1992.
Marín-Ávila, Esteban. "Hope and Trust as Conditions for Rational Actions in Society: A Phenomenological Approach." *Husserl Studies* 37, no. 3 (2021): 229–247.
Marlon, J. R., B. Bloodhart, M. T. Ballew, J. Rolfe-Redding, C. Roser-Renouf, A. Leiserowitz, and E. Maibach. "How Hope and Doubt Affect Climate Change Mobilization." *Frontiers in Communication* 4, no. 20 (2019): 1–15, doi: 10.3389/fcomm.2019.00020.
Masih, Adven. "An Enhanced Seismic Activity Observed Due to Climate Change: Preliminary Results from Alaska." *IOP Conference Series: Earth and Environmental Science* 167 (2018): 1–8.
McGeer, Victoria. "Trust, Hope and Empowerment." *Australasian Journal of Philosophy* 86, no. 2 (2008): 237–254.

McGinnis, Michael, and Elinor Ostrom. "Institutional Analysis and Global Climate Change: Design Principles for Robust International Regimes." *Global Climate Change: Social and Economic Research Issues* (1992): 45–85.
McGuire, Bill. *Waking the Giant: How a Changing Climate Triggers Earthquakes, Tsunamis, and Volcanoes.* New York: Oxford University Press, 2012.
McKirahan, Richard D. *Philosophy before Socrates: An Introduction with Texts and Commentary.* Indianapolis, IN: Hackett, 1994.
"Medical Definition of Atopy." MedicineNet, last reviewed March 29, 2021. https://www.medicinenet.com/script/main/art.asp?articlekey=31081.
Meillassoux, Quentin. *After Finitude: An Essay on the Necessity of Contingency.* Translated by Ray Brassier. London: Continuum, 2008.
Middel, Mark. "Het openen van de subsidiepot leidde in Groningen tot een 'vernederende' tombola." *NRC,* January 13, 2022. https://www.nrc.nl/nieuws/2022/01/13/een-subsidietombola-die-de-groningers-vernederde-a4079235.
Mitchell, Alanna. *Seasick: Ocean Change and the Extinction of Life on Earth.* Chicago: University of Chicago Press, 2009.
Mitman, Gregg. *Breathing Space: How Allergies Shape Our Lives and Landscapes.* New Haven, CT: Yale University Press, 2007.
Morgner, Christian. "Trust and Confidence: History, Theory and Socio-Political Implications." *Human Studies* 36 (2013): 509–532.
Mugerauer, Robert. *Heidegger and Homecoming: The Leitmotif in the Later Writings.* Toronto: University of Toronto Press, 2008.
Mugerauer, Robert. "Language and the Emergence of Environment." In *Dwelling, Place and Environment,* edited by David Seamon and Robert Mugerauer, 51–70. Dordrecht: Springer, 1985.
Mulder, I. M., I. Tulp, and T. Ysebaert. "Ontwikkelingen van bodemgebonden vis en epibenthos in de Oosterschelde in de periode 1970–2018." *Wageningen Marine Research rapport,* no. C024/20 (2020): https://doi.org/10.18174/518404.
National Geographic Society. "Earthquakes." *National Geographic,* last updated May 19, 2022. https://education.nationalgeographic.org/resource/earthquakes/.
National Geographic Society. "Plate Tectonics." *National Geographic,* last updated August 17, 2022. https://education.nationalgeographic.org/resource/plate-tectonics/.
National Trust of Guyana. "Fort Zeelandia." Last modified December 17, 2021. https://ntg.gov.gy/monument/fort-zeelandia.
Neimanis, Astrid. *Bodies of Water: Posthuman Feminist Phenomenology.* London: Bloomsbury, 2017.
Nietzsche, Friedrich. *Nachgelassene Fragmente Frühjahr 1881 bis Sommer 1882.* In *Kritische Gesamtausgabe: Werke,* pt. 5, vol. 2, edited by G. Colli and M. Montinari, 370–371. Berlin: De Gruyter, 1973.
Nietzsche, Friedrich. *On the Genealogy of Morality.* Edited by Keith Ansell-Pearson. Translated by Carol Diethe. Cambridge: Cambridge University Press, 2007.

Nietzsche, Friedrich. "Zarathustra's Prologue." In *Thus Spoke Zarathustra: A Book for All and None*, 9–24. New York: Modern Library, 1995.
Nordman, Erik. *The Uncommon Knowledge of Elinor Ostrom: Essential Lessons for Collective Action*. Washington, DC: Island Press, 2021.
Nordsieck, Robert. "Amazing Facts about Snails." *The Living World of Molluscs*, accessed August 31, 2019. https://molluscs.at/gastropoda/index.html.
Noss, Reed F. *The Redwood Forest: History, Ecology, and Conservation of the Coast Redwoods*. Washington, DC: Island Press, 1999.
Oele, Marjolein. *E-Co-Affectivity: Exploring Pathos at Life's Material Interfaces*. Albany: State University of New York Press, 2020.
Oele, Marjolein. "Folding Nature Back upon Itself: Aristotle and the Rebirth of Physis." In *Ontologies of Nature: Continental Perspectives and Environmental Reorientations*, edited by Gerard Kuperus and Marjolein Oele, 47–66. Dordrecht: Springer, 2017.
Oele, Marjolein. "Priam's Despair and Courage: An Aristotelian Reading of Fear, Hope and Suffering in Homer's *Iliad*." In *Logoi and Muthoi: Further Essays in Greek Philosophy and Literature*, edited by William Wians, 297–317. Albany: State University of New York Press, 2019.
Oele, Marjolein, and Brian Treanor. "Michel Serres and Ecological Crisis: Listening to the World's Expressions." In *Continental Philosophy and the History of Thought: Inaugural Volume*, edited by Antonio Calcagno and Christian Lotz, 79–100. Lanham, MD: Lexington Books, 2023.
Oeser, Erhard. "Historical Earthquake Theories from Aristotle to Kant." In *Historical Earthquakes in Central Europe: Monographs*, 11–31. Vienna: Geologische Bundesanstalt, 1992.
O'Neill, Onora. "Questioning Truth." In *The Routledge Handbook of Trust and Philosophy*, edited by Judith Simon, 17–27. New York: Routledge, 2020.
Oosterlinck, Kim, Ugo Panizza, Mark Weidemaier, and Mitu Gulati. "A Debt of Dishonor." *Boston University Law Review* 102 (2022): 1247–1277.
Oostindie, Gert. "Index of Geographical Names." In *Dutch Colonialism, Migration and Cultural Heritage*, edited by Gert Oostindie, 343–350. Leiden: Brill, 2008.
Oreskes, Naomi. "From Continental Drift to Plate Tectonics." In *Plate Tectonics: An Insider's History of the Modern Theory of the Earth*, edited by Naomi Oreskes, 3–28. New York: CRC Press, 2003.
Ostrom, Elinor. "A Behavioral Approach to the Rational Choice Theory of Collective Action: Presidential Address, American Political Science Association, 1997." *American Political Science Review* 92, no. 1 (1998): 1–22.
Ostrom, Elinor. "Building Trust to Solve Commons Dilemmas: Taking Small Steps to Test an Evolving Theory of Collective Action." In *Games, Groups, and the Global Good*, edited by Simon A. Levin, 207–228. New York: Springer, 2008.
Ostrom, Elinor. "A General Framework for Analyzing Sustainability of Social-Ecological Systems." *Science* 325, no. 5939 (2009): 419–422.

Peperzak, Adriaan. *Modern Freedom: Hegel's Legal, Moral, and Political Philosophy.* Dordrecht: Kluwer Academic, 2001.
Peperzak, Adriaan. *Trust: Who or What Might Support Us?* New York: Fordham University Press, 2013.
Petit, Philippe. *On the High Wire.* Translated by Paul Auster. New York: New Directions Books, 2019.
"Plate Tectonics." *National Geographic*, last accessed April 5, 2023. https://www.nationalgeographic.com/science/article/plate-tectonics?loggedin=true&rnd=1680721122762.
Plato. *Laches, Protagoras, Meno, Euthydemus.* Translated by W. R. M. Lamb. Cambridge, MA: Harvard University Press, 2006.
Posthumus, Stephanie. *French Écocritique: Reading Contemporary French Theory and Fiction Ecologically.* Toronto: University of Toronto Press, 2017.
Poteete, Amy R., Marco A. Janssen, and Elinor Ostrom. *Working Together: Collective Action, the Commons, and Multiple Methods in Practice.* Princeton, NJ: Princeton University Press, 2010.
Preston, Christopher J. *Tenacious Beasts: Wildlife Recoveries That Change How We Think about Animals.* Cambridge, MA: MIT Press, 2023.
Purslow, Neil. *Redwood National Park.* New York: Weigl, 2006.
Pyne, Stephen J. "Consumed by Either Fire or Fire: A Prolegomenon to Anthropogenic Fire." In *Earth, Air, Fire, Water: Humanistic Studies of the Environment*, edited by Jill Ker Conway, Kenneth Keniston, and Leo Marx, 78–101. Amherst: University of Massachusetts Press, 1999.
Pyne, Stephen J. *Fire: A Brief History.* Foreword by William Cronon. London: British Museum Press, 2001.
Ramírez, Miguel Gualdrón. "To 'Stay Where You Are' as a Decolonial Gesture: Glissant's Philosophy of Antillean Space in the Context of Césaire and Fanon." In *Memory, Migration and (De)Colonisation in the Caribbean and Beyond*, edited by Jack Webb, Roderick Westmaas, Maria del Pilar Kaladeen, and William Tantam, 133–152. London: University of London Press, 2020.
Reed, Stanley. "Earthquakes Are Jolting the Netherlands. Gas Drilling Is to Blame." *New York Times*, October 24, 2019. https://www.nytimes.com/2019/10/24/business/energy-environment/netherlands-gas-earthquakes.html.
Reveal News. "Burning Hotter and Faster." November 24, 2018. https://revealnews.org/podcast/burning-hotter-and-faster/.
Ricoeur, Paul. *Memory History Forgetting.* Translated by Kathleen Blamey and David Pellauer. Chicago: University of Chicago Press, 2006.
Roden, David. *Posthuman Life: Philosophy at the Edge of the Human.* London: Routledge, 2015.
Round Taiwan Round. "Fort Zeelandia." Accessed October 31, 2022. https://www.rtaiwanr.com/tainan/fort-zeelandia.

Sallis, John. "The Elemental Earth." In *Rethinking Nature: Essays in Environmental Philosophy*, edited by Bruce V. Foltz and Robert Frodeman, 135–146. Bloomington: Indiana University Press, 2004.

Sallis, John. *The Figure of Nature: On Greek Origins*. Bloomington: Indiana University Press, 2016.

Sallis, John. *The Return of Nature: On the Beyond of Sense*. Bloomington: Indiana University Press, 2016.

Sallis, John. "Return to Nature." *International Journal of Philosophical Studies* 24, no. 3 (July 2016): 381–392.

Sallis, John. *Stone*. Bloomington: Indiana University Press, 1994.

Sandwell, David T. "Plate Tectonics: A Martian View." In *Plate Tectonics: An Insider's History of the Modern Theory of the Earth*, edited by Naomi Oreskes, 331–346. New York: CRC Press, 2003.

San Francisco Ballet. "Pointes of View Lecture Series, *The Promised Land* with Dwight Rhoden and Ariel Osterweis, Ph.D." YouTube. https://www.youtube.com/watch?v=KA9aslpL1hg.

Scarry, Elaine. "On Beauty and Being Just." The Tanner Lectures on Human Values. Delivered at Yale University March 25 and 26, 1998. Accessible online at https://tannerlectures.utah.edu/_resources/documents/a-to-z/s/scarry00.pdf.

Scheman, Naomi. "Trust and Trustworthiness." In *The Routledge Handbook of Trust and Philosophy*, edited by Judith Simon, 28–40. New York: Routledge, 2020.

Schneider-Mayerson, Matthew, and Brent Ryan Bellamy. "Introduction: Loanwords to Live With." In *An Ecotopian Lexicon*, edited by Matthew Schneider-Mayerson and Brent Ryan Bellamy, 1–14. Minneapolis: University of Minnesota Press, 2019.

Scott, James C. *Against the Grain: A Deep History of the Earliest States*. New Haven, CT: Yale University Press, 2017.

Scranton, Roy. *Learning to Die in the Anthropocene: Reflections on the End of a Civilization*. San Francisco, CA: City Lights Books, 2015.

Seitz, Brian. "Grids of Power: Toward a Phenomenology of Fuel." *Environmental Philosophy* 15, no. 2 (Fall 2018): 317–332.

Seneca the Younger. *Natural Questions*. In Seneca the Younger, *Physical Science in the Time of Nero: A Translation of the* Quaestiones Naturales *of Seneca* by John Clarke, MA, Lecturer on Education in the University of Aberdeen, Macmillan and Co., Limited, 1910, a work in the public domain placed online at the Internet Archive, accessed April 24, 2023. https://topostext.org/work/737.

Serres, Michel. *Biogea*. Translated by Randolph Burks. Minneapolis, MN: Univocal, 2012.

Serres, Michel. *Genesis*. Translated by Geneviève James and James Nielson. Ann Arbor: University of Michigan Press, 1995.

Serres, Michel. *The Natural Contract*. Translated by Elizabeth MacArthur and William Paulson. Ann Arbor: University of Michigan Press, 1995.

Serres, Michel. *Times of Crisis: What the Financial Crisis Revealed and How to Reinvent Our Lives and Future*. Translated by Anne-Marie Feenberg-Dibon. New York: Bloomsbury, 2014.

Serres, Michel. *Variations on the Body*. Translated by Randolph Burks. Minneapolis: University of Minnesota Press, 2011.

Serres, Michel, and Bruno Latour. *Conversations on Science, Culture, and Time*. Translated by Roxanne Lapidus. Ann Arbor: University of Michigan Press, 1995.

Shelley, Mary. *Frankenstein: or, The Modern Prometheus*. New York: Modern Library, 1984.

Sims, Caitlin. "About Rhoden's *The Promised Land*." San Francisco Ballet, last accessed April 14, 2023. https://www.sfballet.org/about-rhodens-the-promised-land/.

Sloterdijk, Peter. *Bubbles: Spheres Volume I: Microspherology*. Translated by Wieland Hoban. Los Angeles, CA: Semiotext(e), 2011.

Sloterdijk, Peter. *Foams: Spheres Volume III: Plural Spherology*. Translated by Wieland Hoban. Los Angeles, CA: Semiotext(e), 2016.

Snyder, Gary. *The Practice of the Wild: Essays*. Berkeley, CA: North Point Press, 1990.

SPLIKA. "Ontdek Tambú!" Accessed May 11, 2020. https://splika.nl/ontdek-tambu/.

Stamati, Katerina, Vivek Mudera, and Umber Cheema. "Evolution of Oxygen Utilization in Multicellular Organisms and Implications for Cell Signaling in Tissue Engineering." *Journal of Tissue Engineering* 2, no. 1 (2011): 1–12.

Stanford, Craig. *Upright: The Evolutionary Key to Becoming Human*. Boston, MA: Houghton Mifflin, 2003.

Stein, Edith. "Martin Heidegger's Existential Philosophy." Translated by Mette Lebech. *Maynooth Philosophical Papers* 4 (2007): 55–98.

Stengers, Isabelle. *In Catastrophic Times: Resisting the Common Barbarism*. Translated by Andrew Goffey. London: Open Humanities Press, 2015.

Stephens, Scott L., B. M. Collins, E. Biber, and P. Z. Fulé. "U.S. Federal Fire and Forest Policy: Emphasizing Resilience in Dry Forests." *Ecosphere* 7, no. 11 (2016): https://doi.org/10.1002/ecs2.1584.

Stiegler, Bernard. *Technics and Time, 1: The Fault of Epimetheus*. Translated by Richard Beardsworth and George Collins. Stanford, CA: Stanford University Press, 1998.

Stiegler, Bernard. *What Makes Life Worth Living: On Pharmacology*. Translated by Daniel Ross. Malden, MA: Polity Press, 2013.

Stone, Alison. "Irigaray's Ecological Phenomenology: Towards an Elemental Materialism." *Journal of the British Society for Phenomenology* 46, no. 2 (2015): 117–131.

Struzik, Edward. *Firestorm: How Wildfire Will Shape Our Future*. Washington, DC: Island Press, 2017.

Svec, Carol. *Balance: A Dizzying Journey through the Science of Our Most Delicate Sense*. Chicago: Chicago Review Press, 2017.

Svenaeus, Fredrik. "A Defense of the Phenomenological Account of Health and Illness." *Journal of Medicine and Philosophy* 44 (2019): 459–478.

Svenaeus, Fredrik. "Medicine." In *A Companion to Phenomenology and Existentialism*, edited by Hubert L. Dreyfus and Mark A. Wrathall, 412–424. Hoboken, NJ: Wiley-Blackwell, 2009.

Treanor, Brian. "Mind the Gap: The Challenge of Matter." In *Carnal Hermeneutics*, edited by Richard Kearney and Brian Treanor, 57–73. New York: Fordham University Press, 2015.

"Trust, n." *OED Online*, last accessed May 10, 2023. https://www.oed.com/view/Entry/207004?rskey=787rIv&result=1&isAdvanced=false#eid.

Van Keymeulen, Jacques. "Zeeuws Overzee." *Nehalennia* 198 (2017): 20–21.

Virilio, Paul. *Open Sky*. Translated by Julie Rose. London: Verso, 1997.

Vivante, Paolo. "On the Representation of Nature and Reality in Homer." *Arion: A Journal of Humanities and the Classics* 5, no. 2 (1966): 149–190.

Voltaire. "Poem on the Lisbon Disaster; or an Examination of the Axiom, 'All Is Well' (1755)." In *Toleration and Other Essays by Voltaire*, translated by Joseph McCabe. New York: G. P. Putnam's Sons, 1912.

Voltaire, and S. G. Tallentyre. *Voltaire in His Letters; Being a Selection from His Correspondence, Translated with a Preface and Forewords*. London: John Murray, 1919.

Wall, Derek. *Elinor Ostrom's Rules for Radicals: Cooperate Alternatives Beyond Markets and States*. London: Pluto Press, 2017.

Walters, Vicky, and J. C. Gaillard. "Disaster Risk at the Margins: Homelessness, Vulnerability and Hazards." *Habitat International* 44 (2014): 211–219.

Warren, Louis S. "The California Dream: History of a Myth." *Pacific Historical Review* 92, no. 2 (May 2023): 260–298, doi: https://doi.org/10.1525/phr.2023.92.2.260.

Watkins, Eric. "Editor's Introduction." In Immanuel Kant, *Natural Science*, edited by Eric Watkins. Cambridge: Cambridge University Press, 2012.

Webster, Jane. "The *Zong* in the Context of the Eighteenth-Century Slave Trade." *Journal of Legal History* 28, no. 3 (2007): 285–298, doi:10.1080/01440360701698403.

Wildcat, Daniel R. *Red Alert: Saving the Planet with Indigenous Knowledge*. Wheat Ridge, CO: Fulcrum, 2009.

Wittgenstein, Ludwig. *Philosophical Investigations*. Translated by G. E. M. Anscombe. Oxford: Blackwell, 1958.

Wood, David. *Deep Time, Dark Times: On Being Geologically Human*. New York: Fordham University Press, 2019.

Wrangham, Richard W. *Catching Fire: How Cooking Made Us Human*. London: Basic Books, 2009.

Yanes, Javier. "Will Climate Change Also Trigger Earthquakes, Tsunamis and Volcanic Eruptions?" Last accessed April 5, 2023. https://www.bbvaopen mind.com/en/science/environment/climate-change-trigger-earthquakes-tsunamis-volcanic-eruptions/.

Index

Abram, David, 14
affect: elemental trust and, 6, 15, 109, 114, 116–17, 120, 121–23, 128, 133–34; fire and, 45, 49–55, 57–59
affective habitus, 3–6, 112, 116, 139, 141
Against the Grain (Scott), 48
Aguilera, Abigail Perez, 153n28, 153n38
Ahlzén, Rolf, 164–65n14
air: concept of, 4–5, 59, 61–62; Anaximenes on, 12, 62, 63, 69–73; atopic illness and, 21, 62–69, 73–80, 112; elemental loss and, 21, 63, 80, 112; fire and, 62; home and, 63, 64–69; oxygen and, 14, 61–62, 71, 78–79
air-conditioning, 17, 69, 77–78
airquake, 68
Alaimo, Stacy, 13–14
Albrecht, Glenn, 9, 50, 112, 160n56, 177–78n6
allergic rhinitis, 63. See also atopic illness
American Institute of Architects, 170n65
anarchy, 131–33
Anaxagoras, 171–72n23
Anaximenes, 12, 62, 63, 69–73, 171–72n23

Anthropocene: earth and, 83–84, 98–105; elemental loss and, 12, 15; elemental trust and, 112–13; fire and, 44–45, 48–52; water and, 40–41
anthropogenic climate change: air and, 63–64, 80; earth and, 80, 82–83, 98–99, 101, 103–4, 105, 107; elemental and, 4–6; elemental trust and, 112, 115–16; fire and, 49–51, 54–55; Ostrom's model of collective action and, 132–34; Sixth Great Extinction and, 26–29; theories of loss and, 8–9; water and, 26–29
anthropos, 44
Apollo, 87
Archimedes, 30, 136–37
Arendt, Hannah, 7
Aristotle: Anaximenes and, 163n6; categorical contamination and, 10; on the commons, 129; on earth and earthquakes, 11, 84, 88–91, 92, 97–98; ethics of balance and, 106; on hope, 113
artificial air, 68–69, 75
ashes, 46
asthma, 63, 73–74. See also atopic illness
Athena, 87

atmosphere, 18–19, 40, 44. *See also* air
atopic illness, 21, 62–69, 73–80, 112
Auster, Paul, 108

Bachelard, Gaston, 4, 19–20, 44, 45
bad air, 69, 73–78
Baier, Annette, 115
balance, 83, 88, 90, 105–9
Being and Time (Heidegger), 6–7, 18, 64–65
being-toward-death, 26, 27
Bellamy, Brent Ryan, 39, 154n43
Bennett, Jane, 176n100
Berlant, Lauren, 9, 75–76, 103
Bernstein, Jay, 115–18, 122
Besterman, Theodore, 91
Between the World and Me (Coates), 146n39
Biogea (Serres): elemental trust and, 22, 114, 128, 135–40, 141; on language, 30–33, 34, 36, 38, 39–40, 135; water and, 29–33, 34, 38, 39–40
Bobroff, Kenneth H., 162n68, 162n70
Bos, Oscar Georg, 152n17, 152n19
Boss, Pauline, 8, 112–13
botanical sexism, 168n48
Breathing Space (Mitman), 73–74
Brison, Susan, 116
Brock, Antje, 178n7
Bubbles (Sloterdijk), 26–27
Buber, Martin, 7
Buraniyi, Stephen, 169–70n64
Burkert, Walter, 86–87
Butler, Judith, 7–8, 116, 164n9, 168n45

Callicott, J. Baird, 145n31, 165–66n28
Camp Fire (2018), 54
Capitalocene, 44
Caribbean, 21, 35–38

categorical contamination, 10
Césaire, Aimé, 35–36
chaos, 84–85
cinders, 56, 59
Clare, Stephanie, 14
climate change. *See* anthropogenic climate change
clouds, 62
Coates, Ta-Nehisi, 146n39
co-creation, 4–5, 11–12, 18, 67, 74
co-evolution, 14–15, 67
coexistence, 17–18, 67
Cohen, Jeffrey Jerome, 13–14
Cohen, Paul, 175n79
collective action, 22, 114, 127–36, 139, 142
colonialism: air and, 73–74; fire and, 45, 54–55; water and, 24–25, 35–38
colonialization, 101
common periwinkle (*Littorina littorea*), 28–29
Common Pool Resources (CPR), 129–34
commons, 22, 114, 127–36, 139, 142
community, 121–22, 136–40. *See also* commons
condensation, 62
Covid-19 pandemic: air and, 62–63, 79; elemental trust and, 141; loss and, 8, 177n5; suffering and, 108–9
Cozzoli, Francesco, 157n86
Creole language, 36–37
crisis. *See* anthropogenic climate change; disaster and natural disasters
Critique of Judgment (Kant), 96–97
Crito (Plato), 6

dance, 108–9
Dasein, 64–65
de-cision, 141
deep time, 53

Index | 207

Deltawerken, 23–24, 38–39
Democritus, 171–72n23
Derrida, Jacques, 163n83
Despret, Vinciane, 25, 27–29
Diamond, Jared, 145n31
disaster and natural disasters, 50, 75, 152–53n26. *See also* earth and earthquakes; megafires and wildfires
disorientation, 2, 9, 22, 50. *See also* loss and elemental loss; orientation
disposition (*Gesinnung*), 120–21. *See also* habitus
distrust, 114–15, 122, 124–28. *See also* trust and elemental trust
Drabinski, John E., 37
droughts, 1–2, 5, 89, 103
Duckert, Lowell, 13–14
Dvorak, John, 174n76
Dyl, Joanna, 174–75n78

earth and earthquakes: concept of, 4–5, 79–80, 81–84; elemental loss and, 80, 82–83, 98–99, 101–3, 105–9, 112; ethics of balance and, 105–9; Greek cosmologies on, 11, 83–91, 92, 97–98, 106; Kant on, 11, 91–92, 94–98, 99, 102, 106; plate tectonics and, 11, 83–84, 98–105; Voltaire on, 11, 91–94, 97–98, 99, 106
Earth Emotions (Albrecht), 177–78n6
e-co-affectivity, 10, 170n1
Ecotopian Lexicon (Schneider-Mayerson and Bellamy), 39, 154n43
elemental: Bachelard on, 4, 19–20; Irigaray on, 4, 11, 18–20; Presocratic philosophy on, 4, 11, 12–15, 21–22; Sallis on, 4, 11, 15–17, 19; Sloterdijk on, 11, 17–18, 19; as social-ecological constellation, 3–6, 11–12. *See also* air; earth and earthquakes; fire; water
elemental force, 86–88
elemental loss. *See* loss and elemental loss
elemental trust. *See* trust and elemental trust
Empedocles, 21–22, 136–37
endangered landscapes, 56
Engels, Friedrich, 166–67n41, 167–68n44, 168n52, 169n54
Epimetheus, 46–47
equilibrium, 88, 90–91, 106–7. *See also* balance
extinction, 5, 16–17, 21, 26–29, 112
Exxon-Mobil/Shell, 104

Fanon, Frantz, 35–36
Figueroa Helland, Leonardo E., 153n28, 153n38
fire: concept of, 4–5, 41, 43–44; affect and, 45, 49–55, 57–59; air and, 62; elemental loss and, 1–3, 44, 50, 52, 112; elemental trust and, 52, 54, 56–59; evolution of humanity and, 47–49; Heraclitus on, 12; home and, 43–44; mythological conception of, 44–47, 50–51, 57, 58; prosthetics and, 46–47, 127; pyrophytic practices and, 21, 52–53
Firestorm (Struzik), 50
Fitzgerald, Gerard J., 165n25
flooding, 5, 24, 38–39, 40, 103, 137–38
Foams (Sloterdijk), 27, 165n25
Foucault, Michel, 141–42
fracking, 80, 101, 104–5
Frankenstein (Shelley), 59
Freud, Sigmund, 7–8

Gaia, 84–87
Gaillard, J. C., 75

Garonne (river), 137–39
Gas (Hakkenes), 176n95
gas drilling, 16, 104–5
giant sequoia trees (*Sequoiadendron giganteum*), 45, 52–53, 57
Glissant, Édouard, 25, 35–38
global warming, 26, 132–33. *See also* anthropogenic climate change
Godfrey, Joseph, 118–20
Graham, Daniel, 62, 70
Graham, Stephen, 77–78
Great Oxidation Event, 70–71, 79
grief, 9. *See also* mourning
Grund, Julius, 178n7
Gupta, Saloni, 144n17

Haase, Annegret, 168n45
habits, 45, 57–59
habitus, 3–6, 112, 116, 139, 141
Hades, 86
Haiti earthquake (2010), 102–3
Hakkenes, Emiel, 176n95
Hal, Ralf van, 152n17, 152n19
Haraway, Donna, 9
Hardin, Garrett, 129
hay fever, 73–74
Hegel, Georg Wilhelm Friedrich, 119–23
Heidegger, Martin: on being-in-the-world, 19; on home and illness, 63, 64–68; on loss, 6–7, 26, 27; Sallis and, 15–17; Sloterdijk and, 18
Henry IV (Shakespeare), 172n26
Heraclitus, 12, 51
Heryford, Ryan, 150–51n4
Hesiod, 11, 21, 45–46, 50–51, 85–86, 92, 113
home: air and, 63, 64–69; earth and, 104; elemental trust and, 123; fire and, 1–3, 43–44, 51, 112; loss and, 9; *Unheimlichkeit* and, 65; water and, 24–29, 37–39
Homer, 11, 85–87, 92

hope, 94, 113–14
Houlgate, Stephen, 120, 121–23
Howard, Rachel, 177n110
The Human Condition (Arendt), 7
hybris, 49
hydrosphere, 40. *See also* water

IJsselmeer, 23–24
Iliad (Homer), 86–87
illness: Aristotle on, 90. *See also* atopic illness
Indigenous people: elemental trust and, 114, 128, 139–41; fire and, 21, 45, 52, 53, 55–56, 57; Serres on, 32; water and, 34–35
industrial fire, 3, 49, 51–52, 54, 112
Influx and Efflux (Bennett), 176n100
Ingersoll, Karin Amimoto, 25, 33–35, 36, 38, 39–40
Introduction to Metaphysics (Heidegger), 65
Irigaray, Luce, 4, 11, 18–20, 69, 98, 165n26
isostatic uplift, 103–4

Jak, Robert Gerbrand, 152n17, 152n19
Jonas, Hans, 142
Jones, Rachel, 96, 173n47

Kant, Immanuel, 11, 91–92, 94–98, 99, 102, 106
Katwijk, Marieke van, 156–57n84
Katz, Jonathan M., 175n81
Kennedy, Jennifer, 152n18
Kincade fire (2019), 1–2
Krell, David Farrell, 150n2

landscape: earth and, 83, 107; elemental trust and, 138; fire and, 45, 48, 51, 53–56
language: Glissant on, 25, 35–38; Ingersoll on, 25, 33–35, 36, 38, 39–40; Leonard on, 34, 151n6, 154n50;

Serres on, 30–33, 34, 36, 38, 39–40, 135; Wildcat on, 140; Wittgenstein on, 39
Latour, Bruno, 163n82
Lazzarato, Maurizio, 124–26
Leonard, Wesley Y., 34, 151n6, 154n50
Leopold, Aldo, 31
Levinas, Emmanuel, 7
life: air and, 61–62, 69–72, 77, 79; earth and, 85–86; elemental loss and, 10–11; fire and, 44, 46, 51, 52–53; Serres on, 30–32, 135–36; Voltaire on, 93–94
Lisbon earthquake (1755), 91–98
lithosphere, 40–41. *See also* plate tectonics
Loma Prieta earthquake (1989), 102
loss and elemental loss: concept of, 4, 6–9, 15; air and, 21, 63, 80, 112; Covid-19 pandemic and, 177n5; Despret on, 27–29; earth and, 80, 82–83, 98–99, 101–3, 105–9, 112; elemental change and, 113 (*see also* trust and elemental trust); epistemology of, 10–11; experience of, 2–3; fire and, 1–3, 44, 50, 52, 112; Heidegger on, 26, 27; portals into, 20–22; Sloterdijk on, 25, 26–27; water and, 21, 25–29, 112; Wittgenstein on, 39
loss of trust, 22, 111–13, 126–27

Macauley, David, 21, 82, 148n59, 149n70
Mantz, Felix, 153n28, 153n38
Marín-Ávila, Esteban, 114
Marine Lover (Irigaray), 18–19
Marx, Karl, 20, 124–26
Masih, Adven, 175n90
Matsuo, Amiko, 160n45
McGuire, Bill, 103–4
McKirahan, Richard D., 72

megafires and wildfires, 1–2, 22, 44, 49–51, 54–55
middle voice, 10, 119–20
migration: air and, 63–64, 74–75, 77; water and, 25, 37–38
mistrust, 125–26. *See also* distrust; trust and elemental trust
Mitchell, Alanna, 151n8
Mitman, Gregg, 73–74
Miwok, 45, 52, 53, 57
Monsma, Brad, 160n45
mourning: Butler on, 7–8, 116; Despret on, 27–28; earth and, 82–83; fire and, 50, 52
The Myth of Closure (Boss), 177n5

Native American people, 21, 45, 52, 53, 55–56, 57
The Natural Contract (Serres), 105
nature (*physis*), 10
Nederlandse Aardolie Maatschappij (NAM), 104
Neimanis, Astrid, 40–41
Netherlands, 104–5. *See also* Zeeland
Nicomachean Ethics (Aristotle), 106, 113
Nietzsche, Friedrich, 18–19, 76–77, 108
North Sea Flood (1953), 24

ocean acidification, 5, 26
Odyssey (Homer), 87
On Generation and Corruption (Aristotle), 144–45n25
O'Neill, Onora, 142
Oosterlinck, Kim, 175n80
Oosterschelde, 23–24, 28–29, 38–39
Open Sky (Virilio), 147n45
Oreskes, Naomi, 173–74n60
orientation: earth and, 82–84, 88, 90–94; elemental trust and, 112, 128, 138; ethics of balance and, 105–9; Kant on, 94–98; plate tectonics and, 98–105; Voltaire on, 91–94, 97–98

Ostrom, Elinor, 22, 114, 127–36, 139, 142
otherness, 64
oxygen, 14, 61–62, 71, 78–79

Pacific Gas and Electric Company (PG&E), 1–2, 54
parrhesiastic practice, 141–42
passenger pigeons, 27–28
pathos, 90. *See also* affect
Peperzak, Adriaan, 120–21, 160n47
Petit, Philippe, 108
Phaedo (Plato), 6
Pirquet, Clemens von, 74
plate tectonics, 11, 83–84, 98–105
Plato, 6, 46, 50–51, 58, 163n6
Poe, Edgar Allan, 82
Poetics of Relation (Glissant), 35–38
Politics (Aristotle), 129
Poseidon, 84–87
Posthuman Life (Roden), 158n7, 161n57
posthumanism, 158n7
power: earth and, 85–88, 93–94, 96–98; elemental trust and, 128; fire and, 46, 47–49, 51, 57, 58–59
The Practice of the Wild (Snyder), 181n74
Presocratic philosophy: on air, 12, 62, 63, 69–73; concept of elemental and, 4, 11, 12–15; on earth and earthquakes, 88, 171–72n23; on elemental, 21–22; on fire, 51; scientific thinking and, 136–37
Preston, Christopher, 141
Préval, René, 175n81
Prometheus, 44–47, 57, 58
The Promised Land (ballet), 108–9
prosthetics, 46–47, 127
Protagoras (Plato), 46, 50–51, 58
Proterozoic period, 70–71, 79

The Psychoanalysis of Fire (Bachelard), 148n60
Pyne, Stephen, 47–48, 51, 57
Pyrocene, 45, 49–51, 53, 56–59
Pyrometric (exhibit), 160n45
pyrophytic practices, 21, 52–53

Quevedo, Francisco de, 163n83

Ramírez, Miguel Gualdrón, 36
rarefaction, 62
Red Alert (Wildcat), 139–41
Rhoden, Dwight, 108–9
Ricoeur, Paul, 145n29
Roden, David, 158n7, 161n57

Sallis, John, 4, 11, 15–17, 19, 22, 163–64n8
San Andreas Fault, 101, 174n74
San Bruno Gas explosion (2010), 54
Sandwell, David T., 100
Scheler, Max, 8
Scheman, Naomi, 186n141
Schneider-Mayerson, Matthew, 39, 154n43
scientific thinking, 136–37
Scott, James, 48
Scranton, Roy, 58
The Sea (Krell), 150n2
seagoing pact, 39–40
seascape epistemology, 34
Seismic City (Dyl and Sutter), 174–75n78
Seitz, Brian, 48
Sequoiadendron giganteum (giant sequoia trees), 45, 52–53, 57
Serres, Michel: on Biogea, 22, 29–33, 34, 36, 38, 39–40, 114, 128, 135–40, 141; on earth and earthquakes, 83, 102–3, 105; on elemental trust, 128, 135–40, 141; on home, 25; on

language, 30–33, 34, 36, 38, 39–40, 135; on sky, 16
settler colonialism, 45, 54–55, 73–74
Shakespeare, William, 172n26
shame (*aidōs*), 45, 58
Shelley, Mary, 59
silent disasters, 75
Simondon, Gilbert, 10
Sixth Great Extinction, 26–29
Sloterdijk, Peter: on air, 63, 67–69, 74–75; on elemental, 11, 17–18, 19; on loss, 25, 26–27
slow death, 9, 75–76, 103
Snyder, Gary, 181n74
social justice, 101
society, 7, 67, 102, 114, 124–28, 139
solastalgia, 9
solipsism, 67
Stamati, Katerina, 166n35
Staying with the Trouble (Haraway), 9
Stein, Edith, 151n11
Stengers, Isabelle, 157n3
Stiegler, Bernard, 44–45, 46–47, 48, 58, 126–27
Stone (Sallis), 146–47n44
Stone, Alison, 145n33
Struzik, Edward, 50
suffering: air and, 75–77; anthropogenic climate change and, 6; Covid-19 pandemic and, 62–63, 108–9; elemental trust and, 136; Haiti earthquake (2010) and, 102–3; Voltaire on, 93–94, 97, 99. *See also* loss and elemental loss
Sullivan, Dennis, 141
sustainability, 157–58n5
Svec, Carol, 83
Svenaeus, Fredrik, 64–66

tambú, 37–38
technē, 44–47, 58

Technics and Time (Stiegler), 44–45, 46–47, 48, 58
Tenacious Beasts (Preston), 141
Texas, 104–5
Thales, 171–72n23
Theogony (Hesiod), 21, 45–46, 50–51, 85–86
The Three Characters (Chinese text), 149n64
tightrope walking, 108
Timaeus (Plato), 163n6
"To Vesuvius" (Quevedo), 163n83
tragedy of the commons, 129
transatlantic slave trade, 24, 35–38
trauma, 116, 117
trust and elemental trust: concept of, 3, 4, 22, 113–15; affect and, 6, 15, 109, 114, 116–17, 120, 121–23, 128, 133–34; Bernstein on, 115–18, 122; definition of, 123–24; etymology of, 114; fire and, 52, 54, 56–59; Glissant on, 35; Godfrey on, 118–20; Hegel on, 119–23; home and, 123; Indigenous knowledge and, 114, 128, 139–41; loss of, 22, 111–13, 126–27; Marx on, 124–26; Ostrom's model of collective action and, 22, 114, 127–36, 139, 142; Serres's Biogea and, 22, 114, 128, 135–40, 141; Stiegler on, 126–27; truth and, 141–42; water and, 137–39, 140–41; Wittgenstein on, 39
Trust of People, Words, and God (Godfrey), 118–20
"Trust: On the Real but Almost Unnoticed, Ever-Changing Foundation of Ethical Life" (Bernstein), 115–18, 122
truth, 141–42

Unheimlichkeit, 65

Van Keymeulen, Jacques, 155–56n70
Virilio, Paul, 147n45
Voltaire, 11, 91–94, 97–98, 99, 106

Waking the Giant (McGuire), 103–4
Walters, Vicky, 75
Warren, Louis S., 161n61
water: concept of, 4–5, 23–25; Anthropocene and, 40–41; elemental loss and, 21, 25–29, 112; elemental trust and, 137–39, 140–41; extinction and, 5, 21, 26–29, 112; Glissant's language of the sea and, 25, 35–38; home and, 24–29, 37–39; Ingersoll's aquatic language and, 25, 33–35, 36, 38, 39–40; Serres's Biogea and, 29–33, 34, 38, 39–40

Watkins, Eric, 94, 96
Waves of Knowing (Ingersoll), 33–35, 36, 38, 39–40
Weber, Max, 126
What World Is This? (Butler), 8, 164n9, 168n45
Whitman, Walt, 176n100
Wildcat, Daniel R., 114, 128, 139–41
Wirth, Jason, 184n113
Wittgenstein, Ludwig, 39
Wood, David, 161n57
Works and Days (Hesiod), 113
Wrangham, Richard W., 159n24

Zeeland, 21, 23–24, 28–29, 38–39
Zeelandic (language), 28
Zeus, 45–46, 85–86, 87
Zong (slave ship), 150–51n4

www.ingramcontent.com/pod-product-compliance
Lightning Source LLC
Chambersburg PA
CBHW021840220426
43663CB00005B/341